MILL VALLEY NEW BOOKS
006.5 Samsung Galaxy Tab
by Gookin
WITHDRAWN
Gookin, Dan
Samsung Galaxy Tab 10.1
31111032129809
MAY   2012 N

Samsung
Galaxy Tab® 10.1
FOR
DUMMIES®

P9-CRM-247

by Dan Gookin

WILEY

John Wiley & Sons, Inc.

Samsung Galaxy Tab® 10.1 For Dummies®

Published by
John Wiley & Sons, Inc.
111 River Street
Hoboken, NJ 07030-5774
www.wiley.com

Copyright © 2012 by John Wiley & Sons, Inc., Hoboken, New Jersey

Published by John Wiley & Sons, Inc., Hoboken, New Jersey

Published simultaneously in Canada

No part of this publication may be reproduced, stored in a retrieval system or transmitted in any form or by any means, electronic, mechanical, photocopying, recording, scanning or otherwise, except as permitted under Sections 107 or 108 of the 1976 United States Copyright Act, without either the prior written permission of the Publisher, or authorization through payment of the appropriate per-copy fee to the Copyright Clearance Center, 222 Rosewood Drive, Danvers, MA 01923, (978) 750-8400, fax (978) 646-8600. Requests to the Publisher for permission should be addressed to the Permissions Department, John Wiley & Sons, Inc., 111 River Street, Hoboken, NJ 07030, (201) 748-6011, fax (201) 748-6008, or online at http://www.wiley.com/go/permissions.

Trademarks: Wiley, the Wiley logo, For Dummies, the Dummies Man logo, A Reference for the Rest of Us!, The Dummies Way, Dummies Daily, The Fun and Easy Way, Dummies.com, Making Everything Easier, and related trade dress are trademarks or registered trademarks of John Wiley & Sons, Inc. and/or its affiliates in the United States and other countries, and may not be used without written permission. Samsung Galaxy Tab is a registered trademark of Samsung Electronics Co., Ltd. All other trademarks are the property of their respective owners. John Wiley & Sons, Inc. is not associated with any product or vendor mentioned in this book.

LIMIT OF LIABILITY/DISCLAIMER OF WARRANTY: THE PUBLISHER AND THE AUTHOR MAKE NO REPRESENTATIONS OR WARRANTIES WITH RESPECT TO THE ACCURACY OR COMPLETENESS OF THE CONTENTS OF THIS WORK AND SPECIFICALLY DISCLAIM ALL WARRANTIES, INCLUDING WITHOUT LIMITATION WARRANTIES OF FITNESS FOR A PARTICULAR PURPOSE. NO WARRANTY MAY BE CREATED OR EXTENDED BY SALES OR PROMOTIONAL MATERIALS. THE ADVICE AND STRATEGIES CONTAINED HEREIN MAY NOT BE SUITABLE FOR EVERY SITUATION. THIS WORK IS SOLD WITH THE UNDERSTANDING THAT THE PUBLISHER IS NOT ENGAGED IN RENDERING LEGAL, ACCOUNTING, OR OTHER PROFESSIONAL SERVICES. IF PROFESSIONAL ASSISTANCE IS REQUIRED, THE SERVICES OF A COMPETENT PROFESSIONAL PERSON SHOULD BE SOUGHT. NEITHER THE PUBLISHER NOR THE AUTHOR SHALL BE LIABLE FOR DAMAGES ARISING HEREFROM. THE FACT THAT AN ORGANIZATION OR WEBSITE IS REFERRED TO IN THIS WORK AS A CITATION AND/OR A POTENTIAL SOURCE OF FURTHER INFORMATION DOES NOT MEAN THAT THE AUTHOR OR THE PUBLISHER ENDORSES THE INFORMATION THE ORGANIZATION OR WEBSITE MAY PROVIDE OR RECOMMENDATIONS IT MAY MAKE. FURTHER, READERS SHOULD BE AWARE THAT INTERNET WEBSITES LISTED IN THIS WORK MAY HAVE CHANGED OR DISAPPEARED BETWEEN WHEN THIS WORK WAS WRITTEN AND WHEN IT IS READ.

For general information on our other products and services, please contact our Customer Care Department within the U.S. at 877-762-2974, outside the U.S. at 317-572-3993, or fax 317-572-4002.

For technical support, please visit www.wiley.com/techsupport.

Wiley publishes in a variety of print and electronic formats and by print-on-demand. Some material included with standard print versions of this book may not be included in e-books or in print-on-demand. If this book refers to media such as a CD or DVD that is not included in the version you purchased, you may download this material at http://booksupport.wiley.com. For more information about Wiley products, visit www.wiley.com.

Library of Congress Control Number: 2011945573

ISBN 978-1-118-22833-3 (pbk); ISBN 978-1-118-28017-1 (ebk); ISBN 978-1-118-28018-8 (ebk); ISBN 978-1-118-28019-5 (ebk)

Manufactured in the United States of America

10 9 8 7 6 5 4 3 2 1

WILEY

About the Author

Dan Gookin has been writing about technology for over 20 years. He combines his love of writing with his gizmo fascination to create books that are informative, entertaining, and not boring. Having written more than 120 titles with millions of copies in print translated into over 30 languages, Dan can attest that his method of crafting computer tomes seems to work.

Perhaps his most famous title is the original *DOS For Dummies,* published in 1991. It became the world's fastest-selling computer book, at one time moving more copies per week than the New York Times #1 bestseller (though as a reference, it could not be listed on the NYT Bestseller list). From that book spawned the entire line of *For Dummies* books, which remains a publishing phenomenon to this day.

Dan's most popular titles include *PCs For Dummies, Droid X For Dummies, Word For Dummies,* and *Laptops For Dummies.* He also maintains the vast and helpful website, www.wambooli.com.

Dan holds a degree in Communications/Visual Arts from the University of California, San Diego. Presently, he lives in the Pacific Northwest, where he enjoys spending time with his sons playing video games inside while they watch the gentle woods of Idaho.

Publisher's Acknowledgments

We're proud of this book; please send us your comments at http://dummies.custhelp.com. For other comments, please contact our Customer Care Department within the U.S. at 877-762-2974, outside the U.S. at 317-572-3993, or fax 317-572-4002.

Some of the people who helped bring this book to market include the following:

Acquisitions, Editorial

Senior Project Editor: Nicole Sholly

Senior Acquisitions Editor: Katie Mohr

Copy Editor: Virginia Sanders

Editorial Manager: Kevin Kirschner

Editorial Assistant: Amanda Graham

Sr. Editorial Assistant: Cherie Case

Cover Photo: © iStockphoto.com / Anna Minkevich

Cartoons: Rich Tennant (www.the5thwave.com)

Composition Services

Project Coordinator: Kristie Rees

Layout and Graphics: Claudia Bell, Carl Byers, Joyce Haughey

Proofreaders: Laura Albert, Lauren Mandelbaum, Penny L. Stuart

Indexer: BIM Indexing & Proofreading Services

Publishing and Editorial for Technology Dummies

 Richard Swadley, Vice President and Executive Group Publisher

 Andy Cummings, Vice President and Publisher

 Mary Bednarek, Executive Acquisitions Director

 Mary C. Corder, Editorial Director

Publishing for Consumer Dummies

 Kathleen Nebenhaus, Vice President and Executive Publisher

Composition Services

 Debbie Stailey, Director of Composition Services

Contents at a Glance

Table of Contents

Introduction

*1*t's not a cell phone. It's not a computer. It's the latest craze: the tablet. It exists somewhere between the traditional computer and the newfangled smart phone. That makes the tablet kind of an oddball, but quite a popular oddball.

The Galaxy Tab is Samsung's solution to your mobile, wireless, communications, information, and entertainment needs. Oh, I could blather on and on about how wonderful it is, but my point is simple: The Galaxy Tab does so much, but it comes with such scant documentation that you would merely have to sneeze into the obligatory *Master Your Device* pamphlet and the thing would be ruined.

Anyone wanting more information about how to get the most from the Galaxy Tab needs another source. This book is that source.

About This Book

This book was written to help you get the most from the Galaxy Tab's massive potential. It's a reference. Each chapter covers a specific topic, and the sections within each chapter address an issue related to the topic. The overall idea is to show how things are done on the Galaxy Tab and to help you get the most from the Tab without overwhelming you with information or intimidating you into despair.

Sample sections in this book include

- Making a home for the Tab
- Attaching your Google account to the Galaxy Tab
- Importing contacts from your computer
- Reading an e-mail message
- Running Facebook on your Galaxy Tab
- Talking and video chat
- Making a Skype phone call
- Doing a panoramic shot
- Galaxy Tab travel tips

You have nothing to memorize, no sacred utterances or animal sacrifices, and definitely no PowerPoint presentations. Instead, every section explains a topic as though it's the first thing you read in this book. Nothing is assumed, and everything is cross-referenced. Technical terms and topics, when they come up, are neatly shoved to the side, where they're easily avoided. The idea here isn't to learn anything. This book's philosophy is to help you look it up, figure it out, and get on with your life.

How to Use This Book

This book follows a few conventions for using the Galaxy Tab. First of all, the Galaxy Tab is referred to as the *Galaxy Tab* throughout the book. I might also break down and call it the *Tab* for short, just because, for some reason, typing the word *Galaxy* isn't the easiest thing for me.

The way you interact with the Galaxy Tab is by using its *touchscreen,* the glassy part of the device as it's facing you. The device also has some physical buttons, as well as some holes and connectors. All those items are described in Chapter 1.

There are various ways to touch the screen, which are explained and named in Chapter 3.

Chapter 4 discusses text input on the Galaxy Tab, which involves using an onscreen keyboard. You can also input text by speaking to the Galaxy Tab, which is also covered in Chapter 4.

This book directs you to do things by following numbered steps. Each step involves a specific activity, such as touching something on the screen; for example:

3. Choose Downloads.

This step directs you to touch the text or item labeled *Downloads* on the screen. You might also be told to do this:

3. Touch Downloads.

Some options can be turned off or on, as indicated by a gray box with a green check mark in it, as shown in the margin. By touching the box on the screen, you add or remove the green check mark. When the green check mark appears, the option is on; otherwise, it's off.

The barcodes in the margins are there to help you install recommended apps. They're properly known as QR codes, which describes that type of square barcode. To install the app, scan the QR code using barcode reader software you install on the Galaxy Tab. Chapter 16 discusses how to add software, or *apps,* on the Tab. One of the first apps you get should be a barcode reader. I use the Barcode Scanner app.

Foolish Assumptions

Even though this book is written with the gentle hand-holding required by anyone who is just starting out, or who is easily intimidated, I've made a few assumptions. For example, I assume that you're a human being and not the emperor of Jupiter.

My biggest assumption: You have a Samsung Galaxy Tab of your own. Though you could use this book without owning a Galaxy Tab, I think the people in the Phone Store would grow tired of you reading it while standing in front of the demo model.

There is more than one Galaxy Tab gizmo available. The device covered in this book is the Galaxy Tab 10.1, both the cellular data and Wi-Fi versions. The cellular version is available from Verizon, and potentially from other providers in the near future.

This book doesn't cover the original 7-inch Galaxy Tab, though there is a separate *For Dummies* title specific to that device.

The Wi-Fi Galaxy Tab uses standard computer wireless networking to communicate with the Internet. I call it the Wi-Fi Tab. The Galaxy Tab sold by Verizon uses the digital cellular network to communicate with the Internet, as well as Wi-Fi. I refer to it as the cellular Galaxy Tab.

Only a few subtle differences between the Wi-Fi and cellular Galaxy Tabs exist, and those are noted in the text. Otherwise, whenever I write Galaxy Tab or Tab, the text refers to both models.

I also assume that you have a computer, either a desktop or laptop. The computer can be a PC or Windows computer or a Macintosh. Oh, I suppose it could also be a Linux computer. In any event, I refer to your computer as "your computer" throughout this book. When directions are specific to a PC or Mac, the book says so.

Programs that run on the Galaxy Tab are *apps,* which is short for *applications.* A single program is an app.

Finally, this book doesn't assume that you have a Google account, but already having one helps. Information is provided in Chapter 2 about setting up a Google account — an extremely important part of using the Galaxy Tab. Having a Google account opens up a slew of useful features, information, and programs that make using your Tab more productive.

How This Book Is Organized

This book is divided into five parts, each of which covers a certain aspect of the Galaxy Tab or how it's used.

Part I: The Galaxy in Your Hands

This part of the book is an introduction to the Galaxy Tab. Chapters cover setup and orientation to familiarize you with how the device works. It's a good place to start if you're completely new to the concept of tablet computing, mobile devices, or the Android operating system.

Part II: The Communications Tab

In this part of the book, you read about various ways that the Galaxy Tab can electronically communicate with your online friends. There's texting, e-mail, the web, social networking, and even the much-wanted trick of using the non-phone Galaxy Tab to make phone calls and do video chat.

Part III: The Everything Tab

The Galaxy Tab is pretty much a limitless gizmo. To prove it, the chapters in this part of the book cover all the various and wonderful things the Tab does: It's an eBook reader, a map, a navigator, a camera, a video recorder, a picture book, a portable music player, a calendar, and potentially so much more.

Part IV: Nuts & Bolts

Part IV of this book covers a lot of different topics. Up first is how to connect the Galaxy Tab wirelessly to the Internet as well as to other gizmos, such as a Bluetooth speaker or printer. There's a chapter on sharing and exchanging files with your computer. Then come the maintenance, customization, and troubleshooting chapters.

Part V: The Part of Tens

Things are wrapped up in this book with the traditional *For Dummies* Part of Tens. Each chapter in this part lists ten items or topics. The chapters include tips, tricks, shortcuts, things to remember, and things not to forget, plus a smattering of useful apps that no Galaxy Tab should be without.

Icons Used in This Book

This icon flags useful, helpful tips or shortcuts.

This icon marks a friendly reminder to do something.

This icon marks a friendly reminder not to do something.

This icon alerts you to overly nerdy information and technical discussions of the topic at hand. Reading the information is optional, though it may win you the Daily Double on *Jeopardy!*

Where to Go from Here

Start reading! Observe the table of contents and find something that interests you. Or, look up your puzzle in the index. When those suggestions don't cut it, just start reading Chapter 1.

My e-mail address is dgookin@wambooli.com. Yes, that's my real address. I reply to all e-mail I get, and you'll get a quick reply if you keep your question short and specific to this book. Although I do enjoy saying "Hi," I cannot answer technical support questions, resolve billing issues, or help you troubleshoot your Galaxy Tab. Thanks for understanding.

You can also visit my web page for more information or as a diversion: www.wambooli.com.

Enjoy this book and your Galaxy Tab!

Part I
The Galaxy in Your Hands

I credit Moses with being the first person in history to show mankind how useful tablets can be: Portable. Informative. Great for communications. Valuable to the culture. And despite his tablets' weight, Moses had a good warranty, even though he broke them on purpose.

The Galaxy Tab is the latest, best thing when it comes to tablets. Unlike the stones upon which the Ten Commandments were carved, today's tablets are light-weight and electronic. They're communications devices, dwelling somewhere between the land of cell phones and the realm of computers. Handy. Portable. Chock-full of good information and hours of entertainment. This part of the book introduces you to your new tablet gizmo.

Welcome to Tablet Land

1 thoroughly enjoy getting a new gizmo and opening its box. Expectations build. Joy is released. Then frustration descends like a grand piano pushed out a third-story window. That's because any new electronic device, especially something as sophisticated as the Galaxy Tab, requires a bit of hand-holding. There's a lot of ground to cover, but it all starts with opening the box and with reading this gentle introduction to the Samsung Galaxy Tab.

Set Up Your Galaxy Tab

Odds are good that the folks who sold you the Galaxy Tab have already done some preconfiguration. In the United States, the Tab is available primarily from cellular phone providers, and getting digital cellular service is a usual part of purchasing the Tab.

If you have a cellular (non–Wi-Fi) Tab, it's most likely been unboxed and completely manhandled by the Phone Store people — maybe even in front of your own eyes! That's a necessary step for a 4G Tab, and even though it might have broken your heart (as it did mine), you need that initial setup done before you can unbox and set up the Galaxy Tab for yourself.

✔ If you ordered your Galaxy Tab online, the setup may have been done before the Tab shipped. If not, see Chapter 2.

✔ The initial setup identifies the Tab with the cellular network, giving it a network ID and associating the ID with your cellular bill.

✔ The Wi-Fi Tab doesn't require setup with a cellular provider, but it does require a Wi-Fi signal to use many features. See Chapter 17 for information on configuring your Tab for use with a Wi-Fi network.

✔ Additional software setup is required for the Tab, primarily to link it with your Gmail and other Google accounts on the Internet. See Chapter 2 for the details.

Opening the box

The Galaxy Tab fits snugly inside its box. You'll find it lying right on top. Remove the device by locating and lifting a cardboard tab at the side of the box.

After liberating your Galaxy Tab, remove the plastic sheet that's clinging to the device's front and back. Toss that sheet out, unless you're enrolled in a college art class, in which case you can turn in the sheet for credit as an interpretive sculpture project.

In the box's bottom compartment, you may find

✔ **A USB cable:** You can use it to connect the Tab to a computer or a wall charger.

✔ **A wall charger:** It comes in two pieces. The larger piece has the USB connector, and the smaller piece is customized for your locality's wall sockets.

✔ **Earbud-style earphones:** The Wi-Fi Tab comes with a set of earphones for listening to the Tab's music and other media in the privacy of your own head.

✔ **Pamphlets with warnings and warranty information:** You also receive the brief *Master Your Device* booklet, which you're free to ignore because, honestly, this book puts that thing to shame.

✔ **A Gift Certificate for the Media Hub:** If you're lucky, you might find a $25 gift certificate for the Samsung Media Hub app. Do not throw it away! See Chapter 15.

✔ **The 4G SIM card holder:** For the cellular Tab, you'll need a 4G SIM card. The Phone Store people may have tossed its credit card-sized holder into the box as well. You can throw it out.

✔ **Jimmy Hoffa:** The former labor leader disappeared in 1975, and no one has ever been able to find him. Just in case, look in the bottom of the Galaxy Tab's box to see whether Hoffa's body is there. You never know.

Go ahead and free the USB cable and power charger from their clear plastic cocoons. Assemble the power charger's two pieces, which fit so snugly together that you'll probably never be able to pry them apart.

Keep the box for as long as you own your Galaxy Tab. If you ever need to return the thing or ship it somewhere, the original box is the ideal container. You can shove the pamphlets and papers back into the box as well.

Charging the battery

The first thing that I recommend you do with your Galaxy Tab is give it a full charge. Obey these steps:

1. **Assemble the wall adapter that came with the Tab.**

2. **Attach the USB cable to the Galaxy Tab.**

   The side of the cable end that's labeled *Samsung* faces you as you're looking at the front of the Tab.

3. **Attach the other end of the USB cable to the wall adapter.**

4. **Plug the wall adapter into the wall.**

Upon success, you may see a large Battery icon appear on the Galaxy Tab touchscreen. The icon gives you an idea of the current battery-power level and lets you know that the Galaxy Tab is functioning properly, though you shouldn't be alarmed if the Battery icon fails to appear.

- Your Galaxy Tab most likely came partially charged from the factory, though I still recommend giving it an initial charge just in case, as well as to familiarize yourself with the process.

- The USB cable is used for charging the Galaxy Tab and for connecting it to a computer to share information or exchange files or use the Galaxy Tab as a computer modem. (You find out about this *tethering* process in Chapter 17.)

- You can also charge the Tab by connecting it to a computer's USB port. As long as the computer is on, the Tab charges.

- The battery charges more efficiently if you plug it into a wall rather than charge it from a computer's USB port.

- The Galaxy Tab does not feature a removable battery.

Know Your Way around the Galaxy

"Second star to the right and straight on till morning" may get Peter Pan to Neverland, but for navigating your way around the Galaxy Tab, you need more-specific directions.

Finding things on the Tab

Take heed of Figure 1-1, which is my attempt at illustrating the basic Galaxy Tab hardware features. Follow along on your own Tab as you find key features, described in this section.

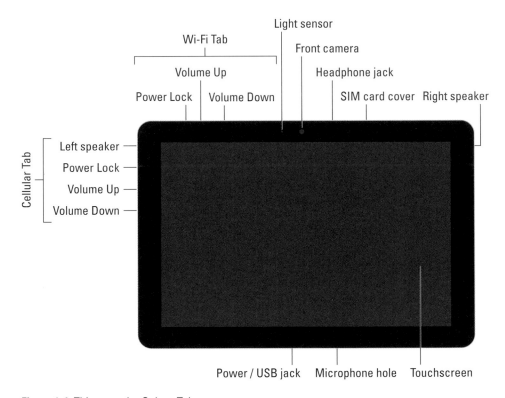

Figure 1-1: Things on the Galaxy Tab.

Dock/USB power connector: The key to discovering things on your Tab is to first find the Power/USB jack, as shown in Figure 1-1. It's a thin slot located on the long side of the Tab, a side I call the *bottom*. Because the Tab has no buttons or other easily identifiable marks on its front, locating the Power/USB jack first helps you orient the Tab as well as locate other goodies, which are illustrated in the figure. The slot is also where the Tab connects to the dock, if you have one. See the later section, "Getting optional accessories."

Touchscreen display: The biggest part of the Tab is its touchscreen display, which occupies almost all the territory on the front of the device. The touchscreen display is a see-touch thing: You look at it and also touch it with your fingers to control the Tab.

Front camera: The Galaxy Tab's front-facing camera is centered above the touchscreen. The camera is used for taking self-portraits as well as for video conferencing.

Light sensor: Though it's difficult to see, just to the left of the front camera is a teensy light sensor. It's used to help adjust the brightness level of the touchscreen.

Around the Galaxy Tab, you find a variety of buttons, holes, connectors, and other doodads, all carefully explained here:

Headphone jack: Atop the Tab case, you see a hole where you can connect standard headphones.

SIM card cover: This spot is used to access the cellular Tab's SIM card, which is inserted into a slot beneath the cover.

Speaker(s): Stereo speakers are located on the left and right sides of the Tab. (Feel free to remove the plastic sticker beneath the right speaker if you find one there.)

Microphone: A tiny hole on the bottom of the Tab (see Figure 1-1) is where you find the device's microphone.

Volume Up/Volume Down: The Tab's volume control is located on the right side of the cellular unit, just below the Power Lock button. On the Wi-Fi Tab, the volume control is on top of the unit, as illustrated in Figure 1-1. The button toward the top of the unit is Volume Up, and the other button is Volume Down.

Power Lock: The Power Lock button is labeled with the universal power icon, shown in the margin. Press this button to turn on the Tab, to lock it (put it to sleep), to wake it up, and to turn it off. Directions for performing these activities are found in Chapter 2.

Figure 1-2 illustrates the back of the Galaxy Tab. It's mostly boring except for the device's main camera, illustrated in the figure. In fact, the entire Tab is physically boring front and back; all the real goodies are found on its edges.

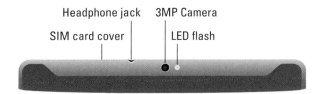

Figure 1-2: Galaxy Tab, upper back.

The back of the Galaxy Tab can be black or white, which is a choice you make when you buy the device. There is no internal difference between the black or white Tab.

- ✔ The Power Lock and Volume buttons are in different locations for the cellular and Wi-Fi Tab models.

- ✔ You'll rarely, if ever, access the SIM card.

- ✔ SIM stands for Subscriber Identity Module. The SIM card is used by your cellular provider to identify your Tab and keep track of the amount of data you access. Yep, that's so you can be billed properly. The SIM also gives your cellular Tab a phone number, though that number is merely an account and not something you can dial into or send a text message.

- ✔ Be careful not to confuse the SIM card with the removable storage media (MicroSD card) used on other tablets and cell phones; they're not the same thing. The Galaxy Tab doesn't use a removable media card.

- ✔ Don't stick anything into the microphone hole. The only things you need to stick into the Tab are the USB cable (or the connector on the dock) or headphones.

Getting optional accessories

You can buy an assortment of handy Galaxy Tab accessories, and I'm sure that the pleasant people at the Phone Store showed you the variety when you bought your Tab. Here are just a few of the items that are available or that you can consider getting in order to complete your Tab experience:

Earphones: You can use any standard cell phone or portable media player earphones with the cellular Galaxy Tab. Simply plug the earphones into the headphone jack at the top of the Tab, and you're ready to go.

Cases: Various cases and case-stands are available for the Galaxy Tab. Some are mere enclosures, like a portfolio. Other cases can also be used as stands to prop up the Tab for easy viewing.

Keyboards: Several different types of keyboards are available for the Galaxy Tab, from the case-keyboard to keyboard docking stands or standard Bluetooth keyboards. They can both prop up the Tab for easy viewing as well as allow for faster typing than can be done on a touchscreen.

Multimedia Dock: The dock is merely a stand you can use to prop up the Tab for easy viewing. It has a speaker jack you can use to connect external speakers.

Galaxy Tab USB Adapter: This USB adapter isn't the same thing as the USB cable that came with your Tab. It's a dongle that plugs into the Tab's Power/ USB jack that allows the Tab to host a USB device, such as a keyboard, mouse, modem, or external storage device (hard drive or optical drive).

HDMI adapter: The adapter plugs into the Power/USB jack. Into the adapter, you can plug an HDMI cable (which is extra) so that you can view the Tab's output on an HDMI-compatible monitor or television.

Screen protectors: These plastic, clingy things are affixed to the front of the Tab, right over the touchscreen. They help protect the touchscreen glass from finger smudges and sneeze globs while still allowing you to use the touchscreen.

Vehicle charger: You can charge the Galaxy Tab in your car when you buy the vehicle charger. This adapter plugs into your car's 12-volt power supply, in the receptacle once known as a cigarette lighter. The vehicle charger is a must-have if you plan to use the Galaxy Tab navigation features in your auto or you need a charge on the road.

Additional accessories may be available. Check the location where your Galaxy Tab was sold to inquire about new items.

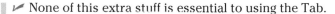

✔ None of this extra stuff is essential to using the Tab.

✔ If the earphones feature a microphone, you can use it for dictation and audio recording on the Tab.

✔ If the earphones feature a button, you can use the button to pause and play music. Press the button once to pause and again to play.

✔ The Galaxy Tab doesn't recognize more than one earphone button. For example, if you use earphones that feature a Volume or Mute button, pressing the extra button does nothing on the Tab.

✔ The set of screen protectors I purchased also came with a microfiber cloth to help clean the Tab's screen, plus a special cleaning-solution wipe. See Chapter 21 for more information about cleaning the Galaxy Tab screen.

✔ See Chapter 17 for more information on pairing your Galaxy Tab with Bluetooth devices, such as a Bluetooth keyboard.

Where to Keep Your Tab

Like your car keys, glasses, wallet, and light saber, you'll want to keep your Galaxy Tab in a place where it's safe, easy to find, and always handy whether you're at home, at work, on the road, or in a galaxy far, far away.

Making a home for the Tab

I recommend keeping the Galaxy Tab in the same spot when you're done using it. My first suggestion is to make a spot next to your computer. Keep the charging cord handy or just plug the cord into the computer's USB port so that you can synchronize information with your computer regularly and keep the Tab charged.

If you have a docking stand, plug your Tab into it when you're not toting it about.

Above all, avoid keeping the Tab in a place where someone might sit on it, step on it, or damage it. For example, don't leave the Tab under a stack of newspapers on a table or counter, where it might get accidentally tossed out or put in the recycle bin.

As long as you remember to return the Tab to the same spot when you're done with it, you'll always know where it is.

Taking the Galaxy Tab with you

If you're like me, you probably carry the Galaxy Tab with you around the house, around the office, at the airport, in the air, or while you're in the car. I hope you're not using the Tab while you're driving! Regardless, have a portable place to store your Tab while you're on the road.

The ideal storage spot for the Tab is a specially designed Galaxy Tab carrying case or pouch, such as the type of pouches mama kangaroos have, but without the expense of owning a zoo. A case keeps the Tab from being dinged, scratched, or even unexpectedly turned on while it's in your backpack, purse, carry-on luggage, or wherever you put the Tab when you aren't using it.

Also see Chapter 19 for information on using the Galaxy Tab on the road.

2

Galaxy Tab On and Off

*1*remember reading my very first computer book, back during the steam-powered "microcomputer" era. The book had very clever and humorous directions for turning on the computer. When it came time to turn off the system, however, there was nothing. No information was written on the proper method for shutting down the computer. No details. No humor. Apparently you just turned off the beastie, either by thunking the big red switch or yanking the plug from the wall socket.

Things are better today, not only with technology but for technology books as well. This chapter not only shows you how to turn on the Galaxy Tab, but it also offers directions on putting the thing to sleep *and* turning it off. As a bonus, there's some setup information tossed in as well. And, no, I didn't forget the humor.

Hello, Tab

In all the effort made by engineers and wizards to make technology easier, one area where they fail is in the basic way you turn on a gizmo. Take the Galaxy Tab: You have two different ways to turn it on, plus special bonus goodies happen the *first* time you turn on the Tab. This section discusses the details.

✔ Initial setup of the Galaxy Tab works best when you already have a Google, or Gmail, account on the Internet. If you lack a Google account, see the section "Setting up a Google account," later in this chapter, for details.

✔ Setup works differently depending on whether you have a cellular Tab or Wi-Fi only. When you have a Wi-Fi–only Tab, the cellular network activation stage is skipped during setup.

✔ See Chapter 17 for information on connecting your Galaxy Tab to a Wi-Fi network.

✔ The Tab doesn't start unless the battery is charged. See Chapter 1.

Turning on your Galaxy Tab (for the first time)

The very, very first time your Galaxy Tab was turned on was most likely at the Phone Store or at a factory if you ordered your Tab online. That process involved hooking up the Tab to the Phone Company's digital network, but that was the extent of the operation.

If the Phone Company hasn't configured your Tab, you have to do it. See the next section, "Activate your Galaxy Tab." Otherwise, skip ahead to the section "Your Google account."

Activate your Galaxy Tab

Follow these steps to turn on your Galaxy Tab for the first time and activate your cellular service:

1. **Press the Power Lock button.**

   You may have to press it longer than you think; when you see the text *Samsung Galaxy Tab 10.1* appear on the screen, the Tab has started.

2. **Unlock the Tab by dragging the Unlock button out toward the unlocking ring, as shown in Figure 2-1.**

   To drag the button, touch it with your finger. Keep your finger on the touchscreen and drag your finger in any direction. The unlocking ring doesn't appear until you move the Unlock button.

   Because you're starting the Tab for the first time, you see the initial screen for the setup program. The first thing to do is to tell the Tab which language to use.

3. **Choose English.**

   Yes, if you're reading this in English, you choose English as the language for your Tab. Если ты говоришь русский, выбрать Русский язык.

4. **If you have a cellular Tab, follow these substeps:**

    a. Touch the Activate button to activate your cellular account.

    b. Obey the directions given by your cellular provider.

    c. Keep reading in the next section, "Your Google account."

5. **If you have a Wi-Fi Tab, follow these substeps:**

    a. Touch the Start button.

    b. Choose a Wi-Fi network from the list displayed.

    c. If prompted, use the onscreen keyboard to type in the Wi-Fi password.

    d. Touch the Connect button.

    e. Touch the Next button

    f. Skip to Step 4 in the next section, "Your Google account."

After you activate the Tab, you see a Congratulations message. Touch the text Proceed with the Setup Process and continue reading with the next section.

If you have trouble activating the cellular Tab, contact your cellular provider. You need to read information from the Galaxy Tab's box, which has activation information printed on a label.

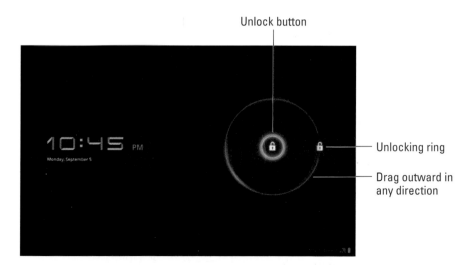

Figure 2-1: The main Galaxy Tab unlock screen.

Your Google account

After your Galaxy Tab has been activated, the next step in configuring it is to synchronize the device with your Google account. Obey:

1. **Start the Galaxy Tab, if you haven't already.**

   Press the Power Lock button until you see the *Samsung Galaxy Tab 10.1* text on the screen.

2. **If necessary, unlock the screen as described in the preceding section.**

3. **Choose your language and touch the Start button.**

4. **Ensure that there is a green check mark by the items listed on the Use Google's Location Service screen.**

   The two items help the Tab find itself on the Planet Earth. If the items aren't selected, touch the little square next to each item to place a green check mark there.

5. **Touch the Next button.**

6. **If prompted, enter the date and time.**

   Wi-Fi tabs that aren't currently connected to a network need to have their time updated.

7. **Touch the Next button again.**

   It's time to set up your Google account.

8. **Touch the Email text box and type your Google account name.**

   Because you read the Tip icon at the start of this section, you've already set up and configured a Google account. Use the onscreen keyboard to type your Google account's e-mail address into the Email text box.

   See Chapter 4 for more information about typing text on your Galaxy Tab.

9. **Touch the Password field and type your Google account password.**

10. **Touch the Sign In button.**

11. **Ensure that there are two green check marks for the items on the Backup and Restore screen.**

    With both check marks in place, the information on your Tab is synchronized with existing information in your Google account on the Internet. It's a good thing.

12. **Touch the Done button.**

The good news is that you're done. The better news is that you need to complete this setup only once on your Galaxy Tab. From this point on, starting the Tab works as described in the next few sections.

✔ The information synchronized on the Galaxy Tab includes the following items from your Google account on the Internet: the contact list, Gmail messages, calendar appointments, and other "Googly" information.

✔ One of the first things you may notice to be synchronized between your Tab and Google is your Gmail inbox. See Chapter 6 for more information on Gmail.

✔ See the later sidebar "Who is this Android person?" for more information about the Android operating system.

Turning on your Galaxy Tab

To turn on your Galaxy Tab, press and hold the Power Lock button. After a few seconds, you see the word *Samsung Galaxy Tab 10.1* and then some hypnotic animation. The Tab is starting.

Eventually, you see the main unlock screen, shown earlier, in Figure 2-1. Use your finger to slide the Unlock button outside the unlocking ring, as indicated in the figure. After your Galaxy Tab is unlocked, you can start using it — and, unlike the first time you turned the thing on, you aren't prompted to complete the setup routine. (well, unless you skipped setup the first time).

✔ Refer to Figure 1-1, in Chapter 1, for the specific location of the Power Lock button.

✔ You probably won't turn on your Galaxy Tab much in the future. Mostly, you'll wake the gizmo from an electronic snooze. See the later section, "Waking up the Tab."

Working the various lock screens

The unlock screen you see when you turn on (or wake up) the Tab isn't a tough lock to pick. In fact, it's known as the Not Secured option in the Set Lock Screen window. If you've added more security, you might see any one of three different lock screens.

The pattern lock, shown in Figure 2-2, requires that you trace your finger along a pattern that includes as many as nine dots on the screen. After you match the pattern, the Tab is unlocked, and you can start using it.

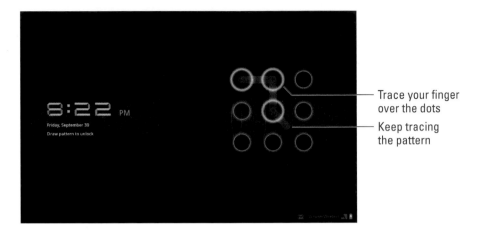

Figure 2-2: The Pattern Lock screen.

The PIN lock is shown in Figure 2-3. It requires that you input a secret number to unlock the Tab. Touch the OK button to accept input, or use the Del button to back up and erase.

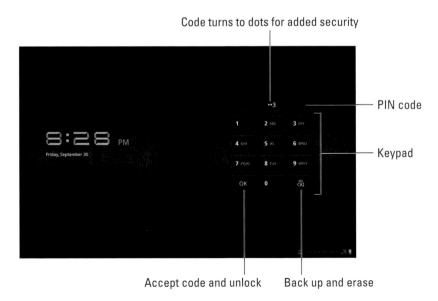

Figure 2-3: The PIN Lock screen.

Finally, the password lock requires that you type a multicharacter password on the screen before the Tab is unlocked. Touch the text box as shown in Figure 2-4 to see the onscreen keyboard and type the password. Touch the OK button to accept the password and unlock the Galaxy Tab.

Figure 2-4: The Password Lock screen.

Whether or not you see these various lock screens depends on how you've configured the Galaxy Tab's security. Specific directions for setting the locks, or for removing them and returning to the standard screen lock, are found in Chapter 20.

- ✔ The pattern lock can start at any dot, not necessarily the upper-left dot, as shown earlier in Figure 2-2.

- ✔ The password lock must contain at least one letter and number, though it can also include a smattering of symbols and other characters.

- ✔ For additional information on working the onscreen keyboard, see Chapter 4.

Waking up the Tab

You'll probably leave your Galaxy Tab on all the time. It was designed that way. The battery lasts quite a while, so when the Tab is bored or when you've ignored it for a while, it falls asleep. Well, it's technically named *Sleep mode*, a special low-power, energy-saving state where the Tab's screen goes blank.

When the Galaxy Tab is sleeping, you wake it up by pressing the Power Lock button. Unlike turning on the Tab, a quick press of the Power Lock button is all that's needed.

After waking the Tab, you see the unlock screen, shown in Figure 2-1. Or, if you've configured the Tab for more security, you see one of the unlocking screens shown in Figures 2-2 through 2-4. Simply unlock the screen, and you can start using the Tab.

- The Galaxy Tab continues to run while it's sleeping. Mail is received, as are text messages. The Tab also continues to play music while it's sleeping, and the display is off.

- Touching the touchscreen when it's off doesn't wake up the Tab.

- Loud noises don't wake up the Tab.

- The Tab doesn't snore while it's sleeping.

- See the section "Putting the Tab to sleep," later in this chapter, for information on manually snoozing the Galaxy Tab.

TECHNICAL STUFF

Who is this Android person?

Just like your computer, your Galaxy Tab has an operating system. It's the main program in charge of all the software (other programs) inside your Tab. Unlike on your computer, however, Android is a mobile device operating system, designed primarily for use in cell phones but also in the Galaxy Tab. (For that reason, you often see the Tab referred to as a *phone* in various apps.)

You find the Android operating system used on many of today's most popular smart phones, including the Droid 3, HTC Thunderbolt, and other phones I can't think of right now. By using Android, the Tab has access to all the Android software — the *apps* or programs — available to Android phones and other mobile devices. You can read how to add those apps to your Tab in Chapter 16.

Android is based on the Linux operating system, which is also a computer operating system, though it's much more stable and bug-free than Windows, so it's not as popular. Google owns, maintains, and develops Android, which is why your online Google information is synced with the Galaxy Tab.

The Android mascot, shown here, often appears on Android apps or hardware. He has no official name, though most folks call him Andy.

Account Creation and Configuration

After you've done the initial configuration as described earlier in this chapter, there's nothing else you need to do to set up the Galaxy Tab. If you've skipped that step or you need to create a Google account, follow the directions in this section to complete the setup process.

Setting up a Google account

To get the most from your Galaxy Tab, you must have a Google account. If you don't already have one, drop everything (but not this book) and follow these steps to obtain one:

1. **Open your computer's web browser program.**

   Yes, it works best if you use your computer, not the Tab, to complete these steps.

2. **Visit the main Google page at** www.google.com.

   Type **www.google.com** into the web browser's address bar.

3. **Click the Sign In link.**

   Another page opens, and on it you can log in to your Google account, but you don't have a Google account, so:

4. **Click the link to create a new account.**

   The link is typically found beneath the text boxes where you would log in to your Google account. As I write this chapter, the link is titled Sign Up for a New Google Account.

5. **Continue heeding the directions until you've created your own Google account.**

Eventually, your account is set up and configured.

To try things out, log off from Google and then log back in. That way, you ensure that you've done everything properly — and remembered your password. (Your web browser may even prompt you to let it remember the password for you.)

I also recommend creating a bookmark for your account's Google page: The Ctrl+D or ⌘+D keyboard shortcut is used to create a bookmark in just about any web browser.

Continue reading in the next section for information on synchronizing your new Google account with the Galaxy Tab.

Attaching your Google account to the Galaxy Tab

Don't fret if you've failed to obey the prompts and neglected to sign in to your Google account when first configuring the Galaxy Tab. You can rerun the configuration setup at any time. Just follow these steps:

1. **Turn on or wake up the Galaxy Tab if it's not already on and eagerly awaiting your next move.**

2. **Unlock the Tab if necessary.**

   You can find directions earlier in this chapter, in the section "Working the various lock screens."

 3. **Touch the Apps Menu button.**

   The Apps Menu button is located in the upper-right corner of the Home screen. Its icon is shown in the margin.

4. **Choose the Settings icon.**

   The Settings screen appears, which contains commands for configuring and setting options for the Galaxy Tab.

5. **Choose Accounts & Sync.**

6. **Touch the Add Account button in the upper-right part of the screen.**

7. **Choose Google Accounts.**

   At this point, you're signing into your Google account on the Galaxy Tab. Refer to the earlier section, "Your Google account," and start reading at Step 7.

Your goal is to synchronize your Google account information on the Internet with the information on your Galaxy Tab.

Adding your personal e-mail account to the Tab, as well as other free online e-mail accounts, is covered in Chapter 6. Refer to Chapter 8 for information on adding social networking accounts, such as Facebook and Twitter.

Goodbye, Tab

I know of three ways to say goodbye to your Galaxy Tab, and only one of them involves training an elephant. The other two methods are documented in this section.

Putting the Tab to sleep

To sleep the Tab, simply press its Power Lock button. The display goes dark; the Tab is asleep.

- ✓ In Sleep mode, the Galaxy Tab still works, still receives e-mail, and can still play music. But it's not using as much power as it would with the display on.

- ✓ The Galaxy Tab will probably spend most of its time in Snooze mode.

- ✓ Snoozing doesn't turn off the Tab.

- ✓ Any timers or alarms you set still activate when the Tab is in Sleep mode. See Chapter 15 for information on setting timers and alarms.

- ✓ To wake up the Tab, press and release the Power Lock button. See the section "Waking up the Tab," earlier in this chapter.

Controlling the sleep timeout

You can manually snooze the Galaxy Tab at any time by pressing the Power Lock button. In fact, some documentation calls it the Power *Lock* button because snoozing the Tab is the same as locking it. When you don't manually snooze the tab, it automatically goes into Sleep mode after a given period of inactivity, just like Uncle Tony does during family gatherings.

You have control over the snooze timeout value, which can be set anywhere from 15 seconds to 1 hour. Obey these steps:

1. **At the Home screen, touch the Apps Menu icon button.**

2. **Choose Settings.**

3. **Choose Screen.**

4. **Choose Timeout.**

5. **Choose a timeout value from the list.**

   I prefer 1 minute, which is also the standard value.

6. **Touch the Home icon button to return to the Home screen.**

The sleep timer begins after a period of inactivity; when you don't touch the screen or tap an icon button, the timer starts ticking. About 5 seconds before the timeout value you set (refer to Step 5), the touchscreen dims. Then it turns off, and the Tab goes to sleep. If you touch the screen before then, the timer is reset.

Turning off the Galaxy Tab

To turn off the Tab, heed these steps:

1. **Press and hold the Power Lock button.**

   You see the Tablet Options menu, shown in Figure 2-5. (The Wi-Fi Tab's Tablet Options menu lacks a Restart command.)

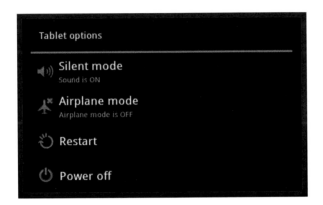

Figure 2-5: The Tablet Options menu.

 If you chicken out and don't want to turn off the Tab, touch the Back icon button to dismiss the Tablet Options menu.

2. **Touch the Power Off item.**

3. **Touch OK.**

   The Galaxy Tab turns itself off.

The Tab doesn't run when it's off, so it doesn't remind you of appointments, collect e-mail, or let you hear any alarms you've set. The Tab also isn't angry with you for turning it off, though you may sense some resentment when you turn it on again.

Be sure to keep the Tab in a safe place while it's turned off. See the section on where to keep your tab in Chapter 1.

Find Your Way around the Galaxy

I'm not certain, but I think the Galaxy Tab is more powerful than all the computers in the bat cave from the 1960s TV show, *Batman*. Those computers were impressive: They had lots of buttons and flashing lights. In today's high-tech world, however, sophisticated devices don't have a lot of buttons and flashing lights. In fact, the more sophisticated the device, such as your Galaxy Tab, the fewer the buttons and lights.

To accommodate for the lack of buttons, the Galaxy Tab features a touchscreen. You use the touchscreen to control the Tab, which is probably a new experience for you. To get you up to speed, and to get Batman up to speed should he be reading this book, I present this chapter on understanding the Galaxy Tab's touchscreen interface.

Basic Operations

It's not a computer. It's not a phone. The Galaxy Tab is truly something different, probably unlike anything you've ever used. To control this unique gizmo, you have to familiarize yourself with some basic tablet operations, as covered in this section.

Touching the touchscreen

Bereft of buttons and knobs, the way you control the Galaxy Tab is for the most part by manipulating things on the touchscreen with one or two fingers. It doesn't matter which fingers you use, and feel free to experiment with other body parts as well, though I find fingers to be handy.

You have specific ways to touch the touchscreen, and those specific ways have names. Here's the list:

Touch: The simplest way to manipulate the touchscreen is to touch it. You touch an object, an icon, a control, a menu item, a doodad, and so on. The touch operation is similar to a mouse click on a computer. It may also be referred to as a *tap* or *press*.

Double-tap: Touch the screen twice in the same location. Double-tapping can be used to zoom in on an image or a map, but it can also zoom out. Because of the double-tap's dual nature, I recommend using the pinch or spread operation instead when you want to zoom.

Long-press: A long-press occurs when you touch part of the screen and keep your finger down. Depending on what you're doing, a pop-up menu may appear, or the item you're long-pressing may get "picked up" so that you can move it around after a long-press. *Long-press* might also be referred to as *touch and hold* in some documentation.

Swipe: To swipe, you touch your finger on one spot and then drag it to another spot. Swipes can go up, down, left, or right, which moves the touchscreen content in the direction you swipe your finger. A swipe can be fast or slow. It's also called a *flick* or *slide*.

Pinch: A pinch involves two fingers, which start out separated and then are brought together. The effect is used to *zoom out,* to reduce the size of an image or see more of a map.

Spread: The opposite of pinch is spread. You start out with your fingers together and then spread them. The spread is used to *zoom in,* to enlarge an image or see more detail on a map.

Rotate: A few apps let you rotate an image on the screen by touching with two fingers and twisting them around a center point. Think of turning a combination lock on a safe, and you get the rotate operation.

You can't manipulate the touchscreen while wearing gloves unless they're gloves specially designed for using electronic touchscreens, such as the gloves that Batman wears.

Changing the orientation

The Galaxy Tab features a gizmo called an *accelerometer*. It determines in which direction the Tab is pointed or whether you've reoriented the device from an upright to a horizontal position, or even upside down. That way, the information on the Tab always appears upright, no matter how you hold it.

To demonstrate how the Galaxy Tab orients itself, rotate the Tab to the left or right. The Tab can be used in either vertical or horizontal orientations. Most apps change their orientation to match however you've turned the Tab, such as the Home screen shown in Figure 3-1.

Vertical orientation

Horizontal orientation

Figure 3-1: Galaxy Tab orientation.

The rotation feature may not work for all apps, especially Android apps designed for use on cell phones and not tablets. Some games present themselves in one orientation only.

 ✔ You can lock the orientation if the rotating screen bothers you. See the section "Making Quick Settings," later in this chapter.

 ✔ This book shows the Home screen, as well as most other apps, in a horizontal orientation. See the later section, "Behold the Home Screen," for more information on the Home screen.

 ✔ A great application for demonstrating the Galaxy Tab accelerometer is the game *Labyrinth*. It can be purchased at the Android Market, or the free version, *Labyrinth Lite,* can be downloaded. See Chapter 16 for more information about the Android Market.

Controlling the volume

There are times when the sound level is too loud. There are times when it's too soft. And, there are those rare times when it's just right. Finding that just-right level is the job of the volume control buttons that cling to the left side of the Galaxy Tab.

Pressing the top part of the Volume button makes the volume louder; pressing the bottom part makes the volume softer. As you press the button, a graphic appears on the touchscreen to illustrate the relative volume level, as shown in Figure 3-2.

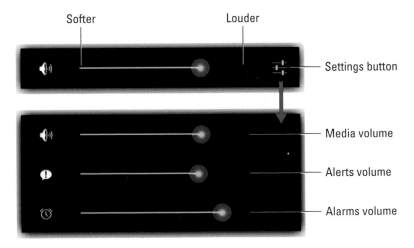

Figure 3-2: Setting the volume.

Touch the Settings button, shown in Figure 3-2, to see more detailed volume controls. You can individually set the volume for media, alerts, and alarms, as shown in the expanded onscreen volume control: Drag the green dot left or right to set the volume.

- When the volume is set all the way down, the Tab is silenced.
- Silencing the Tab by sliding down the volume level places it into Vibration mode.
- The Volume button works even when the Tab is snoozing (in Sleep mode or when the touchscreen display is off). That means you don't need to wake the Tab if you're playing music and need to adjust the volume.
- Refer to Chapter 20 for information on placing the Tab into Vibration mode.

Behold the Home Screen

The main base from which you begin exploration of the Galaxy Tab is the *Home* screen. It's the first thing you see after unlocking the Tab, and the place you go to whenever you quit an application.

Touring the Home screen

The main Home screen for the Galaxy Tab is illustrated in Figure 3-3.

There are several fun and interesting things to notice on the Home screen:

Home screen buttons: Special symbols are found on three corners of the Home screen, as well as in quite a few apps. The symbols identify buttons you touch to activate common Galaxy Tab features.

Notification icons: These icons come and go, depending on what happens in your digital life. For example, new icons appear whenever you receive a new e-mail message or have a pending appointment. The section "Reviewing notifications," later in this chapter, describes how to deal with notifications.

Status icons: These icons represent the Tab's current condition, such as the type of network it's connected to, signal strength, and battery status, as well as whether the Tab is connected to a Wi-Fi network or using Bluetooth, for example.

App icons: The meat of the meal on the Home screen plate is where the action takes place: app (application) icons. Touching an icon runs its program.

Home screen buttons   Widget   Home screen buttons

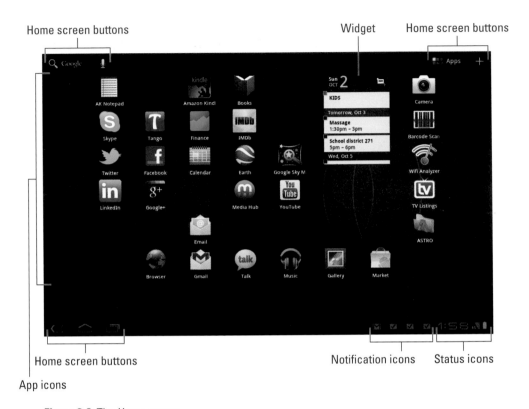

Home screen buttons   Notification icons   Status icons

App icons

Figure 3-3: The Home screen.

Widgets: A widget is a teensy program that can display information, let you control the Tab, access features, or do something purely amusing. You can read more about widgets in Chapter 20.

Ensure that you recognize the names of the various parts of the Home screen, because the terms are used throughout this book and in whatever other scant Galaxy Tab documentation exists. Directions for using the Home screen gizmos are found throughout this chapter.

✔ The Home screen is entirely customizable. You can add and remove icons from the Home screen, add widgets and shortcuts, and even change wallpaper (background) images. See Chapter 20 for more information.

✔ When you rotate the Galaxy Tab, the Home screen changes its orientation to match. (Refer to Figure 3-1.) The horizontal Home screen features all the same gizmos as the vertical Home screen, but because of the narrow width, many of the items shuffle around.

✓ Touching a part of the Home screen that doesn't feature an icon or a control does nothing. That is, unless you're using the *live wallpaper* feature. In that case, touching the screen changes the wallpaper in some way, depending on the wallpaper that's selected. You can read more about live wallpaper in Chapter 20.

Accessing multiple Home screens

The Home screen is more than what you see. It's actually an entire street of Home screens, with only one Home screen *panel* displayed at a time.

To switch from one panel to another, swipe the Home screen left or right. There are two panels to the left of the main Home screen panel, and two panels to the right.

When you touch the Home icon button, you're returned to the last Home screen panel you viewed. To return to the main, center Home screen panel, touch the Home icon button a second time.

Using the icon buttons

Festooning the Galaxy Tab Home screen are various symbols or icons. Those icons identify buttons you can touch. The icon buttons are used to control the Tab, seeing how the device lacks the necessary physical buttons. Table 3-1 lists the most common icon buttons.

Table 3-1		Common Icon Buttons
Button	*Name*	*Function*
🔍	Search	Search the Galaxy Tab or the Internet for some tidbit of information.
🎤	Dictation	Use your voice to dictate text. On the Home screen, dictation is used with the Google Search function.
▦	Apps Menu	Display the Apps Menu.
➕	Add	Add icons, widgets, and shortcuts or change wallpaper.

(continued)

Table 3-1 *(continued)*

Button	Name	Function
	Back	Go back, close, or dismiss the onscreen keyboard.
	Home	Go to the Home screen.
	Recent	Display recently opened apps.

The buttons listed in Table 3-1 are pretty common, available most of the time you use the Galaxy Tab. Beyond those buttons are other buttons and symbols used in the Tab's interface. They're listed in Table 3-2.

Table 3-2 **Other Icon Buttons**

Button	Name	Description
	Menu	This icon button displays the menu for an app. It's often found in the upper-right corner of the screen.
	Old Menu	This icon button is used primarily to display menus for older Android apps. It appears at the bottom of the screen, next to the Recent Apps icon button.
	Favorite	Touch the Favorite icon button to flag a favorite item, such as a contact or web page.
	Gear	The Gear icon button is used to display a settings menu or options for an app or feature.
	Settings	This Settings icon button is the newer version of the Gear icon button.
	Close	This button is used to close a window or clear text from an input field.
	Share	The Share icon button allows you to share information stored on the Tab via e-mail, social networking, or other Internet services.

Not every icon button always performs the actions listed in Table 3-2. For example, if there's no menu to open, pressing the Menu button does nothing.

✔ Various sections throughout this book give examples of using the icon buttons. Their images appear in the book's margins where relevant.

✔ The Google Search button may or may not have the word Google next to it. (Refer to Figure 3-3.) When the button is referenced in this book, only the magnifying glass is referenced, as shown in Table 3-1.

✔ The Add button is also known as the Customize button. Beyond the Home screen, you'll find that button in apps where you can also add or customize items.

 ✔ The Back icon button changes its appearance when the onscreen keyboard or recent apps list is displayed. It's still the Back icon button, but it changes appearance, as shown in the margin. Touch the button to dismiss the item that popped up on the screen.

✔ The little triangle in the lower-right corner of the Menu icon button is used in many apps to denote a pop-up or shortcut menu attached to something on the screen. Touch that triangle to see the shortcut menu.

✔ Other common symbols are used on icon buttons in various apps. For example, the standard Play/Pause icons are used as well as variations on the symbols shown in Tables 3-1 and 3-2.

Home Screen Chores

To become a cat, you must know how to perform several duties: Sleep, eat, catch critters, and cause mischief. A cat's life isn't difficult, and neither is your Galaxy Tab life, as long as you know how to do some basic duties on the Home screen. As with the cat, you have only a few duties to know about.

Starting an application

It's blissfully simple to run an application on the Home screen: Touch its icon. The application starts.

✔ Not all applications appear on the Home screen, but all of them appear when you display the Apps Menu screen. See the section "Visiting the Apps Menu," later in this chapter.

✔ When an application closes or you quit the application, you're returned to the Home screen.

✔ Application is abbreviated as *app*.

Accessing a widget

Like application icons, widgets can appear on the Home screen. To use a widget, touch it. What happens next, of course, depends on the widget and what it does.

For example, the YouTube widget is preset on the first Home screen panel to the left of the main Home screen. You can swipe your finger across that widget to peruse videos like you're flipping the pages in a book; touch a video to view it.

Other widgets do interesting things, display useful information, or give you access to the Galaxy Tab's features.

See Chapter 20 for details on working with widgets.

Reviewing notifications

Notifications appear as icons at the bottom right of the Home screen, as illustrated earlier, in Figure 3-3. You can check out notifications individually or look at the whole swath of them all at once.

To review an individual notification, touch its icon at the bottom right of the screen, as illustrated in Figure 3-4. The notification pop-up disappears rather quickly, so to act on the notification, you must touch it, as indicated in the figure. Or you can dismiss the notification by touching the X (Close) button.

Figure 3-4: Reviewing a single notification.

After acting upon or closing a notification, it disappears from the list. Or just touch anywhere else on the Home screen to dismiss the pop-up window.

Only a maximum of the last five most recent notifications are shown on the bottom of the screen. To see the rest, you must pop up the full notification list.

To see all notifications, touch the time display in the lower-right corner of the Home screen. You see a scrolling list of all notifications, as shown in Figure 3-5.

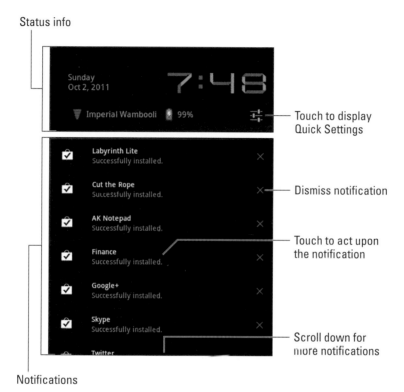

Status info

Sunday
Oct 2, 2011

7:48

Imperial Wambooli 99%

Touch to display
Quick Settings

Labyrinth Lite
Successfully installed.

Cut the Rope
Successfully installed.

Dismiss notification

AK Notepad
Successfully installed.

Finance
Successfully installed.

Touch to act upon
the notification

Google+
Successfully installed.

Skype
Successfully installed.

Scroll down for
more notifications

Twitter

Notifications

Figure 3-5: All the notifications.

You can scroll through the list, as shown in Figure 3-5. To peruse a specific notification, touch it. To close a notification, touch the X (Close) button on the right.

To hide the notification list, touch the Back icon button. Or you can touch anywhere else on the Home screen.

  ✔ The notifications at the bottom of the Home screen might not show up if the Notifications Quick Settings has been turned off. See the next section.

  ✔ If you don't deal with the notifications, they can stack up!

  ✔ Notification icons disappear after they've been chosen.

  ✔ Dismissing some notifications doesn't prevent them from appearing again in the future. For example, notifications to update your programs continue to appear, as do calendar reminders.

  ✔ Some programs, such as Facebook and the various Twitter apps, don't display notifications unless you're logged in. See Chapter 8.

  ✔ The Galaxy Tab plays a sound, or *ringtone,* when a new notification floats in. You can choose which sound plays; see Chapter 20 for more information.

  ✔ See Chapter 15 for information on dismissing calendar reminders.

Making Quick Settings

The Quick Settings are a clutch of popular Tab features, each of which can be quickly accessed from the notifications pop-up. To see the Quick Settings, pop up the notifications list as described in the preceding section. Then touch the Settings icon button, as shown in the margin. The Quick Settings are shown in Figure 3-6.

You can use several items in the Quick Settings list to manipulate various options on the Galaxy Tab:

Airplane Mode/Flight Mode: Turns off the Tab's wireless radios that are not allowed to be on during an airplane trip. See Chapter 19 for more information on using the Galaxy Tab while aloft.

Wi-Fi: Displays the Wireless & Networks, Wi-Fi Settings window. See Chapter 17 for information on accessing wireless networks.

Auto-Rotate Screen: Enables the Tab's ability to rotate and reorient the touchscreen based on which way you're holding the Galaxy Tab. See the section "Changing the orientation," earlier in this chapter.

Brightness: Specifies how bright the touchscreen appears. Touch the word Auto to enable automatic brightness based on ambient light. Otherwise, drag the dot left or right to make the screen brighter or darker, respectively.

Notifications: Turns on or off the notification icon display at the bottom of the touchscreen.

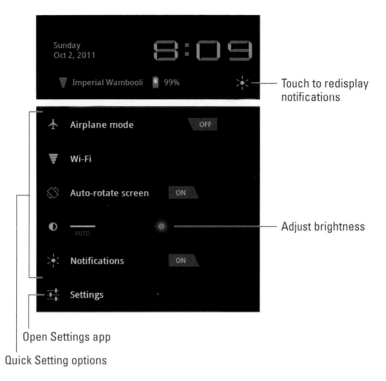

Sunday
Oct 2, 2011

8:09

Imperial Wambooli   99%   Touch to redisplay
notifications

✈ Airplane mode   OFF

▼ Wi-Fi

◇ Auto-rotate screen   ON

◐ ————   Adjust brightness
AUTO

✳ Notifications   ON

Settings

Open Settings app

Quick Setting options

Figure 3-6: Galaxy Tab Quick Settings.

The last item in the Quick Settings list is titled Settings. It's not an on-off item, but rather a shortcut to the Settings app on the Apps Menu screen. You use the Settings app to control everything on the Galaxy Tab, not just the few items on the Quick Settings list.

Visiting the Apps Menu

The application icons you see on the Home screen don't represent all the apps in your Galaxy Tab. Those icons aren't even applications themselves; they're shortcuts. To see all applications installed on your Galaxy Tab, you must visit the Apps Menu screen. To do so, touch the Apps button on the Home screen. You see the first panel of the Apps Menu, as shown in Figure 3-7.

You can find any additional apps by swiping the Apps Menu screen to the left.

View only apps you've installed   Get more apps at the Market

Another page of apps

Scroll right to see more apps

Figure 3-7: The Apps Menu screen.

As you install apps, they're added to the Apps Menu. New apps are inserted into the Apps Menu alphabetically, which means that any time you add an app the Apps Menu gets re-sorted. That makes it difficult to locate apps by memory, though my advice in Chapter 20 is to place apps you use most often on the Home screen.

To view only apps you've installed on your Galaxy Tab, touch My Apps at the top of the Apps Menu screen, as shown in Figure 3-7.

✔ See Chapter 16 for information on getting more apps for your Galaxy Tab.

✔ The terms *program, application,* and *app* all mean the same thing.

Reviewing recent apps

If you're like me, you probably use the same apps over and over on your Galaxy Tab. You can easily access that list of recent apps by touching the Recent Apps icon button on the Home screen. When you do, you see a pop-up list of apps most recently accessed, similar to the list shown in Figure 3-8.

Scroll up for more

App thumbnails

Hide list

Recently opened apps

Figure 3-8: Recently used apps.

To reopen an app, choose it from the list. Otherwise you can hide the recently used apps list by touching the Back (or Back-Hide) icon button.

  For the programs you use all the time, consider creating shortcuts on the Home screen. Chapter 20 describes how to create shortcuts for apps, as well as shortcuts to popular contacts, shortcuts for e-mail, and all sorts of fun stuff.

4

Typing and Text on the Tab

*B*elieve it or not, the interface to the first computers had no monitor. Nope, computer scientists and proto-nerds of the 1960s used teletype machines. That was if they were lucky; before then punch cards were popular. But historically speaking, a physical keyboard has always been a part of the high tech scene. Until now.

Your Galaxy Tab lacks a real, live keyboard. All it has is a touchscreen, though you can use that touchscreen for typing. It works because of something called the *onscreen keyboard*. Not only that, but you can use your finger to edit and manipulate the text you type. Tab typing is a new concept. It can be frustrating. It can be strange. It can be understood and accepted if you follow my advice in this chapter.

The Old Hunt-and-Peck

The old mechanical typewriters required a lot of effort to press their keys. It was forceful: clackity-clack-clack. Electronic typewriters made typing easier. And, of course, the computer is the easiest thing to type on. A tablet? That device takes some getting used to because its keys are merely flat rectangles on a touchscreen. If this concept doesn't drive you nuts, typing on a tablet is something you should master with relative ease.

Using the onscreen keyboard

For text communications on the Galaxy Tab, you touch an onscreen keyboard. That keyboard pops up whenever the Tab requires text input or when you have an opportunity to type something.

The basic onscreen keyboard is officially known as the Samsung keypad. Its layout is shown in Figure 4-1. You'll be relieved to see that it's similar to the standard computer keyboard, though some of the keys change their function depending on what you're typing.

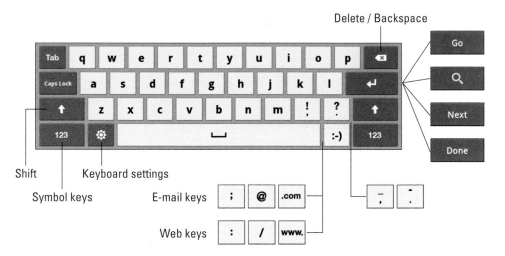

Figure 4-1: The Samsung keypad onscreen keyboard.

Figure 4-1 illustrates the onscreen keyboard in Alphabetic mode. You see keys from A through Z in lowercase. You also see a Shift key for producing capital letters, and a Delete key, which works to backspace and erase.

The Enter key below the Delete key changes its look depending on what you're typing. Five variations are shown in Figure 4-1. Here's what each one does:

> **Enter/Return:** Just like the Enter or Return key on your computer keyboard, this key ends a paragraph of text. It's used mostly when filling in long stretches of text or when multiline input is available.

> **Go:** This action key directs the app to proceed with a search, accept input, or perform another action.

Search: You see the Search key appear when you're searching for something on the Tab. Touching the key starts the search.

Next: This key appears when you're typing information into multiple fields. Touching this key switches from one field to the next, such as when typing a username and password.

Done: This key appears whenever you've finished typing text in the final field of a screen that has several fields. Sometimes it dismisses the onscreen keyboard, sometimes not.

The large U key at the bottom center of the onscreen keyboard is the Space key. Next to it is the Smiley key, which inserts the colon, dash, and right parenthesis characters into your text, commonly known as the *smiley*.

Between the Space and Smiley keys, you'll occasionally see two sets of three additional keys. These sets of keys are used to assist when typing e-mail and web page addresses. The .com and www. keys insert all those characters with one key press.

The ! and ? keys also change, as shown in Figure 4-1: When typing in some situations, the exclamation point changes to an underline, and the question mark changes to a hyphen. When does that happen? I don't know, but watch out for it.

Also see the next section for accessing the number-and-symbol keys on the onscreen keyboard.

- ✔ If you pine for a real keyboard, one that exists in the fourth dimension, you're not stuck. See the nearby sidebar, "A real keyboard?"

- ✔ To dismiss the onscreen keyboard, touch the Back-Hide icon button that replaces the standard Back icon button on the touchscreen.

- ✔ To re-summon the keyboard, touch any text field or spot on the screen where typing is permitted.

- ✔ Touch the Keyboard Settings (Gear) key to make adjustments to the onscreen keyboard.

- ✔ The keyboard reorients itself when you turn the Tab to a vertical position, though it's narrower and it may not be as easy on your fingers for typing.

- ✔ Some folks feel that the onscreen keyboard isn't complete unless there is a dictation button. See the section "Activating voice input on the keyboard," later in this chapter, for the secret instructions.

A real keyboard?

If typing is your thing and the onscreen keyboard doesn't do it for you, consider getting the Galaxy Tab *keyboard dock:* This docking stand props up the Tab at a good viewing angle but, unlike the multimedia dock, features a laptop-size keyboard.

Another choice for typing in the real world is to get a Bluetooth keyboard. I feel it's a better option than the keyboard dock because Bluetooth is wireless, which kind of goes well with the whole mobile computing paradigm. The Galaxy Tab works with any Bluetooth keyboard, and you can read more about Bluetooth in Chapter 17.

Accessing other symbols

You're not limited to typing only the symbols you see on the alphabetic keyboard, shown in Figure 4-1. The onscreen keyboard has many more symbols available, which you can see by touching the 123 key. Touching this key gives you access to three additional keyboard layouts, as shown in Figure 4-2.

Touch the 1/3, 2/3, or 3/3 key to switch between various symbol keyboards, as illustrated in Figure 4-2.

To return to the standard "alpha" keyboard (refer to Figure 4-1), touch the ABC key.

You can access special character keys from the main alphabetic keyboard, providing you know a secret: Long-press (touch and hold) a key. When you do, you see a pop-up palette of additional characters, similar to the ones shown for the A key in Figure 4-3.

Choose a character from the pop-up palette or touch the X button to close the pop-up palette.

Not every character has a special pop-up palette.

Typing duties

It's cinchy to type on the onscreen keyboard: Just press a letter to produce the character. It works just like a computer keyboard in that respect. Plus the keyboard is large enough in the Tab's horizontal orientation that you can almost touch-type.

Switch to symbol keyboards   Switch to alpha keyboard

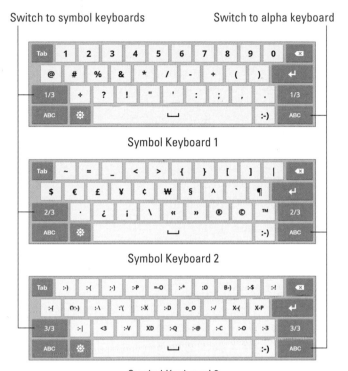

Symbol Keyboard 1

Symbol Keyboard 2

Symbol Keyboard 3

Figure 4-2: Number and symbol keyboards.

As you type, the key you touch is highlighted. The Tab may give a wee bit of tactile feedback. It's easy to get used to, but I still find using a physical keyboard is the best way to type.

Figure 4-3: Special symbol pop-up palette thing.

 ✔ Above all, it helps to *type slowly* until you get used to the keyboard.

 ✔ When you make a mistake, press the Delete key to back up and erase.

 ✔ A blinking cursor on the touchscreen shows where new text appears, which is similar to how text input works on your computer.

 ✔ When you type a password, the character you type appears briefly, but for security reasons, it's then replaced by a black dot.

 ✔ See the later section, "Text Editing," for more details on editing your text.

Adding spell check and typing correction

Anyone can type, but it's the rare individual who can spell. In fact, if it weren't for my word processor's spell checker (and my adept editor), my spelling would be ~~uhtrohshush~~ atrocious. So, with great relief and joy, I present to you the method you use to add typing correction to the onscreen keyboard. Follow these steps:

1. **Touch the Keyboard Settings key to summon the Samsung Keypad Settings screen.**

   The Keyboard Settings key looks like a gear and is just to the left of the Space key. (Refer to Figure 4-1.)

2. **Ensure that a check mark appears by the option XT9.**

   To place a check mark by that option, touch the gray check mark box.

3. **Ensure that a check mark appears by the option Automatic Full Stop.**

   Setting this option directs the Galaxy Tab to add a period anytime you press the Space key twice.

4. **Ensure that a check mark appears by the option Auto-Capitalization.**

   When this option is set, the Tab automatically capitalizes any character you type after typing a period and a space.

5. **Touch the Back icon button to return to whatever you were doing earlier.**

When the XT9 option is on, you see a list of text suggestions appear as you use the onscreen keyboard, as shown in Figure 4-4. Choose a word from the list by touching it with your finger, or choose the first (fully highlighted) word by touching the Space key.

To undo an automatic word selection, press the Delete key on the keyboard.

- ✔ If you find the XT9 setting annoying (and many do), repeat the steps in this section to disable it.

- ✔ I have no idea why it's XT9 and not something easier to remember, like Word-Suggestion-o-Rama.

- ✔ Well, actually, XT9 comes from T9, a predictive-text technology designed for cell phones. *T9* stands for typing *text* on *nine* keys, which is what you would find on a phone. The XT9 is an extension of that predictive-typing technology.

Suggestions

Text you're typing   Show more suggestions

Accept highlighted suggestion

Figure 4-4: Automatic word selection.

Text Editing

You'll probably do more text editing on your Galaxy Tab than you realize. That includes the basic stuff, such as spiffing up typos and adding a period here or there as well as complex editing involving cut, copy, and paste. The concepts are the same as you find on a computer, but without a keyboard and mouse, the process can be daunting. This section irons out the text-editing wrinkles.

A great app on which to test your text-editing skills is the AK Notepad. You can find it at the Android Market (see Chapter 16), or scan the QR code in the margin for a quick download link.

Moving the cursor

The first part of editing text is to move the cursor to the right spot. The *cursor* is that blinking, vertical line where text appears. On most computing devices, you move the cursor by using a pointing device. The Galaxy Tab has no pointing device, but you do: your finger.

To move the cursor, simply touch the spot on the text where you want to move the cursor. To help your precision, a cursor tab appears below the text, as shown in the margin. You can move that tab with your finger to move the cursor around in the text.

After you move the cursor, you can continue to type, use the Delete key to back up and erase, or paste in text copied from elsewhere.

You may see a pop-up by the cursor tab with a Paste command button in it. That button is used to paste in text, as described in the later section, "Cutting, copying, and pasting."

Selecting text

Selecting text on the Galaxy Tab works just like selecting text in a word processor: You mark the start and end of a block. That chunk of text appears highlighted on the screen.

Text-selection starts by long-pressing a chunk of text. Sometimes you have to press for a while, but eventually you see the Text Selection toolbar appear on the top of the screen. You also see a chunk of text selected, as shown in Figure 4-5.

Close the Text Selection toolbar   Text selection commands

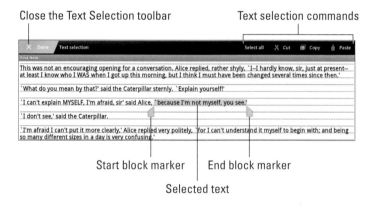

Start block marker   End block marker

Selected text

Figure 4-5: Tab text selection.

Drag the start and end markers around the touchscreen to define the block of selected text. Or you can touch the Select All command at the top of the screen to mark all the text as a single block. (Refer to Figure 4-5.)

After you select the text, you can delete it by touching the Delete key on the keyboard. You can replace the text by typing something new. Or you can cut or copy the text. See the section "Cutting, copying, and pasting," later in this chapter.

To cancel text selection, touch the Done button, or just touch anywhere on the touchscreen outside of the selected block.

 ✔ Seeing the onscreen keyboard is a good indication that you can edit and select text.

 ✔ Sometimes you may see a pop-up menu when you long-press text. If so, choose the Select Text command. You'll then see the Text Selection toolbar and be able to select text on the screen.

Selecting text on a web page

It's possible to select text from a web page even though the text there isn't "editable" text. Because the text isn't editable, or even edible, you need to follow these steps:

1. **Long-press the web page near the text you want to copy.**

   The start and end block markers appear, as does the Text Selection toolbar, though it doesn't look exactly like Figure 4-5: In addition to the Copy and Select All commands, there are Share, Find, and Web Search commands.

2. **Move the cursor tabs to mark the beginning and end of the block.**

   If you move the tabs bcyond a text region on the page, they disappear and are replaced by an area-selection tool, as shown in Figure 4-6. Use the four arrows to select a region of text on the web page.

3. **Choose Copy from the Text Selection toolbar.**

Close the Text Selection toolbar   Text selection and other commands

Resize selected text

Figure 4-6: Selecting text on a web page.

The text is copied into the Galaxy Tab clipboard. From there, it can be pasted into any app that accepts text input. See the next section.

- ✔ You can only copy text from a web page. Obviously, you cannot cut text.

- ✔ Copying text from a web page allows you to paste that text into an e-mail message or Facebook status update or into any field where you can paste text on the Galaxy Tab.

- ✔ The two other commands on the text-selection pop-up menu are Search and Share. Choose Search to look for text within the selected block. Choose the Share command to share the block as text or as an image via e-mail, instant message, Facebook, or any other sharing app installed on your Tab.

- ✔ Refer to Chapter 7 for more information on surfing the web with your Galaxy Tab.

Cutting, copying, and pasting

Selected text is primed for cutting or copying, which works just like it does in your favorite word processor. After you select the text, choose the proper command from the Text Selection toolbar: To copy the text, choose the Copy command. To cut the text, choose Cut.

Just like on your computer, cut or copied text on the Galaxy Tab is stored in a clipboard. To paste any previously cut or copied text, move the cursor to the spot where you want the text pasted.

If you're lucky, you'll see a Paste command button appear above the blinking cursor, as shown in Figure 4-7. Touch that command to paste in the text.

When you can't seem to summon the Paste command button or it vanishes before you can touch it, long-press the text again. When the Text Selection toolbar appears, touch the Paste command.

The Paste command can be anywhere text is input on the Tab, such as in an e-mail message, a Twitter tweet, or any text field. Then touch the Paste icon that appears, as shown in Figure 4-7.

Figure 4-7: The Paste command button.

- ✔ The Paste command button shows up only when there's text to paste.

- ✔ You can paste text only into locations where text is allowed. Odds are good that if you can type, or whenever you see the onscreen keyboard, you can paste text.

Galaxy Tab Dictation

The Galaxy Tab has the amazing ability to interpret your dictation as text. It works almost as well as computer dictation in science fiction movies, though I can't seem to find the command to launch photon torpedoes.

Activating voice input on the keyboard

To use diction instead of typing, you need to activate voice input for the Samsung keypad. Obey these steps:

1. **Display the onscreen keyboard.**

   Touch a text box or somehow get the onscreen keyboard to appear.

2. **Touch the Settings button, the one with the Gear icon.**

3. **Touch the check box by Voice Input to place a green check mark there.**

4. **Touch the Yes button to confirm.**

   You can touch the Home icon button to return to the Home screen when you're done.

 A new button now appears on the onscreen keyboard, near the bottom right. It's the Microphone button, as shown in the margin. Touch that button to dictate text instead of typing it.

Using voice input

Talking to your Tab really works, and works quite well, providing that you touch the Microphone key on the keyboard and properly dictate your text.

After touching the Microphone key, you see a special window appear on the bottom of the screen. When the text Speak Now appears, dictate your text; speak directly at the Tab.

As you speak, a Microphone graphic on the screen flashes. The flashing doesn't mean that the Galaxy Tab is embarrassed by what you're saying. No, the flashing merely indicates that the Tab is listening, detecting the volume of your voice.

After you stop talking, the Tab digests what you said. You see your voice input appear as a wavelike pattern on the screen. Eventually, the text you spoke — or a close approximation — appears on the screen. It's magical and sometimes comical.

- ✒ The first time you try voice input, you might see a description displayed. Touch the OK button to continue.

- ✒ The better your diction, the better your results. Also, it helps to speak only a sentence or less.

- ✒ You can edit your voice input just as you edit any text. See the section "Text Editing," earlier in this chapter.

- ✒ Speak the punctuation in your text. For example, you would say, "I'm sorry comma and it won't happen again" to have the Galaxy Tab produce the text `I'm sorry, and it won't happen again` (or similar wording).

- ✒ Common punctuation you can dictate includes the comma, period, exclamation point, question mark, and colon.

- ✒ Pause your speech before and after speaking punctuation.

- ✒ There is no way presently to capitalize words you dictate.

- ✒ Dictation may not work where no Internet connection exists.

Uttering s**** words

The Galaxy Tab features a voice censor. It replaces those naughty words you might utter, placing the word's first letter on the screen, followed by the appropriate number of asterisks.

For example, if *spatula* were a blue word and you uttered *spatula* when dictating text, the dictation feature would place `s******` on the screen rather than the word *spatula*.

Yeah, I know: silly. Or "s****."

The Tab knows a lot of blue terms, including the infamous "Seven Words You Can Never Say on Television," but apparently the terms *crap* and *damn* are fine. Don't ask me how much time I spent researching this topic.

Searching with your voice

You can say "Here kitty" all you like, but the cat may never come. On the Galaxy Tab, however, you can use the Voice Search app to find things with your voice and actually meet with some decent results.

Start the Voice Search app by locating it on the Apps Menu. You can also access Voice Search from the Home screen by touching the Microphone icon in the upper-left corner.

After starting the app, you see the Voice Search input box. Dictate what you want, such as "Restaurants near me." In a few moments, the Galaxy Tab runs the proper app and finds what you're looking for.

Examples of what you can utter into the Voice Search app include

> *Find a good Chinese restaurant*
>
> *Send e-mail to Obama*
>
> *Set alarm for o'dark thirty*
>
> *Listen to The Monkees*

I admit that this feature is a tad unreliable, especially compared with how well the Dictation feature works overall. Still, it's worth a try if you truly want to play Mr. Spock and dictate your commands to a cold, impersonal piece of electronics.

Part II
The Communications Tab

The 5th Wave   By Rich Tennant

"Ironically, he went out there looking for a 'hot spot.'"

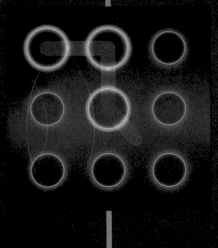

*S*ome say that technology isolates people, but a valid argument can be made that never before has everyone been so connected. Sure, we may not get together in person, and it's probably been a really long time since you've hand-written a letter to someone. That is, if you've ever written anyone a letter. Studies show that most kids prefer to text each other than to talk on the phone.

Welcome to electronically connected life in the 21st century. I'm sure that you've heard of e-mail. You've probably also heard of the World Wide Web. And that Facebook thing? Well, whether or not you know about any of that stuff, it's all covered in this part of the book. The topic here is communications. It's something that the Galaxy Tab does well.

Tablet options

🔊 **Silent mode**
Sound is ON

✈ **Airplane mode**
Airplane mode is OFF

⟳ **Restart**

⏻ **Power off**

You Have Friends

When I was a kid, I kept a dozen or so phone numbers in my head. That was enough to phone someone in a pinch. Beyond that, there was the address book or numbers written down on the kitchen cabinet. Today, things are different. Not only do people typically have more than one phone number, but there are e-mail addresses, websites, and a host of other information. Why cram all that stuff inside your head when you have something handy like the Galaxy Tab to store it for you?

As a communications device, your Galaxy Tab has a need to harbor information about all the people you know — specifically, those with whom you want to communicate electronically. From sending e-mail to social networking, you want to have access to your list of friends, pals, and cohorts. This chapter explains how do that on your Galaxy Tab.

Meet the Contacts App

You may already have some friends in your Galaxy Tab. That's because your Google account was synchronized with the Tab when you first set things up. Because all your Gmail and other types of contacts on the Internet were duplicated on the Tab, you already have a host of friends available. The place where you can access those folks is the Contacts app.

- If you haven't yet set up a Google account, refer to Chapter 2.

- Adding more contacts is covered later in this chapter, in the section "Adding contacts."

- Most apps on the Galaxy Tab use contact information from the Contacts app. Those apps include Email, Gmail, Latitude, as well as any app that lets you share information, such as photographs or videos.

- Information from your social networking apps is also coordinated with the Contacts app. See Chapter 8 for more information on using the Galaxy Tab as your social networking hub.

Using the Contacts app

To peruse the Galaxy Tab address book, start the Contacts app: Touch the Apps Menu icon button on the Home screen; then touch the Contacts app icon.

The Contacts app shows a list of all contacts in your Galaxy Tab, organized alphabetically by first name, similar to the ones shown in Figure 5-1.

Scroll the list by swiping with your finger. Or, you can drag the blue thumb button on the left side of the screen to quickly scan through the list, as shown in Figure 5-1.

To do anything with a contact, you first have to choose it: Touch a contact name, and you see detailed information in the right side of the screen, as shown in Figure 5-1. The list of activities you can do with the contact depends on the information shown and the apps installed on the tab. Here are some options:

Place a phone call: Yes, the Tab is not a phone, but when you install Skype, touching a contact's phone number activates that app, and you can use the Tab to make a call. See Chapter 9 for details.

Send e-mail: Touch the contact's e-mail address to compose an e-mail message using either the Gmail or Email app. When the contact has more than one e-mail address, you can choose to which one you want to send the message. Chapter 6 covers using e-mail on your Tab.

View address: When the contact has a home or business address, you can choose that item to view the address using the Maps app. You can then get directions, look at the place using the Street View tool, or do any of a number of interesting things, covered in Chapter 10.

View social networking status: Contacts who are also your social networking buddies show their current status, as shown in Figure 5-1. The status might also appear at the bottom of the info list, there may be a View Profile item to choose, or you may see a Social Network Feeds button, which lets you see all of the contact's social networking status updates. See Chapter 8 for more information on social networking with the Galaxy Tab.

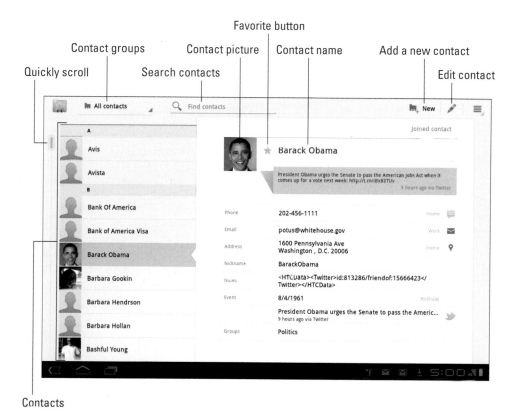

Figure 5-1: Your Galaxy Tab address book.

Some tidbits of information that show up for a contact don't have an associated action. For example, the Tab doesn't sing *Happy Birthday* when you touch a contact's birthday information.

✔ Not every contact has a picture, and the picture can come from a number of sources (Gmail or Facebook, for example). See the section "Add an image for a contact" for more information.

✔ In Figure 5-1, the contact is referred to as a *joined contact*. That means that the information you see comes from multiple sources, such as Gmail and Facebook. See the section "Joining identical contacts" for information on joining contacts.

Sorting your contacts

Your contacts are displayed in the Contacts app in a certain order: alphabetically by first name, first name first. You can change that order if you like. Here's how:

1. **Start the Contacts app.**

2. **Touch the Menu icon button.**

3. **Choose Settings.**

   The Display Options screen appears, which shows you the settings for viewing your contacts.

4. **Choose the List By command to specify how contacts are sorted: by first name or last name.**

   The Contacts app is configured to show contacts by first name.

5. **Choose Display Contacts By to specify how the contacts appear in the list: first name first or last name first.**

   The Contacts app shows the contacts listed by first name first.

There's no right or wrong way to display your contacts — only whichever method you're used to. I prefer them sorted by last name and listed first name first.

Searching contacts

You can have a massive number of contacts. Though the Contacts app doesn't provide a running total, I'm certain that I have more than 500 contacts on my Tab. That number combines my Facebook, Gmail, Twitter, and other accounts. I have a lot of contacts, and I have the potential for even more contacts.

Rather than endlessly scroll the Contacts list and run the risk of rubbing your fingers to nubs, you can employ the Galaxy Tab's powerful Search command. Type the name you want to locate in the Find Contacts text box at the top of the screen, as shown in Figure 5-1. The list of contacts quickly narrows to show only the contacts that contain the text you type.

> ✔ To clear a search, touch the X button, found at the right side of the Find Contacts text box.

> ✔ No, there's no correlation between the number of contacts you have and how popular you are in real life.

All Your Friends in the Galaxy Tab

There are two primary things you can do with the Contacts app besides looking up the people you know. The first thing, and possibly the most rewarding thing personally, is to add more contacts. The second thing, which is necessary when the first thing becomes wildly successful, is organizing those people. This section covers both duties.

Adding contacts

There are more ways to put contacts into your Galaxy Tab than you're probably aware of. This section lists a few of the more popular and useful methods.

Create a new contact from scratch

Sometimes it's necessary to create a contact when you actually meet another human being in the real world, or maybe you finally got around to transferring information into the Tab from your old, paper address book. In either instance, you have information to input, and it starts like this:

1. **Open the Contacts app.**

2. **Touch the New Contact button.**

   Refer to Figure 5-1 for the button's specific location.

3. **Fill in the information on the New Contact screen as best you can.**

   Fill in the text fields with the information you know, as illustrated in Figure 5-2.

Touch to add photo   Save and close

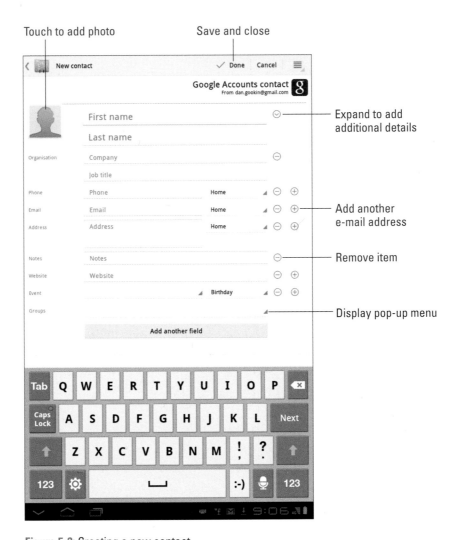

Expand to add additional details

Add another e-mail address

Remove item

Display pop-up menu

Figure 5-2: Creating a new contact.

Use the chevron (down-arrow) button to expand an area to see more details. To add fields, touch the Plus button; touch the Minus button to remove a field.

4. Touch the Done button to complete editing and add the new contact.

The new contact is automatically synched with your Google account. That's one beauty of the Android operating system used by the Galaxy Tab: You have no need to duplicate your efforts; contacts you create on the Tab are instantly updated with your Google account on the Internet.

- ✔ Use the chevron (down-arrow) buttons when you don't see enough fields to add information required for a contact.

- ✔ Touching the triangle buttons (refer to Figure 5-2) displays pop-up menus from which you can choose various options, such as setting whether a phone number or an e-mail address is Home, Business, or what have you.

- ✔ Information from social networking sites is stirred into the Contacts list automatically, though sometimes the process creates duplicate entries. See the section "Joining identical contacts" for how to remedy such a situation.

Create a contact from an e-mail message

Perhaps one of the easiest ways to build up the Contacts list is to create a new contact from an e-mail message. Follow these steps when you receive a message from someone not already in the Contacts list:

1. **Long-press the new contact's name or e-mail address found at the top of the message.**

2. **Touch the OK button in the Add Contact dialog box.**

   The Select a Contact dialog box appears.

3. **Choose an existing contact if you merely want to add the e-mail address to someone already in the list; otherwise, choose Create a New Contact.**

4. **Fill in the blanks on the New Contact screen, as shown in Figure 5-2.**

5. **Touch the Done button to finish adding the contact.**

Importing contacts from your computer

Your computer's e-mail program is doubtless a useful repository of contacts you've built up over the years. You can export these contacts from your computer's e-mail program and then import them into the Galaxy Tab. It's not easy, but it's possible.

The key is to save or export your computer e-mail program's records in the *vCard* (.vcf) file format. These records can then be imported by the Galaxy Tab into the Contacts app. The method for exporting contacts varies depending on the e-mail program:

✔ **In the Windows Live Mail program,** choose Go⟹Contacts and then choose File⟹Export⟹Business Card (.VCF) to export the contacts.

✔ **In Windows Mail,** choose File⟹Export⟹Windows Contacts and then choose vCards (Folder of .VCF Files) from the Export Windows Contacts dialog box. Click the Export button.

✔ **On the Mac,** open the Address Book program and choose File⟹Export⟹Export vCard.

After the vCard files are created on your computer, connect the Galaxy Tab to the computer and transfer them. Transferring files from your computer to the Galaxy Tab is covered in Chapter 18.

After the vCard files have been copied to the Tab, follow these steps in the Contacts app to complete the process:

1. **Touch the Menu icon button.**

2. **Choose the Import/Export command.**

3. **Choose Import from USB Storage.**

4. **Choose the option Import All vCard Files**

5. **Touch the OK button.**

   The contacts are saved on your Tab but will also be synchronized to your Gmail account, which instantly creates a backup copy.

The importing process may create some duplicates. That's okay: You can join two entries for the same person in the Contacts app. See the section "Joining identical contacts," later in this chapter.

Grab contacts from your social networking sites

You can pour your whole gang of friends and followers into the Galaxy Tab from your social networking sites. The operation is automatic: Simply add the social networking site to the Tab's inventory of apps as described in Chapter 8. The social networking contacts are instantly added to the Contacts app list.

Find a new contact on the map

When you use the Maps app to locate a coffee house, apothecary, or parole office (or all three in one place), you can quickly create a contact for that location. Here's how:

1. **After searching for your location, touch the cartoon bubble that appears on the map.**

   You see more details for the location on the left side of the screen, as shown in Figure 5-3.

2. **Touch the More button, shown in Figure 5-3.**

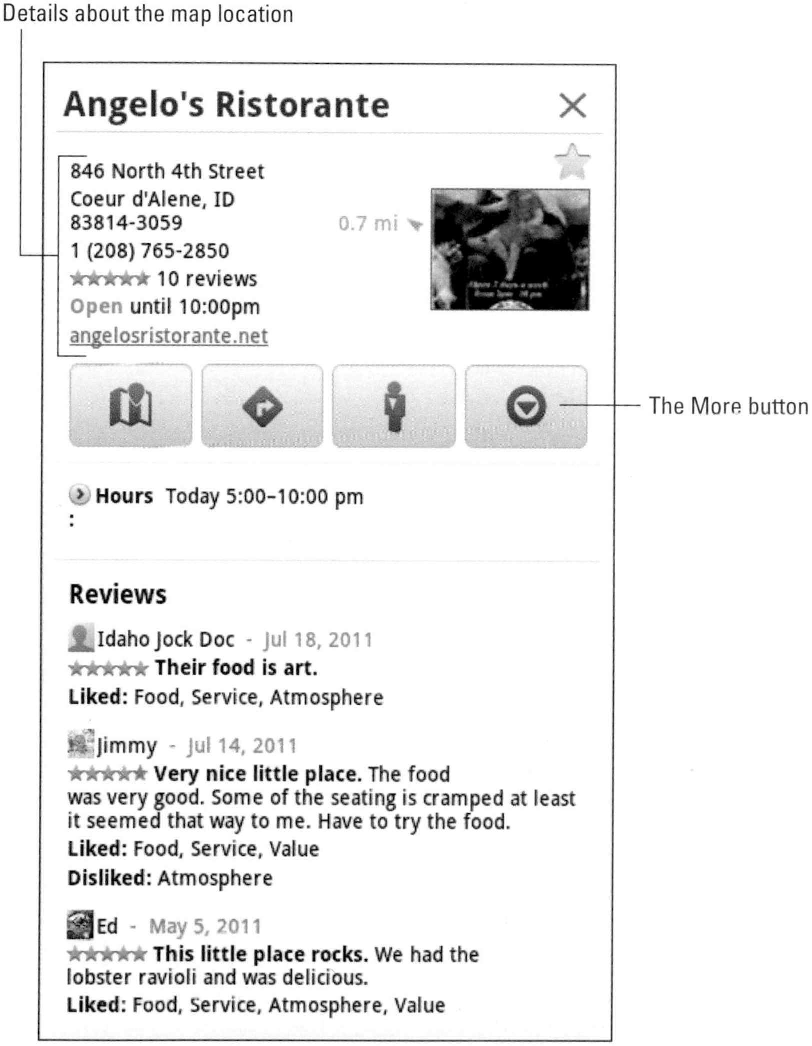

Details about the map location

Figure 5-3: Adding a contact from the Maps app.

3. **Choose Add As a Contact.**

   You see the New Contact screen with much of the information already filled-in. That's because the Maps app shared that info with the Contacts app. It's good when the apps play together nicely.

4. **Optionally, add more information if you know it.**

5. **Touch the Done button.**

   The new contact is created.

See Chapter 10 for detailed information on how to search for a location using the Maps application.

Editing a contact

To make minor touch-ups on any contact, start by locating and displaying the contact's information. Touch the Edit Contact icon button, shown in the margin, and start making changes.

Change or add information by touching a field and typing on the onscreen keyboard. You can edit information as well: Touch the field to edit and change whatever you want.

Some information cannot be edited. For example, fields pulled in from social networking sites can be edited only by that account holder on the social networking site.

When you're finished editing, touch the Done button.

Add an image for a contact

Nothing can be more delicious than snapping an inappropriate picture of someone you know and using the picture as his contact picture on your Galaxy Tab. Then, every time he calls you, that embarrassing, potentially career-ending photo comes up.

Oh, and I suppose you could use nice pictures as well, but what's the fun in that?

The simplest way to add a picture to one of your Galaxy Tab contacts is to have the image already stored in the Tab. You can snap a picture and save it (covered in Chapter 11), grab a picture from the Internet (covered in Chapter 7), or use any image already stored in the Tab's Gallery app (covered in Chapter 12). The image doesn't even have to be a picture of the contact — any image will do.

After the contact's photo, or any other suitable image, is stored on the Tab, follow these steps to update the contact's information:

1. **Locate and display the contact's information.**

2. **Touch the Edit Contact icon button.**

3. **Touch the Contact Picture icon.**

   Refer to Figure 5-1 for its location.

4. **Choose the option Select Photo from Gallery.**

   If you have other image management apps on your Tab, you can instead choose the app's command from the list.

5. **Choose Gallery.**

   The photo gallery is displayed. It lists all photos and videos stored on your Galaxy Tab.

6. **Browse the photo gallery to look for a suitable image.**

   See Chapter 12 for more information on using the Gallery app.

7. **Touch the image you want to use for the contact.**

8. **Crop the image.**

   Use Figure 5-4 as a guide for how to crop the image.

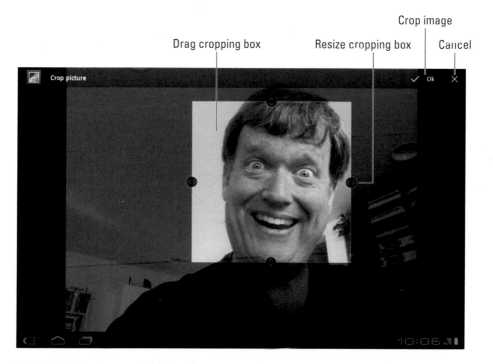

Figure 5-4: Cropping a contact's image.

9. **Touch the OK button.**

The image is cropped but not yet assigned:

10. **Touch the Done button to finish editing the contact.**

The image is now assigned, and it appears whenever the contact is referenced on your Galaxy Tab.

You can add pictures to contacts on your Google account by using any computer. Just visit your Gmail Contacts list to edit a contact. You can then add to that contact any picture stored on your computer. The picture is eventually synced with the same contact on your Galaxy Tab.

- ✓ If the contact is in your presence, you can always take her picture using the Galaxy Tab. After Step 3 in the preceding list, choose the command Take Photo or Take New Photo. See Chapter 11 for details on using the Galaxy Tab's camera.

- ✓ Pictures can also be added by your Gmail friends and contacts when they add their own images to their accounts.

- ✓ Some images in the Gallery app may not work for contact icons. For example, images synchronized with your online photo albums may be unavailable.

- ✓ To remove or change a contact's picture, follow Steps 1 through 3 in the preceding list. Choose Remove Photo to get rid of the existing image.

Make a favorite

A *favorite* contact is someone you stay in touch with most often. The person doesn't have to be someone you like — just someone you (perhaps unfortunately) contact often, such as your bookie.

The favorite contacts are kept in the Starred group, which can be chosen from the Contact Groups menu. (Refer to Figure 5-1.) There are also other apps and widgets that make use of your favorite contacts.

To add a contact to the Starred group, display the contact's information and touch the Star button by the contact's image, as shown in Figure 5-1. When the star is blue, the contact is one of your favorites and stored in the Starred group.

To remove a favorite, touch the contact's star again, and it loses its color. Removing a favorite doesn't delete the contact but instead removes it from the Starred group.

By the way, a contact has no idea whether he's one of your favorites, so don't believe that you're hurting his feelings by not making him a favorite.

Manage Your Friends

Nothing is truly perfect the first time, especially when you create things on a Galaxy Tab while typing with your thumbs at 34,000 feet during turbulence. You can do a whole slate of things with your Galaxy Tab contacts. This section covers the more interesting and useful things.

Joining identical contacts

Because the Galaxy Tab can pull contacts from multiple sources (Facebook, Gmail, Twitter), you may discover duplicate contact entries in the Contacts app. Rather than fuss over which entry to use, you can join the contacts. Here's how:

1. **Wildly scroll the Contacts list until you locate a duplicate.**

   Well, maybe not *wildly* scroll, but locate a duplicated entry. Because the Contacts list is sorted, the duplicates appear close together (though that may not always be the case).

2. **Select one of the contacts to view it on the right side of the screen.**

3. **Touch the Edit Contact button.**

4. **Touch the Menu icon button.**

5. **Choose Join.**

   The Join Contact(s) window appears. It lists any potential matches right away based on name matches.

6. **Choose an account to join.**

   The accounts are merged. Well, they appear together on your Galaxy Tab.

7. **Touch the Done button to complete the joining.**

If you don't see a matching contact in Step 6, choose the command Show All Contacts from the bottom of the Join Contacts window. You can then scroll through the entire Contacts list to find a match.

Separating contacts

The topic of separating contacts has little to do with parenting, though separating bickering children is the first step to avoiding a fight. Your Galaxy Tab contacts might not be bickering, but occasionally the Tab may automatically join two contacts that aren't really the same person. When that happens, you can split them by following these steps:

1. **Display the contact that comes from two separate sources.**

   Sometimes it's difficult to spot such a contact. The easiest way for me is to see two diverse e-mail addresses for the contact, which usually indicates a mismatch.

2. **Edit the contact by touching the Edit Contact button.**

3. **Touch the Menu icon button and choose the Separate command.**

4. **Touch the OK button to confirm that you're separating the contacts.**

   Where there was one contact, there are now two.

You don't really need to look for improperly joined contacts as much as you'll just stumble across them. When you do, feel free to separate them, especially if you detect any bickering.

Removing a contact

Every so often, consider reviewing your contacts. Purge those folks whom you no longer recognize or you've forgotten. It's simple:

1. **Locate the contact in your Contacts list and display the contact's information.**

2. **Touch the Menu icon button.**

3. **Choose Delete Contact.**

4. **Touch OK to remove the contact from your Galaxy Tab.**

Because the Contacts list is synchronized with your Gmail contacts for your Google account, the contact is also removed there.

For some linked accounts, such as Facebook, deleting the account from your Tab doesn't remove the human from your Facebook account. The warning that appears (before Step 4 in the preceding list) explains as much.

Removing a contact doesn't kill the person in real life.

6

Mail of the Electronic Kind

1'll bet it's been a long time since you've asked someone for his e-mail address and he didn't have one. Probably longer still since someone responded, "E-mail? What's that?" It would probably be odder still if people asked why there's a dash in "e-mail" now, when in my books published before 2010 there wasn't, but I'm getting sidetracked.

To help keep you electronically connected, the Galaxy Tab features the ability to collect and send your electronic missives. You can read and compose just about anywhere you go, peruse attachments, forward messages, and do the entire e-mail e-nchilada all in one spot.

Galactic E-Mail

Electronic mail is handled on the Galaxy Tab by two apps: Gmail and Email.

The Gmail app hooks directly into your Google Gmail account. In fact, they're exact echoes of each other: The Gmail you receive on your computer is also received on your Tab.

You can also use the Email app to connect with non-Gmail electronic mail, such as the standard mail service provided by your ISP or a web-based e-mail system such as Yahoo! Mail or Windows Live Mail.

Regardless of the app, electronic mail on the Galaxy Tab works just like it does on your computer: You can receive mail, create new messages, forward e-mail, send messages to a group of contacts, and work with attachments, for example. As long as there's a data connection, e-mail works just peachy.

 ✔ Both the Gmail and Email apps are located on the Apps Menu.

 ✔ There is a shortcut to the Gmail app on the main panel of the Home screen. Adding the Email app icon to the Home screen is easy: See Chapter 20.

 ✔ The Email app can be configured to handle multiple e-mail accounts, as discussed later in this section.

 ✔ Although you can use your Tab's web browser to visit the Gmail website, you should use the Gmail app to pick up your Gmail.

 ✔ If you forget your Gmail password, visit this web address:

      www.google.com/accounts/ForgotPasswd

Setting up an Email account

The Email app is used to access web-based e-mail, or *webmail,* such as Yahoo!, Windows Live, and others. It also lets you read e-mail provided by your Internet service provider (ISP), office, or other large, intimidating organization. To get things set up regardless of the service, follow these steps:

 1. **Start the Email app.**

    Look for it on the Apps Menu, along with all other apps on your Tab.

    If you haven't yet run the Email app, the first screen you see is Account Setup. Continue with Step 2. Otherwise you're taken to the Email inbox.

    See the next section for information on adding additional e-mail accounts.

 2. **Type the e-mail address you use for the account.**

 3. **Type the password for that account.**

 4. **Touch the Next button.**

    If you're lucky, everything is connected smoothly. Otherwise you'll have to specify the details as provided by your ISP. That includes the incoming and outgoing server information, often known by the bewildering acronyms POP3 and SMTP. Plod through the steps on the screen, though you'll primarily need to specify only the incoming and outgoing server names.

Eventually you'll end up at the Account Options screen.

5. **Set the account options on the aptly named Account Options screen.**

   You might want to reset the Inbox Checking Frequency to something other than 15 minutes.

   If the account is to be your main e-mail account, place a green check mark by the option Send Email from this Account by Default.

6. **Touch the Next button.**

7. **Give the account a name and check your own name.**

   The account is given the name of the mail server, which may not ring a bell with you when it comes to receiving your e-mail. I name my ISP's e-mail account Main because it's my main account.

   The Your Name field lists your name as it's applied to outgoing messages. So if your name is really Wilma Flagstone and not `wflag4457`, you can make that change now.

8. **Touch the Next button.**

   You're done.

The next thing you'll see will be your e-mail account inbox. See the section "You've Got E-Mail" for what to do next.

Adding even more e-mail accounts

The Email app can be configured to pick up mail from multiple sources. If you have a Yahoo! Mail or Windows Live account, or maybe your corporate account, in addition to your ISP's account, you can add them. Follow through with these steps:

1. **Visit the Apps Menu and start the Settings app.**

2. **Choose Accounts & Sync.**

3. **Touch the Add Account button.**

4. **If your account type is shown in the list, such as Yahoo! Mail, choose it. Otherwise, choose the Email icon.**

5. **Type the account's e-mail address.**

6. **Type the password for the account.**

7. **Touch the Next button.**

   In a few magical moments, the e-mail account is configured and added to the account list.

   If you goofed up the account name or password, you're warned: Try again. Or if the account requires additional setup, use the information provided by the ISP or other source to help you fill in the appropriate fields.

8. **Set account options.**

   Most of the preset choices are fine for a web-based e-mail account.

   If the account is your primary e-mail account, place a green check mark by the option Send Email from this Account by Default.

   You might also consider a more frequent update interval, especially if you get a lot of mail or need to respond to it quickly.

9. **Touch the Next button.**

10. **Name the account and confirm your name.**

    Feel free to change both the account name and your own name.

11. **Touch the Next button.**

    The account is added to the list on the My Accounts screen.

You can repeat the steps in this section to add more e-mail accounts. All the accounts you configure will be made available through the Email app.

You've Got E-Mail

The Galaxy Tab works flawlessly with Gmail. In fact, if Gmail is already set up to be your main e-mail address, you'll enjoy having access to your messages all the time by using your Tab.

Non-Gmail e-mail, handled by the Email app, must be set up before it can be used, as covered earlier in this chapter. After completing the quick and occasionally painless setup, you can receive e-mail on your Tab just as you can on a computer.

Getting a new message

You're alerted to the arrival of a new e-mail message in your Tab by a notification icon. The icon differs depending on the e-mail's source.

For a new Gmail message, you see the New Gmail notification, shown in the margin, appear at the top of the touchscreen.

For a new e-mail message, you see the New Email notification.

Touch the notification icon at the bottom of the screen to see a summary of the most recent message. When multiple messages are waiting, you'll see a number indicating how many. Touching the notification's pop-up window takes you to either the Gmail or Email app where you can read the message.

To deal with the new-message notification, drag down the notifications and choose the appropriate one. You're taken directly to your inbox to read the new message.

Checking the inbox

To peruse your Gmail, start the Gmail app. You can find it on the main Home screen or on the Apps Menu. The Gmail inbox is shown in Figure 6-1.

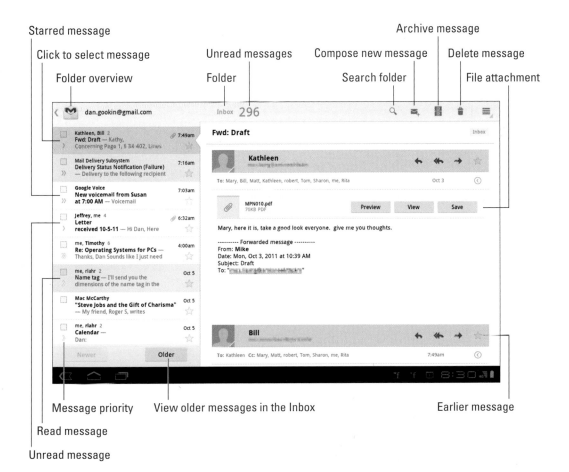

Figure 6-1: The Gmail inbox.

To check your Email inbox, open the Email app. You're taken to the inbox for your primary e-mail account.

When you have multiple e-mail accounts accessed through the Email app, you can view your universal inbox by choosing the Combined View command from the Account menu, as shown in Figure 6-2.

Click to select message

Unread message

Delete message

Mailbox overview

Move to folder

View mailboxes

Account menu   Account color codes   Compose new message   File attachment

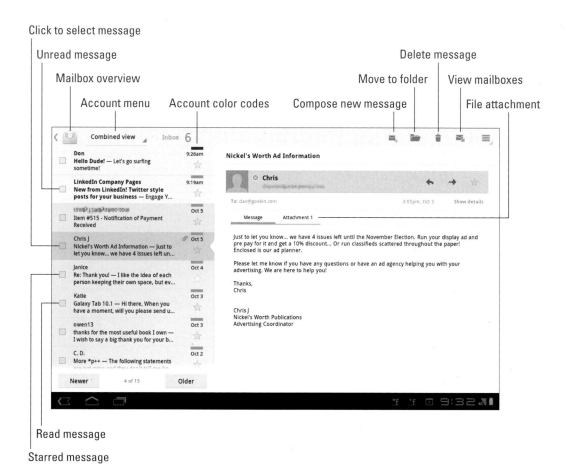

Read message

Starred message

Figure 6-2: Messages in the Email app.

Notice that your Gmail inbox is missing from the Combined View window. (Refer to Figure 6-2.) Gmail is its own app; your Gmail messages don't show up in the universal inbox.

- ✔ See the section "Setting the primary e-mail account" for information on setting the primary e-mail account.

- ✔ Search your Gmail messages by pressing the Search button, as shown in Figure 6-1.

- ✔ Gmail is organized using labels, not folders. To see your Gmail labels from the inbox, touch the Folder Overview button. It's found in the upper-left corner of the screen.

- ✔ The Email app is used to access your primary non-Gmail e-mail account. The Messaging app is used to access all non-Gmail accounts.

- ✔ Multiple e-mail accounts gathered in the Email app are color coded. When you view the combined inbox (refer to Figure 6-2), you see the color codes to the right of each message.

- ✔ Scroll the message list in the Email app to view older messages. The Newer and Older buttons move you through the messages one at a time.

Reading an e-mail message

As mail comes in, you can read it by choosing a new e-mail notification, as described earlier in this chapter. Reading and working with the message operate much the same whether you're using the Gmail or Email app.

Choose a message to read by touching the message on the left side of the screen, as illustrated in Figures 6-1 and 6-2. The message text appears on the right side of the window, which you can scroll up or down by using your finger.

Use the Newer and Older buttons to page through your messages one at a time.

Table 6-1 lists common e-mail activities and their associated icon buttons.

Table 6-1		Gmail and Email Icon Buttons
Command	*Icon*	*Function*
Reply	←	Reply to the current message.
Reply All	⇐	Reply to everyone.
Forward	→	Forward the message to someone else.
Star	☆	Mark the message.
Delete	🗑	Move the message to the Trash folder.

To access additional e-mail commands, touch the Menu icon button. The commands available depend on what you're doing in the Gmail or Email app at the time you touch the button.

✔ Use Reply All only when everyone else must get a copy of your reply. Because most people find endless Reply All e-mail threads annoying, use the Reply All option judiciously.

✔ Starred messages can be viewed or searched separately, making them easier to locate later.

✔ If you properly configure the Email program, there's no need to delete messages you read. See the section "Configuring the manual delete option," later in this chapter.

✔ I find it easier to delete (and manage) Gmail using a computer.

Write That Message

Every so often, someone comes up to me and says, "Dan, you're a computer freak. You probably get a lot of e-mail." I generally nod and smile. Then the person ponders, "How can I get more e-mail?" The answer is simple: To get mail, you have to send mail. Or, you can just be a jerk on a blog and leave your e-mail address there. That method works too, though I don't recommend it.

Composing a new message

Crafting an e-mail epistle on your Tab works exactly like creating one on your computer. Figure 6-3 shows the basic setup.

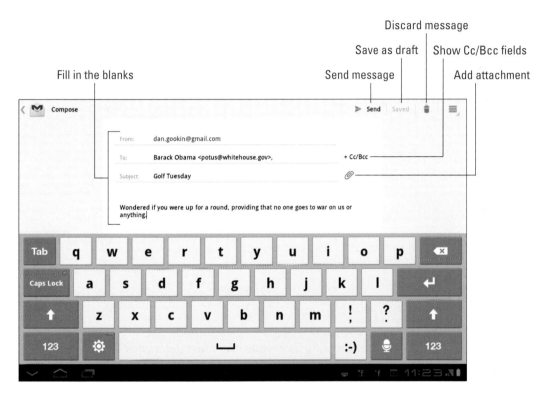

Figure 6-3: Writing a new e-mail message.

Here's how to get there:

1. **Start an e-mail app, either Gmail or Email.**

2. **Touch the Compose icon button.**

   The button is shown in the margin; it's the same icon for both apps, as is the Compose window, shown in Figure 6-3.

3. **Touch the To field and type the e-mail address.**

   You can type the first few letters of a contact name and then choose a matching contact from the list that's displayed.

4. **Type a subject.**

5. **Type the message.**

6. **Touch the Send button to whisk your missive to the Internet for immediate delivery.**

   Or you can touch the Save Draft button (refer to Figure 6-3), and the message is stored in the Drafts folder. You can open this folder to edit the message. Touch Send to send it.

Copies of the messages you send in the Email program are stored in the Sent mailbox. If you're using Gmail, copies are saved in your Gmail account, which you can access from your Galaxy Tab or from any computer or mobile device connected to the Internet.

✔ To cancel a message, touch the Trash button, as shown in the margin. Touch the OK button to confirm.

✔ To summon the Cc field in Gmail, press the +Cc/Bcc button, as shown in Figure 6-3. The Cc (Carbon Copy) and Bcc (Blind Carbon Copy) fields appear, eager for you to fill them in.

✔ Refer to Chapter 5 for more information on the Contacts list.

✔ Chapter 4 covers typing, voice input, and text editing.

Sending e-mail to a contact

A quick and easy way to compose a new message is to find a contact and then create a message using that contact's information. Heed these steps:

1. **Open the Contacts app.**

   See Chapter 5 for details.

2. **Locate the contact to whom you want to send an electronic message.**

   Review Chapter 8 for ways to hunt down contacts in a long list.

3. **Touch the contact's e-mail address.**

4. **Choose Gmail to send the message using Gmail or touch Email to compose an e-mail message using your main e-mail account.**

   Other options may appear on the complete Action Using menu. For example, a custom e-mail app you've downloaded may show up there as well.

At this point, creating the message works as described in the preceding section; refer there for additional information.

Message Attachments

Attachments on the Galaxy Tab work pretty much the same in both the Gmail and Email apps. The key is the paperclip icon, not only for receiving attachments, but for sending them as well.

Dealing with attachments

The Galaxy Tab lets you view or save most e-mail attachments, depending on what's attached. You can also send attachments, though it's more of a computer activity, not something that's completely useful on a mobile device; the Tab isn't really designed for creating or manipulating information.

Email messages with attachments are flagged in the inbox with the paperclip icon, which seems to be the standard I-have-an-attachment icon for most e-mail programs. When you open one of these messages, you may see the attachment right away, specifically if it's a picture.

When you don't see the attachment right away, you may see one of the attachment options illustrated in the earlier Figures 6-1 and 6-2.

- ✔ Touch the Preview button to witness the attachment on your Tab.
- ✔ Touch the View button to download and see the attachment.
- ✔ Touch the Save button to save the attachment without viewing it.

What happens after you touch the Preview or View button depends on the type of attachment. Sometimes you see a list of apps from which you can choose one to open the attachment. Many Microsoft Office documents are opened by the Quickoffice app.

Some attachments cannot be opened. In these cases, use a computer to fetch the message and attempt to open the attachment. Or, you can reply to the message and inform the sender that you cannot open the attachment on your Galaxy Tab.

- ✔ Sometimes, pictures included in an e-mail message aren't displayed. You find the Show Pictures button in the message, which you can touch to display the pictures.
- ✔ See Chapter 12 for more information on the Gallery app and how image and video sharing works on your Galaxy Tab.

Sending an attachment

The most common thing to send from the Galaxy Tab as an e-mail attachment is a picture of video. You're not limited to only pictures, though. You can attach documents you've previously saved on the Tab, music, even random files if you're so bold.

The key to adding an attachment to an outgoing message is to touch the paperclip icon in the Compose window. This technique works in both the Gmail and Email apps. After touching the paperclip icon, you see the Choose Attachment menu. The number of items on that menu depends on what's installed on your Galaxy Tab. There are a few basic items:

Gallery: Pluck a picture of video from the Tab's Gallery app.

Quickoffice: Choose a document that you've saved on your Galaxy Tab.

Select music track: Choose music saved on your Galaxy Tab.

Other items: If you've installed another photo manager or a file manager, it also appears on the list.

The number of items you see depends on what's installed on the Galaxy Tab. Also the variety is different between the Gmail and Email apps.

You'll use the program you've chosen to locate the specific file or media tidbit you plan on sending. That item is attached to the outgoing message.

To select more than one attachment, touch the paperclip icon again.

 It's also possible to send an attachment by using the various Share commands and buttons located in apps throughout the Galaxy Tab. After choosing the Share command, select Gmail or Email as the app to use for sharing whatever it is you want to share.

E-Mail Configuration

You can have oodles of fun and waste oceans of time confirming and customizing the e-mail experience on your Galaxy Tab. The most interesting things you can do are to modify or create an e-mail signature, specify how mail you retrieve on the Tab is deleted from the server, and assign a default e-mail account for the Email app.

Creating a signature

I highly recommend that you create a custom e-mail signature for sending messages from your Galaxy Tab. Here's my signature:

```
DAN

This was sent from my Galaxy Tab.
Typos, no matter how hilarious, are unintentional.
```

To create a signature for Gmail, obey these directions:

1. **Start the Gmail app.**
2. **Touch the Menu icon button.**
3. **Choose Settings.**
4. **Choose your Gmail account from the left side of the window.**
5. **Choose Signature from the bottom part of the scrolling list on the right side of the window.**
6. **Type or dictate your signature.**
7. **Touch OK.**

You can obey these same steps to change your signature; the existing signature shows up after Step 5.

To set a signature for the Email app, heed these steps:

1. **In the Email app, touch the Menu icon button.**
2. **Choose Account Settings.**

    If you don't see the Account Settings command, choose a specific account from the Account menu (refer to Figure 6-2) or just choose the account from the list on the left side of the screen.

3. **Choose Signature.**
4. **Type or dictate your new outgoing e-mail signature.**
5. **Touch the OK button.**

When you have multiple e-mail accounts, repeat these steps to configure a signature for each one.

Configuring the manual delete option

Non-Gmail e-mail you fetch on your Galaxy Tab is typically left on the e-mail server. That's because, unlike your computer's e-mail program, the Email app doesn't delete messages after it picks them up. The advantage is that you can retrieve the same messages later using your computer. The disadvantage is that you end up retrieving mail you've already read and possibly replied to.

You can control whether the Email app removes messages after they're picked up. Follow these steps:

1. **In the Email app, touch the Menu icon button.**

2. **Choose Account Settings.**

3. **If you're looking at the Combined View, choose a specific account from the left side of the Window.**

   Specifically, choose the account you use for your ISP. If not, ensure that you're viewing the inbox for the ISP's e-mail account and then start over with Step 1.

4. **Choose the command Incoming Settings.**

5. **Touch the menu next to the item Delete Email From Server.**

6. **Choose the option When I Delete From Inbox.**

7. **Touch the Done button.**

When you delete a message in the Email app on your Galaxy Tab, the message is also deleted from the mail server. It isn't picked up again, not by the Tab, another mobile device, or any computer that fetches e-mail from that same account.

- Mail you retrieve using your computer's mail program is deleted from the mail server after it's picked up. That's normal behavior. Your Galaxy Tab cannot pick up mail from the server if your computer has already deleted it.

- Deleting mail on the server isn't a problem for Gmail. No matter how you access your Gmail, from your Tab or from a computer, the inbox lists the same messages.

Setting the primary e-mail account

When you have more than one e-mail account, the main account — the default — is the one used by the Email app to send messages. To change that primary mail account, follow these steps:

1. **Start the Email app.**

2. **From the Account menu, choose Combined View.**

3. **Touch the Menu icon button and choose Account Settings.**

4. **Choose the e-mail account you want to mark as your favorite from the left side of the screen.**

5. **On the right side of the screen, place a green check mark by the Default Account item.**

The messages you compose and send using the Email app are sent from the account you specified in Step 4.

Tablet Web Browsing

In This Chapter

▶ Browsing the web on your Tab

▶ Adding a bookmark

▶ Working with tabs

▶ Sharing and saving web pages

▶ Downloading images and files

▶ Setting a new home page

▶ Configuring the Browser app

The World Wide Web was designed to be viewed on a computer. The monitor is big and roomy. Web pages are displayed amply, like Uncle Jeff on the sofa watching a ballgame. The smaller the screen, however, the more difficult it is to view web pages designed for those roomy monitors. The web on a cell phone? Tragic. But on the Galaxy Tab, the web just seems to fit.

The Galaxy Tab has a nice, roomy screen. Viewing the web on the Tab is like seeing a younger, thinner version of Uncle Jeff sitting in the Hepplewhite. It's enjoyable, especially when you've read the good information in this chapter on surfing the web with your Galaxy Tab.

✔ If possible, activate the Galaxy Tab's Wi-Fi connection before you venture out on the web. Though you can use the Tab's cellular data connection, the Wi-Fi connection incurs no data usage charges.

✔ Many places you visit on the web can instead be accessed directly and more effectively by using specific apps. Facebook, Gmail, Twitter, and YouTube, and potentially other popular web destinations, have apps that are either preinstalled on the Tab or can be downloaded for free from the Android Market. Use them instead of the Browser app.

Mobile Web Browsing

Rare is the person these days who has had no experience with the World Wide Web. More common is someone who has used the web on a computer but has yet to taste the Internet waters on a mobile device. If that's you, consider this section your quick mobile web orientation.

Viewing the web

Your Galaxy Tab's web-browsing app is named Browser. You can find its icon on the main Home screen or, like all the other apps on the Tab, it's on the Apps Menu. Figure 7-1 illustrates the Browser app's interface.

Figure 7-1: The Browser.

Here are some handy Galaxy Tab web-browsing tips:

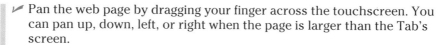

✔ Pan the web page by dragging your finger across the touchscreen. You can pan up, down, left, or right when the page is larger than the Tab's screen.

✔ Pinch the screen to zoom out or spread two fingers to zoom in.

✔ You can orient the Tab vertically to read a web page in Portrait mode. Doing so may reformat some web pages, which can make long lines of text easier to read.

Visiting a web page

To visit a web page, type its address into the Address box. (Refer to Figure 7-1.) You can also type a search word or phrase if you don't know the exact address of a web page. Touch the Go button on the onscreen keyboard or the Go button by the Address box (see the margin) to search the web or visit a specific web page.

If you don't see the Address box, touch the web page's tab atop the screen. The Address box, along with the various buttons left and right, appears on the screen.

You "click" links on a page by touching them with your finger. If you have trouble stabbing the right link, zoom in on the page and try again.

✔ When typing a web page address, use the www. key to instantly type those characters for the address. The www. key changes to the .com key to assist you in rapidly typing those characters as well.

✔ To reload a web page, touch the Refresh symbol on the left end of the Address bar.

✔ To stop a web page from loading, touch the X that appears to the left of the Address bar. The X replaces the Refresh button and appears only when a web page is loading.

Browsing back and forth

To return to a web page, you can touch the Browser's Back button, shown here and in Figure 7-1, or press the Back icon button at the bottom of the screen.

Touch the Browser's Forward button to go forward or to return to a page you were visiting before you touched the Back button.

To review the long-term history of your web-browsing adventures, touch the Bookmarks button in the upper-left corner of the Browser window, as shown in Figure 7-2. Choose History to view your web-browsing history.

Menu icon button (clear history)

History list

Bookmarked site

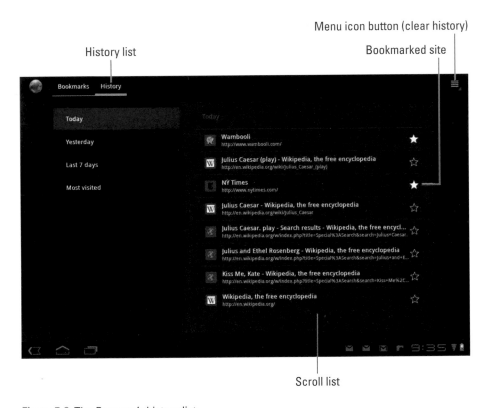

Scroll list

Figure 7-2: The Browser's history list.

To view a page you visited weeks or months ago, you can choose a web page from the History list.

To clear the History list, touch the Menu icon button, shown in Figure 7-2, and choose the Clear History command.

Using bookmarks

Bookmarks are those electronic breadcrumbs you can drop as you wander the web. Need to revisit a website? Just look up its bookmark. This advice assumes, of course, that you bother to create (I prefer *drop*) a bookmark when you first visit the site.

The cinchy way to bookmark a page is to touch the Favorite (star) icon on the right end of the Address bar. Tap that icon, and you see the Bookmark This Page window, shown in Figure 7-3.

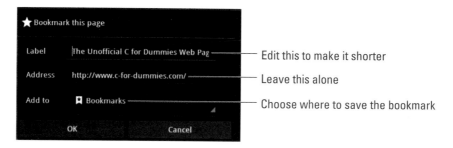

★ Bookmark this page

Label	The Unofficial C for Dummies Web Pag ——	—— Edit this to make it shorter
Address	http://www.c-for-dummies.com/ ——	—— Leave this alone
Add to	🔖 Bookmarks ——	—— Choose where to save the bookmark

OK   Cancel

Figure 7-3: Adding a bookmark.

I edit the Label to something shorter, especially if the web page's title is long. Shorter names look better on the Bookmarks window. (Refer to Figure 7-3.) Touch the OK button and you've added the bookmark.

After the bookmark is set, it appears in the list of bookmarks. To see the list, touch the Bookmarks button on the Browser app's main window. (Refer to Figure 7-1.) You see a list of web page thumbnails with their labels or titles beneath. Swipe the list downward to see more bookmarks and thumbnails.

Touch a bookmark to visit that page.

✔ You can add a bookmark to the Home screen by touching the Add To menu in the Bookmark This Page window. Choose Home Screen from the menu.

✔ Remove a bookmark by long-pressing its entry in the Bookmarks list. Choose the command Delete Bookmark. Touch the OK button to confirm. The bookmark is gone.

✔ Bookmarked websites can also be placed on the Home screen: Long-press the bookmark thumbnail and choose the command Add Shortcut to Home.

✔ The MyBookmarks app, available at the Android Market, can import your Internet Explorer, Firefox, and Chrome bookmarks from your Windows computer into the Galaxy Tab. See Chapter 16 for more information on the Android Market.

✔ Refer to Chapter 4 for information on editing text on the Galaxy Tab.

Managing web pages in multiple tabs

The Browser app uses a tabbed interface to display more than one web page at a time. Refer to Figure 7-1 to see various tabs marching across the Browser app's screen, just above the Address bar.

Here's how you work the tabbed interface:

- ✒ *To open a blank tab,* touch the plus button to the right of the last tab, as shown in Figure 7-1.

- ✒ *To open a link in a new tab,* long-press that link. Choose the command Open in New Tab from the menu that appears.

- ✒ *To open a bookmark in a new window,* long-press the bookmark and choose the command Open in New Tab.

You switch between tabs by choosing one from the top of the screen.

Close a tab by touching its X (Close) button; you can close only the tab you're currently viewing.

- ✒ The tabs keep marching across the screen, left to right. You can scroll the tabs to view the ones that have scrolled off the screen.

- ✒ New tabs open using the home page that's set for the Browser application. See the section "Setting a home page," later in this chapter, for information.

- ✒ For secure browsing, you can open an *incognito tab:* Press the Menu icon button and choose the command New Incognito Tab. When you go incognito, the Browser app won't track your history, leave cookies, or other evidence of which web pages you've visited in the incognito tab. A short description appears on the incognito tab page describing how it works.

Searching the web

The handiest way to find things on the web is to use the Google widget, shown in Figure 7-4. That widget doesn't come preinstalled on any Home screen panel, so you'll have to add it per the fine directions found in Chapter 20.

Figure 7-4: The Google widget.

To search for something anytime you're viewing a web page in the Browser app, touch the Search icon button, found on the right end of the Address bar. Type the search term into the Address box. You can choose from a list of suggestions.

To find text on the web page you're looking at, as opposed to searching the entire Internet, follow these steps:

1. **Visit the web page where you want to find a specific tidbit o' text.**

2. **Press the Menu icon button.**

3. **Choose Find on Page.**

4. **Type the text you're searching for.**

5. **Use the left- or right-arrow button to locate that text on the page — backward or forward, respectively.**

   The found text appears highlighted in green.

6. **Touch the X (Done) button when you're done searching.**

The Google Search app, found on the Apps Menu, works like a full-screen version of the Google widget. Use the app to search the web.

Sharing a page

There it is! That web page that you just *have* to talk about to everyone you know. The gauche way to share the page is to copy and paste it. Because you're reading this book, though, you know the better way to share a web page. Heed these steps:

1. **Go to the web page you want to share.**

2. **Press the Menu icon button and choose the Share Page command.**

   The Share Via menu appears, listing apps and methods by which you can share the page, as shown in Figure 7-5.

   The variety and number of items on the Share Via menu depend on the applications installed on your Tab. For example, you might see Twitter or Facebook appear, if you've set up those social networking sites as covered in Chapter 8.

3. **Choose a method to share the link.**

   For example, choose Email to send the link by mail, or Twitter to share the link with your followers.

4. **Do whatever happens next.**

   Whatever happens next depends on how you're sharing the link: Compose the e-mail, create a comment in Facebook, or whatever. Refer to various chapters in this book for specific directions.

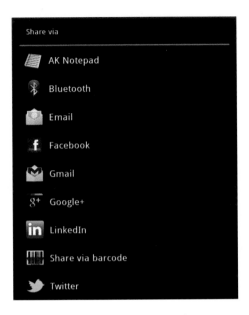

Figure 7-5: Options for sharing a web page.

Saving a web page

I like to save some web pages for later reading. It's not an obvious thing to do, but I save the web pages of long diatribes or interesting text so that I can read them later, such as when I'm cooped up in an airplane for a cross-country trip, sitting around bored at the car repair shop, or visiting other locations where time slows and boredom grows.

To save a web page, follow these steps:

1. **Visit the page you want to save.**

2. **Touch the Menu icon button and choose the command Save Page.**

    The page is downloaded to the Tab's internal storage.

The web page is saved in the `download` folder. You can view the page by opening the Downloads app and then choosing the page from the Downloads list.

✔ Web pages you save are given the same name or title as the web page itself. Look for that title in the list presented when you open the Downloads app.

> ✔ See the later section "Reviewing your downloads" for more information about the Downloads app.
>
> ✔ Refer to Chapter 19 for information on using your Galaxy Tab on an airplane.

The Art of Downloading

There's nothing to downloading, other than understanding that most people use the term without knowing exactly what it means. Officially, a *download* is a transfer of information over a network from another source to your gizmo. For your Galaxy Tab, that network is the Internet, and the other source is a web page.

> ✔ The Downloading complete notification appears after the Galaxy Tab has downloaded something. You can choose that notification to view the download.
>
> ✔ There's no need to download program files to the Galaxy Tab. If you want new software, you can obtain it from the Android Market, covered in Chapter 16.
>
> ✔ Most people use the term *download* to refer to copying or transferring a file or other information. That's technically inaccurate, but the description passes for social discussion.
>
> ✔ The opposite of downloading is *uploading.* That's the process of sending information from your gizmo to another location on a network.

Grabbing an image from a web page

The simplest thing to download is an image from a web page. It's cinchy: Long-press the image. You see a pop-up menu appear, from which you choose the command Save Image.

To view images you download from the web, you use the Gallery app. Downloaded images are saved in the Download album.

> ✔ Refer to Chapter 12 for information on the Gallery.
>
> ✔ Technically, the image is stored on the Tab's internal storage. It can be found in the `download` folder. You can read about Galaxy Tab file storage in Chapter 18.

Downloading a file

The web is full of links that don't open in a web browser window. For example, some links automatically download, such as links to PDF files or Microsoft Word documents or other types of files that can't be displayed by a web browser. Such links are automatically downloaded.

To save other types of links that aren't automatically downloaded, long-press the link and choose the command Save Link from the menu that appears. If the Save Link command doesn't appear, the Galaxy Tab is unable to save the file, either because the file is of an unrecognized type or because there could be a security issue.

✔ You can view the saved file by using the Downloads app. See the next section.

✔ The Quickoffice app is used on the Galaxy Tab to display PDF and Microsoft Office files.

Reviewing your downloads

The Browser app keeps a list of all the stuff you download from the web. To review your download history, open the Downloads app on the Apps Menu screen. You'll see the list of downloads sorted by date, as shown in Figure 7-6.

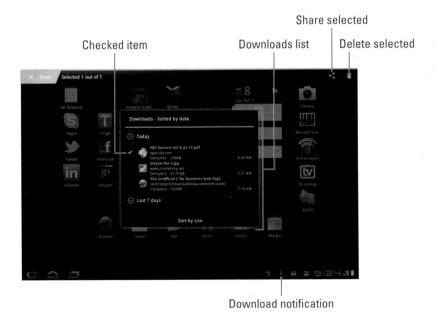

Figure 7-6: The Download Manager.

To view a download, choose it from the list. The Galaxy Tab opens the appropriate app to view the download.

- ✔ The Download Manager also lists any web pages you've downloaded.

- ✔ To remove an item from the Downloads list, place a green check mark in its box, as shown in Figure 7-6. Touch the Trash icon at the top of the screen to remove that download.

- ✔ Sharing a downloaded item is done by placing a green check mark by the downloaded file and choosing the Share icon button at the top of the screen. (Refer to Figure 7-6.)

- ✔ You can quickly review any download by choosing the Download notification.

Browser Controls and Settings

More options and settings and controls exist for the Browser app than just about any other app I've used on the Galaxy Tab. It's complex. Rather than bore you with every dang doodle detail, I thought I'd present just a few of the options worthy of your attention.

Setting a home page

The *home page* is the first page you see when you start the Browser app, and it's the first page that's loaded when you fire up a new tab. To set your home page, heed these directions:

1. **Browse to the page you want to set as the home page.**

2. **Touch the Menu icon button.**

3. **Choose Settings.**

   The Settings screen appears.

4. **Choose General on the left side of the screen.**

5. **Choose Set Home Page.**

6. **Touch the Current Page button.**

7. **Touch OK.**

   The home page is set.

I changed the home page on my Tab because it was preset to my cellular provider's page, and that page took forever to load. Remember: You don't have to use your cellular provider's home page.

If you want your home page to be blank (not set to any particular web page), type **about:blank** in the text box instead of touching the Current Page button. (Refer to Step 6.) That's the word *about,* a colon, and then the word *blank,* with no period at the end and no spaces in the middle. I prefer a blank home page because it's the fastest web page to load. It's also the web page with the most accurate information.

Changing the way the web looks

You can do a few things to improve the way the web looks on your Galaxy Tab. First and foremost, don't forget that you can orient the device horizontally and vertically, which rearranges the way a web page is displayed.

From the Settings screen, you can also adjust the zoom setting used to display a web page. Heed these steps when using the Browser app:

1. **Touch the Menu icon button.**

2. **Choose Settings.**

3. **Choose Advanced from the left side of the screen.**

4. **On the right side of the screen, choose Default Zoom.**

5. **Choose a setting.**

    There are three options: Far, Medium, and Close for tiny, normal, and larger sized web pages, respectively.

The Close setting might not be "big" enough, so remember that you can spread your fingers to zoom in on any web page.

You can also choose the Text Size command from the Advanced screen. That command changes the way text appears on a web page. There are five settings: Tiny through Huge.

Setting privacy and security options

With regard to security, my advice is always to be smart and think before doing anything questionable on the web. Use common sense. One of the most effective ways that the Bad Guys win is by using *human engineering* to try to trick you into doing something you normally wouldn't do, such as click a link to see a cute animation or a racy picture of a celebrity or politician. As long as you use your noggin, you should be safe.

As far as the Galaxy Tab's browser settings go, most of the security options are already enabled for you, including the blocking of pop-up windows (which normally spew ads).

If web page cookies concern you, you can clear them from the Settings window. Follow Steps 1 and 2 in the preceding section and choose Privacy & Security from the left side of the screen. Touch the option Clear All Cookie Data.

You can also choose the command Clear Form Data and remove the check mark from Remember Forum Data. These two settings prevent any text you've typed into a text field from being summoned automatically by someone who may steal your Tab.

You might be concerned about various warnings regarding location data. What they mean is that the Galaxy Tab can take advantage of your location on Planet Earth (using the GPS or satellite position system) to help locate businesses and people near you. I see no security problem in leaving that feature on, though you can disable location services from the Browser app's Settings screen, Privacy & Security page: Remove the check mark by Enable Location. You can also choose the item Clear Location Access to wipe out any information saved in the Tab and used by certain web pages.

See the earlier section, "Browsing back and forth," for steps on clearing your web-browsing history.

8

The Digital Social Life

In This Chapter

▶ Accessing social updates for your contacts

▶ Getting Facebook on the Galaxy Tab

▶ Sharing your life on Facebook

▶ Sending pictures to Facebook

▶ Tweeting on Twitter

▶ Exploring other social networking opportunities

*A*t the dawn of the Internet, there was no reason to use the Internet. Well, yes: It was a time-killer. Then came the glory of e-mail, the thrill of online shopping, the tedium of blogging. At the end of the first decade of the 21st century, there was another reason: online social networking.

Armed with your Galaxy Tab, you can keep your digital social life up-to-date wherever you go. You can communicate with your friends, followers, and buddies; let them know where you are; upload pictures and videos you take on the Tab; or just share your personal, private, intimate thoughts with all of humanity.

In Your Facebook

Of all the social networking sites, Facebook is the king. It's the online place to go to catch up with friends, send messages, express your thoughts, share pictures and video, play games, and waste more time than you ever thought you had.

✔ Though you can access Facebook on the web by using the Browser app, I highly recommend that you use the Facebook app described in this section.

✔ You can access updates to your contacts' Facebook statuses from the Contacts app. See Chapter 5.

✔ Facebook is one of the most popular sites on the Internet at the time this book goes to press. On some days, it sees more Internet traffic than Google.

✔ The Galaxy Tab is supposed to ship with a social networking app called the Social Hub. As this book goes to press, that app is not available. If it becomes available in the future, check my website for an update:

    www.wambooli.com/help/galaxytab

Setting up your Facebook account

The best way to use Facebook is to have a Facebook account, and the best way to do that is to sign up at www.facebook.com by using your computer. Register for a new account by setting up your username and password.

Don't forget your Facebook username and password!

Eventually, the Facebook robots send you a confirmation e-mail. You reply to that message, and the online social networking community braces itself for your long-awaited arrival.

After you're all set up, you're ready to access Facebook on your Galaxy Tab. To get the most from Facebook, you need a Facebook app. Keep reading in the next section.

Getting the Facebook app

The Galaxy Tab doesn't come with a Facebook app, but you can get the Facebook app for free from the Android Market. That app is your red carpet to the Facebook social networking kingdom.

To get the Facebook app, you can scan the barcode shown in the margin. Or, you can go to the Android Market and search for the Facebook for Android app. See Chapter 16.

Running Facebook on your Galaxy Tab

You access Facebook by running the Facebook app. If you can't find the Facebook app, you need to install it; refer to the preceding section.

The first time you behold the Facebook app, you'll probably be asked to log in. Do so: Type the e-mail address you used to sign up for Facebook and then type your Facebook password. Touch the Login button.

If you're asked to sync your contacts, do so. I recommend choosing the option Sync All, which brings in all your Facebook friends to the Tab's Contacts list. Touch the Finish button to begin using Facebook.

Eventually, you see the Facebook news or status updates feed. To go to the main Facebook page, shown in Figure 8-1, touch the Back icon button.

News Feed and status updates

Status update

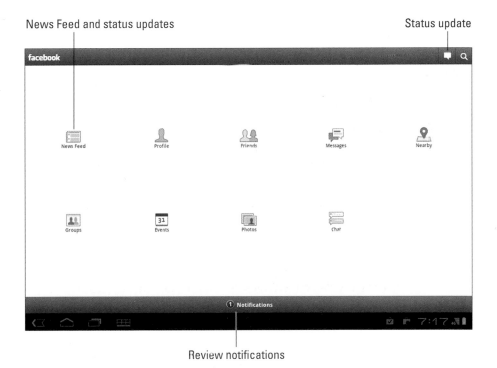

Review notifications

Figure 8-1: Facebook on the Galaxy Tab.

When you're done using Facebook, touch the Home icon button to return to the Home screen.

The Facebook app continues to run until you either sign out or turn off the Galaxy Tab. To sign out of Facebook, touch the Menu icon button (at the bottom of the screen) and choose the Logout command.

  ✔ Refer to Chapter 20 for information on placing a Facebook app shortcut on the Home screen.

  ✔ Also see Chapter 20 for information on adding a widget to the Home screen. The Facebook app comes with a widget that displays recent status updates and allows you to share your thoughts directly from the Home screen.

  ✔ To see more details on an item in the News Feed, choose that item. It appears on another screen, along with the details.

  ✔ The News Feed is updated when you swipe down on the screen.

  ✔ Notifications for Facebook appear at the bottom of the screen, as shown in the margin.

Setting your status

The primary thing you live for on Facebook, besides having more friends than anyone else, is to update your status. It's the best way to share your thoughts with the universe, far cheaper than skywriting and far less offensive than a robocall.

To set your status on the Galaxy Tab, follow these steps in the Facebook app:

  1. **View the News Feed.**

  2. **Touch the Status button at the top of the screen.**

     You see the Update Status screen, where you can type your musing, similar to what's shown in Figure 8-2.

  3. **Type something pithy, newsworthy, or typical of the stuff you read in Facebook.**

  4. **Touch the Post button.**

You can also set your status by using the Facebook widget on the home page, if it's been installed: Touch the What's on Your Mind text box, type your important news tidbit, and touch the Share button.

Choose friends to join you

Share your location

Upload photo

Choose sharing audience

Status update text

Share status

Figure 8-2: Updating your Facebook status.

Uploading a picture to Facebook

One of the many things your Galaxy Tab can do is take pictures. Combine that feature with the Facebook app, and you have an all-in-one gizmo designed for sharing the various intimate and private moments of your life with the ogling throngs of the Internet.

The key to sharing a picture on Facebook is to locate the wee Camera icon, which is found on the Update Status screen. (Refer to Figure 8-2.) There's also a Photo button on the News Feed screen. Sharing a picture works similarly no matter where you start.

Here's how to work that button and upload an image or a video to Facebook:

1. **Touch the big Photo button on the News Feed screen.**

2. **Choose Photo.**

3. **Choose an option from the Upload Photo menu.**

    You have two options for uploading a picture:

    Choose from Gallery: If you choose this option, browse the Gallery app to look for the picture you want to upload. (See Chapter 12 for more information on how the Gallery app works.)

Capture a Photo: Use the Galaxy Tab's camera to snap a picture of whatever is around you. Touch the Shutter button to snap the picture; touch Save to continue or Discard to start over and take a new picture. (See Chapter 11 for more information on how to use the Camera app.)

After selecting or taking a picture, the image appears as a thumbnail on the Write Post screen, which looks nearly identical to the Update Status screen, shown earlier in Figure 8-2.

4. **Optionally, type some text to accompany the image.**

5. **Touch the Post button.**

The image is posted as soon as it's transferred over the Internet and digested by Facebook.

The image can be found as part of your status update/News Feed, but it's also saved to the Mobile Uploads album.

When you choose Video in Step 2, things work pretty much the same; refer to Chapter 11 for more details on using the Galaxy Tab as a video camera.

✔ You can use the Facebook app to view the image in Facebook, or you can use Facebook on any computer connected to the Internet.

✔ To view your Facebook photo albums, choose Profile from the main Facebook screen and then choose Photos from the bottom of your profile page. Choose an album to view the photos.

✔ Facebook also appears on the various Share menus you find on the Galaxy Tab. Choose Facebook from the Share menu to send to Facebook whatever it is you're looking at. (Other chapters in this book give you more information about the various Share menus and where they appear.)

Configuring the Facebook app

The commands that control Facebook are stored on the Settings screen, which you access by touching the Menu icon button while viewing the main Facebook screen and choosing the Settings command.

Choose Refresh Interval to specify how often the Tab checks for new Facebook activities. You might find the one-hour value to be too long for your active Facebook social life, so choose something quicker. Or, to disable Facebook notifications, choose Never.

The following two options determine how the Galaxy Tab reacts to Facebook updates:

Vibrate: Vibrates the Tab

Notification Ringtone: Plays a specific ringtone

For the notification ringtone, choose the Silent option when you want the Tab not to make noise upon encountering a Facebook update.

 Touch the Back icon button to close the Settings screen and return to the main Facebook screen.

Tweet Suite

Twitter is a social networking site, similar to Facebook but far briefer. On Twitter, you write short spurts of text that express your thoughts or observations, or you share links. Or, you can just use Twitter to follow the thoughts and twitterings, or *tweets,* of other people.

- ✔ A message posted on Twitter is a *tweet.*
- ✔ A tweet can be no more than 140 characters long. That number includes spaces and punctuation.
- ✔ You can post messages on Twitter and follow others who post messages.
- ✔ They say that of all the people who have accounts on Twitter, only a small portion of them actively use the service.
- ✔ I'm not a big fan of Twitter. Even more so than Facebook, Twitter seems to exist to sate some people's craving for attention. It provides the bricks that pave the road to pseudo-fame, so a lot of what I read on Twitter seems to me to be self-centered junk. Then again, I've seen some good news feeds on Twitter, so I don't dislike it completely.

Setting up Twitter

The best way to use Twitter on the Galaxy Tab is to already have a Twitter account. Start by going to `http://twitter.com` on a computer and following the directions there for creating a new account.

 After you've established a Twitter account, obtain the Twitter app for your Galaxy Tab. The app can be obtained from the Android Market. Use the QR code in the margin to get a quick link to the app. (Refer to Chapter 16 for additional information on downloading apps to your Galaxy Tab.)

When you start the Twitter app for the first time, touch the Sign In button. Type your Twitter username or e-mail address and then type your Twitter password. After that, you can use Twitter without having to log in again — until you turn off the Tab or exit the Twitter app.

Figure 8-3 shows the Twitter app's main screen, which shows the current tweet feed.

Create new tweet

Updates   Timeline   Mentions   Messages   Lists

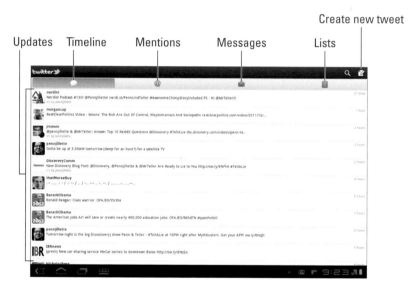

Figure 8-3: The Twitter app.

See the next section for information on *tweeting,* or updating your status using the Twitter app.

Tweeting

The Twitter app provides an excellent interface to the many wonderful and interesting things that Twitter does. Of course, the two most basic tasks are reading and writing tweets.

To read tweets, choose the Timeline as shown in Figure 8-3. Recent tweets are displayed in a list, with the most recent information at the top. Scroll the list by swiping it with your finger.

To tweet, touch the New Tweet icon. (Refer to Figure 8-3.) Use the New Tweet screen, shown in Figure 8-4, to compose your tweet.

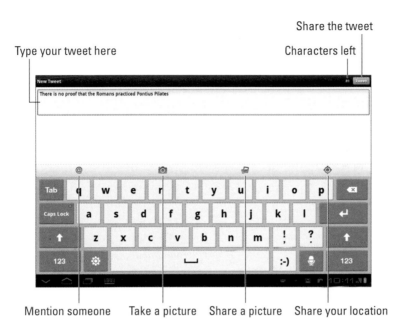

Figure 8-4: Creating a tweet.

Touch the Tweet button to share your thoughts with the Twitterverse.

- You have only 140 characters for creating your tweet. That includes spaces.

- The character counter in the Twitter app lets you know how close you're getting to the 140-character limit.

- Twitter itself doesn't display pictures, other than your account picture. When you send a picture to Twitter, you use an image-hosting service and then share the link, or URL, to the image. All that complexity is handled by the Twitter app.

- The Twitter app appears on various Share menus in other apps on your Galaxy Tab. You use those Share menus to send to Twitter whatever you're looking at.

Even More Social Networking

The Internet is nuts over social networking. Facebook may be the king, but there are lots of landed gentry out for that crown. It almost seems as though a new social networking site pops up every week. Beyond Facebook and Twitter, other social networking sites include, but are not limited to,

- Google+
- Latitude
- LinkedIn
- Meebo
- Myspace

I recommend first setting up the social networking account on your computer, similar to the way I describe it earlier in this chapter for Facebook and Twitter. After that, obtain an app for the social networking site using the Android Market. Set up and configure that app on your Galaxy Tab to connect with your existing account.

- See Chapter 16 for more information on the Android Market.

- Latitude is Google's social networking app that lets you share your location with your Google friends. You can also use Latitude to find your Google friends, meet up, or avoid them completely.

- As with Facebook and Twitter, you may find your social networking apps appearing on various Share menus on the Galaxy Tab. That way, you can easily share your pictures and other types of media with your online social networking pals.

9

Phone Calls and Video Chat

*E*ven though it's not a phone, your Galaxy Tab has a phone number. Well, if it's a non–Wi-Fi Tab, then it has a phone number. That number was assigned when you first bought the Tab, and it's used for billing purposes only. Such a situation might lead you to believe that the Galaxy Tab is utterly incapable of making phone calls. Oh, boy. Is that assumption ever incorrect.

Armed with the proper app, your Galaxy Tab can indeed make phone calls. Not only that, it can make *video* phone calls as well. They're not really true video calls, like the ones Walt Disney promised people in the 1960s, but they're a way to chat with other human beings while seeing them live on the Galaxy Tab screen. This chapter explains how it all works.

Google Can Talk and Look and Listen

I blame that front-facing camera. I mean, what's the point of having a front-facing camera unless you can do video chat? Sure, you can take pictures of yourself (self-portraits), which is covered in Chapter 11. But video chat is the new rage on mobile devices.

To answer the video chat call, you run the Google Talk app. It's rather limited in that you can video (and text) chat only with your Google contacts who've also configured Google Chat, but hey: That's good enough for me!

Google Talk started out as an extension of Gmail on the Internet, primarily as a way to instantly text chat with your Google friends. Eventually they added video chat and, lo, over all these years, video chat is now available on the Galaxy Tab.

Using Google Talk

Get started with Google Talk by starting the Talk app on your Galaxy Tab. Like all the apps, it's located on the Apps Menu, though you may be lucky and find a Talk app shortcut right on the main Home screen.

When you start the Talk app the first time, you're prompted to sign in using your Google account: Touch the Sign In button. That's it for the not-quite-painful setup.

After signing in, you see the main Talk screen, shown in Figure 9-1. Your Google contacts who have activated Google Talk, either on their computer or on a mobile gizmo like the Galaxy Tab, appear on the left side of the screen.

You can do three things with your friends while using the Talk app: Text chat, voice chat, and video chat. But before you do any of that, you need to get some friends.

To sign out of Google Talk, touch the Talk icon button in the upper-left corner of the screen. On the main Talk screen, touch the Sign Out button.

- You can redisplay your account Status by choosing your account from the Friends list, such as my account being chosen in Figure 9-1.

- You can touch the gray Status Message box to type in a new status for your account. For example, when I was writing this book, my status was, "I'm writing a book! Please chat with me!" Though that status wasn't very effective.

✔ Set your status icon by touching the menu just below the gray Status Message box. There are three status icons: Available, Busy, and Invisible.

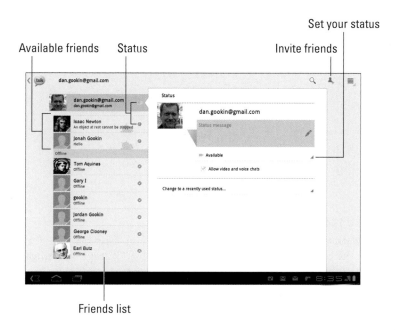

Figure 9-1: Google Talk.

Getting friends on Google Talk

Yeah, it happens: You don't have any friends. Well, at least you don't have any friends showing up in the Friends list in Google Talk. You can easily fix that problem: Touch the Invite Friends button, as shown in Figure 9-1. Type the friend's e-mail address and touch the Send Invitation button to send that person an invite.

You'll receive a reply to your invitation on a mobile device running the Talk app or on a computer with the Gmail web page open. When you receive the invitation, you find it listed in the Friends list. Initiations have the heading Chat Invitation.

To accept an incoming invitation, touch the Chat Invitation item in your Friends list. You see the Accept Invitation dialog box. Touch the Accept button to confirm your friendship and, eventually, chat with that person.

Your friends can be on a computer or mobile device to use Google Talk; it doesn't matter which. But they must have a camera available to enable video chat.

Typing at your friends

The most basic form of communications with the Talk app is text chatting. That means typing at another person, which is probably one of the oldest forms of communications on the Internet. It's also the most tedious, so I'll be brief.

You start text chatting by touching a contact in the Friends list. Type your message as shown in Figure 9-2. Touch the Send button to send your comment.

Current chat friend   Conversation

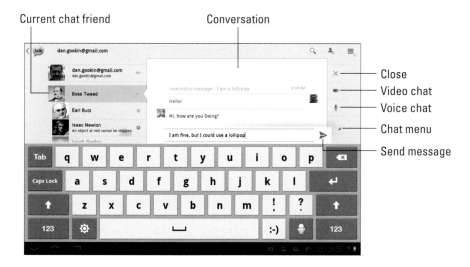

Close

Video chat

Voice chat

Chat menu

Send message

Figure 9-2: Text chatting.

You type, your friend types, and so on until you get tired or the Tab runs out of battery juice.

When you're done talking, touch the X (Close) button, as illustrated in Figure 9-2. Or you can just choose another friend from the list and chat with him. Or you can touch your own name on the list, which shows your current status.

Resume any conversation by choosing that same contact from the Friends list.

Talking and video chat

Take the conversation up a notch by touching the Voice or Video button on the right side of the text chat window. (Refer to Figure 9-2.) When you do, your friend receives an invite pop-up and Talk notification. Or if a friend is asking you to voice or video chat, you see the pop-up. Touch the Accept button to begin talking.

Figure 9-3 shows a video chat. The person you're talking with appears in the big window; you're in the smaller window. With the connection made and the invite accepted, you can begin enjoying video chat.

Figure 9-3: Video chat on the Galaxy Tab.

The controls in the upper-right corner of the screen may vanish after a second; touch the screen to see the controls again.

To end the conversation, touch the X (Close) button. Well, say "Goodbye" first and then touch the X button.

- ✔ When you're nude or just don't want to video chat, touch the Decline button for the video chat invite. Then choose that contact and reply with a text message or voice chat instead.

- ✔ You can disable incoming voice and video chats by deselecting the Allow Video and Voice Chats item on your Talk account's Status screen. Refer to Figure 9-1.

✔ The Galaxy Tab's front-facing camera is at the top center of the Tab. If you want to make eye contact, look directly into the camera, though when you do you won't be able to see the other person.

Connect to the World with Skype

Perhaps the most versatile app for converting the phoneless Galaxy Tab into a phone is Skype. It's one of the most popular Internet communications programs, allowing you to text, voice, or video chat with others on the Internet as well as use the Internet to make real, honest-to-goodness phone calls.

Obtaining a Skype account

Get started with Skype by creating an account. I recommend visiting www.skype.com on a computer, where you can enjoy the full screen and keyboard, though you can use the Browser on the Galaxy Tab if you've completely shunned computers.

At the Skype website, click the Join Skype button or, if the page has been updated since this book went to press, find and click a similar-sounding button. Sign up according to the directions offered on the website.

After you have a Skype account, the next step is to obtain a copy of the Skype app for your Galaxy Tab, as covered in the next section.

✔ As with other web services, you create a Skype name to identify your user account. It's the name you use to identify yourself to others who use Skype.

✔ If you want to use Skype to place phone calls, you need to stuff some cash into your account. Log in to the Skype website and follow the directions for getting Skype Credit.

✔ There's no charge for using Skype to chat with other Skype users. As long as you know the other party's Skype name, connecting and chatting is simple. See the later section, "Chatting with another Skype user."

Getting Skype for the Galaxy Tab

Your Galaxy Tab doesn't come with Skype software preinstalled. To get Skype, saunter on over to the Android Market and download the app. If you have a barcode–scanning app, you can also scan the icon in the margin, as described in this book's Introduction.

After installing Skype on your Tab, follow these steps to get started:

1. **Start the Skype app.**

2. **Read through the initial, informational screens.**

   You can't make emergency calls using Skype.

3. **Type in your account name and password.**

4. **Touch the Sign In button.**

   You may be asked to accept the terms of agreement; do so. There may be a tour presented that previews how Skype works. Feel free to skip the tour.

One of the biggest questions you're asked when you first run the Skype app on your Galaxy Tab is whether you want to synchronize your contacts. I recommend choosing the preset option, Sync With Existing Contacts. Touch the Continue button.

The main Skype screen is shown in Figure 9-4. The Contacts button lists people and phone numbers you've connected with on Skype. The later section, "Building your Skype Contacts list," describes how to get more contacts than just Skype Test Call.

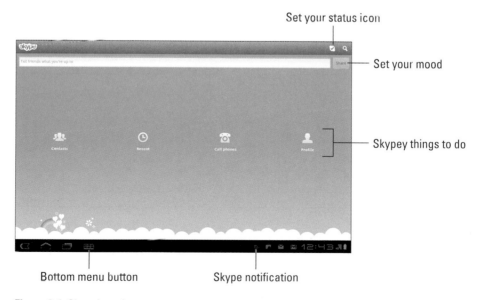

Set your status icon

Set your mood

Skypey things to do

Bottom menu button

Skype notification

Figure 9-4: Skype's main screen.

The Skype app stays active the entire time your Tab is on. If you desire to sign out of Skype, follow these steps:

1. **Touch the Profile button on the Skype app's main screen.**

   Refer to Figure 9-4.

2. **Touch the bottom Menu icon button.**

3. **Choose Sign Out.**

4. **Touch the Yes button.**

You're prompted to sign back in to Skype the next time you run the app.

  ✔ To quickly access Skype, touch the Skype notification, shown in the margin.

  ✔ You can make calls to phones on Skype only when you've added Skype Credit to your account.

Managing your Skype status

You have two ways to present yourself to the Skype universe. The first is your Skype mood, a message that's always displayed. The second is the Skype status, which tells the Skype-o-verse how open you are to receiving new calls.

To set either your mood or status, touch the Profile button on the main Skype screen. (Refer to Figure 9-4.)

Set your mood by touching the mood message next to your account picture. Type in some text using the onscreen keyboard.

Set your status by touching the Status button at the top of the screen, illustrated earlier in Figure 9-4. A toolbar with a variety of status icons appears, describing whether you're open for calls, away, or prefer not to be bothered.

The Profile screen also lists how much Skype Credit you have. To purchase more credit, touch the Skype Credit button, whip out your credit card, and follow the directions on the screen.

Building your Skype Contacts list

Text, voice, and video chat on Skype over the Internet are free. If you can use a Wi-Fi connection, you can chat without incurring a loss of your cellular plan's data quota. Before you can talk, however, you need to connect with another Skype user.

Yes, the other person must have a Skype account. Further, the person must agree to your request to become a Skype contact.

The Skype app can scan your Galaxy Tab's address book (the Contacts list) for any potential Skype subscribers you may have missed. The operation can take some time — like over an hour — though it's worthwhile. To find your friends on Skype, follow these steps:

1. **Touch the Contacts button on the Skype app's main screen.**

2. **Touch the bottom Menu icon button.**

3. **Choose Search Address Book.**

   You most likely already have a gaggle of contacts in your Tab. The Skype app can scour your Contacts list and discover which ones are already on Skype.

4. **Touch the Continue button.**

   This operation can take some time. (I'm serious — more than an hour.) Be patient.

   You can snooze the Tab while Skype is plowing through your Contacts list.

   Eventually, you see a list of Skype contacts that the Skype app has found in your Contacts list.

5. **Touch the Continue button.**

   The Skype app lists all contacts it could find who have Skype accounts.

6. **Remove the check marks by the contacts you don't want to add.**

   If you add all the contacts (done in Step 7), a Skype request is sent to each one. If you don't want to send a request to someone in the list, remove the check mark by that contact's name.

   Be sure to check the list! Skype searches for matching text, not for individuals, so random and unusual Skype contacts doubtlessly show up in the list, especially ones that list multiple Skype names; look for `Customer Care` and `noreply`, and be sure to remove them.

7. **Touch the Add button.**

8. **Type an introductory message.**

   The contact has to approve you as a Skype buddy, so make the message sound important but not urgent, wanting but not desperate.

9. **Touch the Add Contacts button.**

   The contacts are added to the Contacts tab, but they sport a question mark status until they agree to accept your Skype invitation.

If scanning the Galaxy Tab's Contacts list doesn't do the job, you search for a specific contact:

1. **Touch the Contacts button on the Skype app's main screen.**

2. **Touch the bottom Menu icon button.**

3. **Choose Add Contacts.**

4. **Type the contact's name or phone number.**

5. **Touch the Search icon button to start the search.**

6. **Scroll the list of results to find the exact person you're looking for.**

   If your friend has a common name, the list will be quite extensive. You can use city information to help narrow the list, but not every Skype user specifies a current city. The Skype username may also help you identify specific people.

7. **Touch an entry to add it to your Contacts list.**

   You see a full-page description for the contact, where you can choose to call him, chat on Skype, or add him to your Contacts list.

8. **Touch the Add button.**

No matter how you add people to your list, you see the question mark icon as a person's status until he agrees to accept your request.

✔ You can always e-mail people you know and ask them whether they're on Skype.

✔ Some people may not use Skype often, so it takes a while for them to respond to your friend request.

✔ If you accidentally add unusual or odd Skype contacts, my advice is to delete them. To remove a contact, long-press that contact's name in the list and choose the command Remove Contact from the pop-up menu.

✔ You can block a contact by long-pressing his entry and choosing the command Block Contact from the pop-up menu.

✔ If the Skype app crashes during a contact-searching operation, it's probably because you've collected some bogus Skype contacts. It happens. A good way to get out of this situation is to use the Skype program on a computer to clean up and remove unwanted contacts. You may also need to uninstall and then reinstall the Skype app. See Chapter 16 for information on uninstalling apps.

Chatting with another Skype user

You can text chat with any Skype user, which works similarly to texting, though with no maximum-character limitations. The only restriction is that you can chat only with other Skype users.

To chat, choose a contact from the Contacts list. (Refer to Figure 9-4.) You see a screen with more detailed information about the contact. Choose the option Send IM, where the IM stands for instant message. Providing that your Skype friend is online and eager, you'll be chatting in no time, as shown in Figure 9-5.

Type your text in the box, as illustrated in Figure 9-5. Touch the Send button to publish your comment. You can also use the Smiley button to insert a cute graphic into your text. The conversation unfolds similar to what's shown in Figure 9-5.

✔ The Skype Chat notification, shown in the margin, appears whenever someone wants to chat with you. It's handy to see, especially when you may have switched away from the Skype app to do something else on the Galaxy Tab. Simply touch that notification to get into the conversation.

✔ You can add more people to the conversation, if you like: Touch the bottom Menu icon button and choose the command Add. Select the contacts you want to join with your chat session, and then touch the Add Selected button. It's a gang chat!

✔ To stop chatting, touch the Back icon button. The conversation is kept in the Skype app, even after the other person has disconnected.

✔ For the chat to work, the other user must be online and available.

Stuff they write

Go to main Skype screen

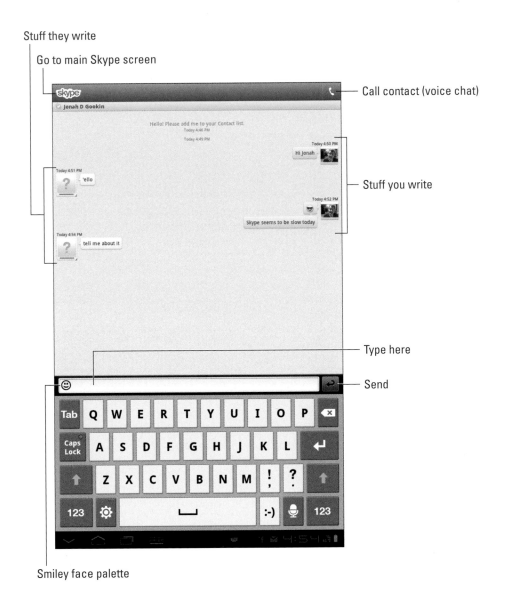

Call contact (voice chat)

Stuff you write

Type here

Send

Smiley face palette

Figure 9-5: Chatting on Skype.

Speaking on Skype (voice chat)

Perhaps the number-one reason for getting Skype is to transmogrify your Galaxy Tab into a phone. The trick works: As long as your pal has a Skype account, you can chat it up all you want, pretending all the while that the Tab is a phone. Follow these steps:

1. **Touch the Contacts icon on the Skype app's main screen.**

2. **Choose a contact.**

   Chatting works best when the contact is available: Look for a green check mark icon by her name.

3. **Choose Skype Call from the Actions tab on the contact's information screen.**

   If prompted, choose the contact's Skype account, not her phone number. (Calling a phone with Skype is covered in the next section.)

   In a few Internet seconds, the other person picks up, and you're speaking with each other. You see the In-Call screen, lovingly illustrated in Figure 9-6.

Skype contact to whom you're chatting   Silence speaker

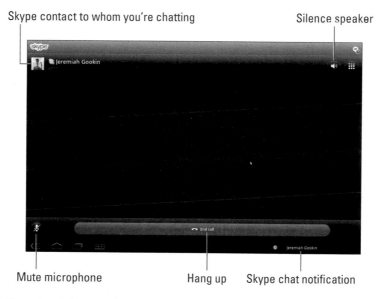

Mute microphone   Hang up   Skype chat notification

Figure 9-6: A Skype voice chat.

4. **Talk.**

   Blah-blah-blah. There's no time limit, though Internet connection problems may inadvertently hang you up.

To disconnect the call, touch the red End Call button, shown in Figure 9-6.

If someone calls you on Skype, you see the Skype incoming call screen, similar to the one shown in Figure 9-7. Touch the Answer button to accept the call and start talking. Touch Decline to dismiss the call, especially when it's someone who annoys you.

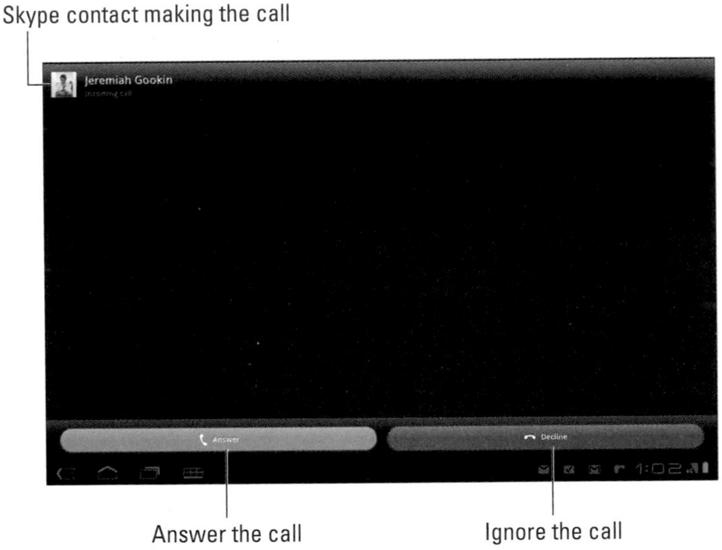

Skype contact making the call

Answer the call   Ignore the call

Figure 9-7: An incoming Skype voice call.

The Incoming Call screen (see Figure 9-7) appears even when the Galaxy Tab is sleeping. The incoming call wakes up the Tab.

- Voice chat on Skype over the Internet is free. When you use a Wi-Fi connection, you can chat without incurring a loss of your cellular plan's data minutes.
- You can chat with any user in your Skype contacts list, by using a mobile device, a computer, or any other gizmo on which Skype is installed.
- To mute the microphone, touch the Mute Mic button, illustrated earlier, in Figure 9-6.
- If you plan to use Skype a lot, get a good headset.
- When a headset is plugged in, the self-speaker Mute button switches between headphones and the Tab's built-in speakers.

Seeing on Skype (video call)

Your Galaxy Tab may be blessed with the ability to make Skype video calls. (The Skype app may not allow video chat on all Tabs.) If so, you can see your Skype contact while you yack with him. Well, it works providing that the other person also is using Skype on a gizmo that features video chat.

A video call works similarly to a Skype Call, covered in the preceding section. But instead of choosing Skype Call in Step 3, you choose Skype Video Call. And in Step 4, in addition to "Talk," you can make funny faces or show the other person around the room.

Use the Camera button (in the lower-right part of the screen) to turn the Galaxy Tab's video camera on or off or to switch between front and rear cameras.

Making a Skype phone call

Voice chat is okay on Skype, and it comes a close second to the real thing: making a phone call. Yep, you can use Skype to call any phone number on the planet, but most easily you can call people's phone numbers as listed in the Galaxy Tab's Contacts list. Here's what to do:

1. **Ensure that you have Skype Credit.**

   You can't make a "real" phone call unless you have Skype Credit on your account. You add Skype Credit by touching the Profile button (refer to Figure 9-4) and choosing Skype Credit.

2. **From the Skype app's main screen, touch the Call Phones button.**

   You see a big dial pad for typing phone numbers, just like you would if the Galaxy Tab were a huge cell phone.

3. **Type the phone number to dial.**

   Or, use the Contacts button in the upper-right corner of the screen to summon a contact. Choosing a contact places his number on the Call tab.

   Always input the full phone number when making a Skype phone call, including the country code, shown as +1 for the United States, as well as the area code.

4. **Touch the Done button to dismiss the onscreen dial pad.**

5. **Touch the Call button to place the call.**

This step works just like using a cell phone. Indeed, at this point, the Galaxy Tab has been transformed by the Skype app into a cell phone (albeit a cell phone that uses Internet telephony to make the call).

6. **Talk.**

   The In-Call screen looks nearly identical to Figure 9-6. The biggest difference is the per-minute price listed beneath the contact's name in the upper-left corner of the screen.

7. **To end the call, touch the End Call button.**

8. **If the number you dialed isn't a current Skype contact, touch the Add Contact button to create a Skype contact for that person.**

   Skype contacts are separate from Galaxy Tab contacts. By touching the Add Contact button, you create a phone number contact for the number you just dialed.

Lamentably, you can't receive a phone call using Skype on your Galaxy Tab from a cell phone or landline unless you pay for a Skype online number. In that case, you can use Skype to both send and receive regular phone calls. This book doesn't cover the Online Number option.

- ✔ You can check the Skype website for a current list of call rates, for both domestic and international calls: www.skype.com.

- ✔ Unless you've paid Skype to have a specific phone number, the phone number shown on the recipient's Caller ID screen is something unexpected, often merely the text Unknown. Because of that, you might want to e-mail or text the person you're calling and let her know that you're placing a Skype call. That way, she won't skip the call because she doesn't recognize the Caller ID number.

Sending a text message with Skype

One other cell phone–like thing you can do with Skype on your Galaxy Tab is to send a text message. If you have a teenager or are one, you recognize that text messaging is perhaps the only way young people use their cell phones. It's *rad*. (Or some other word similar to *rad* but more in sync with the current generation.)

To send a text message using the Skype app on your Galaxy Tab, heed these directions:

1. **Ensure that you have some Skype credit.**

Text messages aren't free, as any parent without an unlimited text messaging cellular plan can attest. As this book goes to press, it costs 11.2 cents to send a text message using Skype.

2. **Summon a contact from the list of Skype contacts.**

   Touch the Contacts icon on the main Skype screen and then choose a contact, hopefully one who also has his cell phone number listed.

3. **On the contact's info screen, choose SMS.**

   You see a text message composition screen, which is far too spacious and boring to illustrate in this book. Do note, however, the per-message cost listed in the upper-right corner of the screen.

4. **Touch the text box at the bottom of the screen.**

   The onscreen keyboard appears.

5. **Type your missive.**

   You have only 160 characters to make your point.

6. **Touch the Send button.**

   The text message is sent.

The cell phone you messaged receives the text just like any other text message. The sender information, however, might be only a cryptic number. So do make sure that you identify yourself when sending the text message.

The recipient can reply to the message. The reply is received in the Skype app, and it's tracked like a text conversation, similar to what's shown in Figure 9-5. The message may not be received instantly, as it is on a cell phone. Eventually you'll get the message. And you'll be charged for it.

   ✔ To get Skype Credit, touch the Profile icon on the main Skype screen. Touch the Skype Credit item and follow the directions on screen to buy more credit.

   ✔ It's possible to compose a text message from the Contacts app: When a contact's information is displayed, touch his phone number. Providing that the Skype app is running and you're signed in, you're whisked off to the text message composition screen, described earlier in this section.

   ✔ Text messages are also known by the scary and bewildering acronym *SMS*. I believe that means Short Message Service. Most people just say "text message."

Part III
The Everything Tab

Alice's
Adventures in
Lewis Carroll

Great
Expectations
Charles Dickens

*M*y favorite scenes from the original *Star Trek* TV show were when Mr. Spock would whip out his tricorder. It was a gizmo that could do everything. It recorded, analyzed, plus it could tap into the computer to recall information. I'm sure it could play music and remind Mr. Spock of upcoming appointments as well, but those scenes were never shown on TV.

Boy! Would Mr. Spock be jealous of the Galaxy Tab. It does just about everything that his old tricorder did — and more. Plus it does all those things without making a distracting whistling noise. If you'd like to do those things, too, just read this part of the book, which covers those wonderful, unusual, and potentially great things the Galaxy Tab can do.

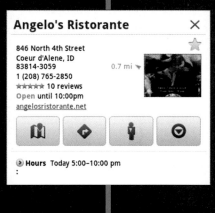

Angelo's Ristorante ✕

846 North 4th Street
Coeur d'Alene, ID
83814-3059
1 (208) 765-2850
★★★★★ 10 reviews
Open until 10:00pm
angelosristorante.net   0.7 mi ▾

🗺 ◈ 👤 ◉

② **Hours** Today 5:00–10:00 pm
:

Getting from Here to There

In This Chapter

▶ Exploring your world with Maps

▶ Adding layers to the map

▶ Finding your location

▶ Sharing your location

▶ Searching for places

▶ Using the Galaxy Tab as a navigator

▶ Adding a navigation Home screen shortcut

S tupid kidnappers. They frisked me for a phone but left the Galaxy Tab. I suppose they thought it might be a picture frame. Or perhaps they didn't even look inside the leatherette case, figuring it was portfolio. That was a mistake.

Even from inside the trunk, I could use the Tab. The signal was clear. The Maps app told me that I was in Seattle.

Seattle! Had they driven that far? It wasn't that important: Using the Tab, I knew not only where I was, but where a fancy Hungarian restaurant was nearby. I could send an e-mail with my location to the authorities and then be chowing down on a hot bowl of goulash in no time. Thank heavens for the Maps app!

There's a Map for That

Your location, as well as the location of things near and far, is found on the Galaxy Tab by using the Maps app. Good news: You run no risk of improperly folding the Maps app. Better news: The Maps app charts the entire country, including freeways, highways, roads, streets, avenues, drives, bike paths, addresses, businesses, and points of interest.

Using the Maps app

You start the Maps app by choosing Maps from the Apps Menu. If you're starting the app for the first time or it has been recently updated, you can read its What's New screen; touch the OK button to continue.

The Galaxy Tab communicates with global positioning system (GPS) satellites to hone in on your current location. (See the later sidebar, "Activate your locations!") It's shown on the map, similar to Figure 10-1. The position is accurate to within a given range, as shown by a blue circle around your location on the map.

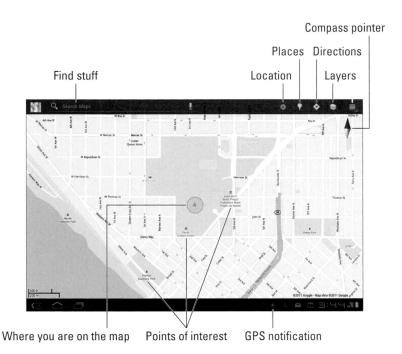

Figure 10-1: Your location on a map.

Here are some fun things you can do when viewing the basic street map:

Zoom in: To make the map larger (to move it closer), double-tap the screen or spread your fingers on the touchscreen.

Zoom out: To make the map smaller (to see more), pinch your fingers on the touchscreen.

Pan and scroll: To see what's to the left or right or at the top or bottom of the map, drag your finger on the touchscreen; the map scrolls in the direction you drag your finger.

Rotate: Using two fingers, rotate the map clockwise or counterclockwise. Touch the Compass Pointer (shown in Figure 10-1) to reorient the map with north at the top of the screen.

 Perspective: Tap the Location button to switch to Perspective view, where the map is shown at an angle. Touch the Location button again (though now it's really the Perspective button) to return to flat-map view or, if that doesn't work, touch the Compass Pointer.

The closer you zoom in to the map, the more detail you see, such as street names, address block numbers, and businesses and other sites — but no tiny people.

✔ The blue triangle (refer to Figure 10-1) shows in which general direction the Tab is pointing.

✔ When the Tab's direction is unavailable, you see a blue dot as your location on the map.

 ✔ When all you want is a virtual compass, similar to the one you lost as a kid, you can get the Compass app from the Android Market. See Chapter 16 for more information about the Android Market.

✔ You can enter Perspective view for only your current location.

Activate your locations!

The Maps app works best when you activate all the Galaxy Tab location technology. I recommend that you turn on three location settings. From the Apps Menu, open the Settings icon. Choose Location & Security. In the Location and Security settings, ensure that green check marks appear by these two items:

Use Wireless Networks: Allows the Tab to use signals from the Verizon cell towers to triangulate your position and refine the data received from GPS satellites.

Use GPS Satellites: Allows your Tab to access the GPS (global positioning system) satellites, but it's not that accurate. That's why you need to activate more than this service to fully use your Tab's location abilities.

Further, you can activate the Tab's Wi-Fi radio for even more exact location information. See Chapter 17 for information on turning on the Galaxy Tab Wi-Fi setting.

Adding layers

You add details from the Maps app by applying *layers:* A layer can enhance the map's visual appearance, provide more information, or add other fun features to the basic street map, such as Satellite view, shown in Figure 10-2.

Layers button

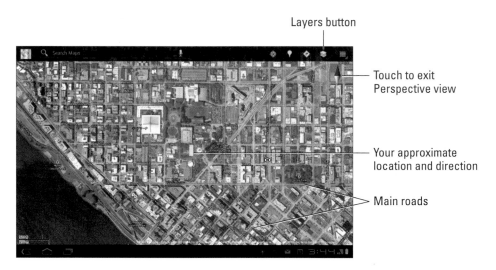

Touch to exit
Perspective view

Your approximate
location and direction

Main roads

Figure 10-2: The Satellite layer.

The key to accessing layers is to touch the Layers button, illustrated in Figure 10-2. Choose an option from the Layers menu to add that information to the Map app's display.

You can add another layer by choosing it from the Layers menu, but keep in mind that some layers obscure others. For example, the Terrain layer overlays the Satellite layer so that you see only the Terrain layer.

To remove a layer, choose it from the Layers menu; any active layer appears with a green check mark to its right. To return to Street view, remove all layers.

✔ Most of the features found on the Layers menu originated in the Google Labs. To see new features that may be added to the Maps app, visit the Labs by touching the Menu icon button in the Maps app. Choose Labs to pore over potential new features.

✔ The Galaxy Tab warns you whenever various applications access the Tab's Location feature. The warning is nothing serious — the Tab is just letting you know that an app is accessing the device's physical location.

Some folks may view this action as an invasion of privacy; hence the warnings. I see no issue with letting the Tab know where you are, but I understand that not everyone feels that way. If you'd rather not share location information, simply decline access when prompted.

It Knows Where You Are

You can look at a physical map all day long, and unless you have a sextant or a GPS, how would you know where you are? Never fear! The Galaxy Tab knows where you are. Not only does it have a GPS, but by using the Maps app, you can also instantly find out where you are and what's nearby and even send your location to someone else.

Finding out where you are

The Maps app shows your location as a compass arrow or blue dot on the screen. But *where* is that? I mean, if you need to phone a tow truck, you can't just say, "I'm the blue triangle on the orange slab by the green thing."

Well, you *can* say that, but it probably won't do any good.

To find your current street address, or any street address, long-press a location on the Maps screen. Up pops a bubble, similar to the one shown in Figure 10-3, that gives your approximate address.

Information about your current location

Figure 10-3: Finding an address.

If you touch the address bubble, you see a pop-up window full of interesting things you can do, also shown in Figure 10-3.

- ✔ When you're searching for a location, distance and general direction are shown in the pop-up window. Otherwise, as shown in Figure 10-3, the distance and direction information isn't necessary.

- ✔ The What's Nearby command displays a list of nearby businesses or points of interest, some of them shown on the screen and others available if you touch the What's Nearby command.

- ✔ Choose the Search Nearby item to use the Search command to locate businesses, people, or points of interest near the given location.

- ✔ What's *really* fun to play with is the Street View command. Choosing this option displays the location from a 360-degree perspective. In Street view, you can browse a locale, pan and tilt, or zoom in on details to familiarize yourself with an area, for example — whether you're familiarizing yourself with a location or planning a burglary.

Helping others find your location

It's possible to use the Maps app to send your current location to a friend. If your pal has a mobile device (phone or tablet) with smarts similar to the Galaxy Tab, he can use the coordinates to get directions to your location. Maybe he'll even bring some goulash!

To send your current location in an e-mail message, obey these steps:

1. **Long-press your current location on the Map.**

   You see a pop-up bubble.

2. **Touch the pop-up bubble.**

3. **Choose the command Share This Place from the pop-up window.**

   The pop-up window is shown in Figure 10-3.

4. **Choose either the Gmail or Email item from the Share This Place menu.**

   The Gmail or Email app starts, with a preset subject and message. The subject is your street address or the address of the bubble you touched in Step 2. The message content is the address again, but it's also a link to the current location.

5. **Type one or more recipients into the To field.**

6. **Touch the Send button to whisk off the message.**

When the recipient receives the e-mail, she can touch the link to open your location in the Maps app — providing that she has a Galaxy Tab or some other mobile Android device. When the location appears, she can follow my advice in the later section, "Getting directions," for getting to your location. And don't loan her this book either; have her buy her own copy. And bring goulash. Thanks.

Find Things

The Maps app can help you find places in the real world, just like the Browser app helps you find places on the Internet. Both operations work basically the same:

Open the Maps app and type something to find into the Search Maps text box, as illustrated in Figure 10-1. You can type a variety of terms into the Search box, as explained in this section.

Looking for a specific address

To locate an address, type it into the Search box; for example:

```
1600 Pennsylvania Ave., Washington, D.C. 20006
```

Touch the Search button on the keyboard, and that location is then shown on the map. The next step is getting directions, which you can read about in the later section, "Getting directions."

- You don't need to type the entire address. Oftentimes, all you need is the street number and street name and then either the city name or zip code.
- If you omit the city name or zip code, the Galaxy Tab looks for the closest matching address near your current location.

Finding a business, restaurant, or point of interest

You may not know an address, but you know when you crave sushi or Hungarian or perhaps the exotic flavors of Freedonia. Maybe you need a hotel or a gas station, or you have to find a place that buys old dentures. To find a business entity or a point of interest, type its name in the Search box; for example:

```
Movie theater
```

This command flags movie theaters on the current Maps screen or nearby.

Specify your current location, as described earlier in this chapter, to find locations near you. Otherwise, the Maps app looks for places near the area you see on the screen.

Or, you can be specific and look for businesses near a certain location by specifying the city name, district, or zip code, such as

```
Hungarian 98001
```

After typing this command and touching the Search button, you see a smattering of Hungarian restaurants found near Seattle, similar to the ones shown in Figure 10-4.

Search text

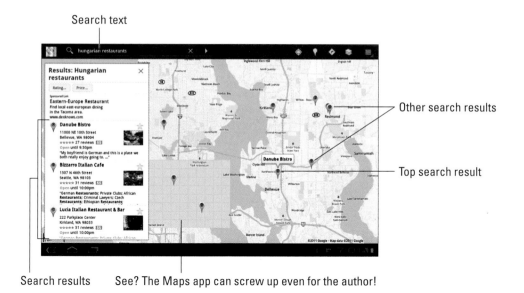

Other search results

Top search result

Search results   See? The Maps app can screw up even for the author!

Figure 10-4: Finding Hungarian restaurants near Seattle, Washington.

To see more information about a result, touch its cartoon bubble, such as the one for the Danube Bistro in Figure 10-4. The screen that appears offers more information, plus perhaps even a web address and Tab number.

 You can touch the Get Directions button on the restaurant's (or any location's) details screen to get directions; see the later section, "Getting directions."

- ✔ Every letter or dot on the screen represents a search result. (Refer to Figure 10-4.)
- ✔ Spread your fingers on the touchscreen to zoom in to the map.
- ✔ You can create a contact for the location, keeping it as a part of your Contacts list: After touching the location balloon, touch the More button and choose the command Add As a Contact. The contact is created using data known about the business, including its location and Tab number and even a web page address — if that information is available.

Searching for interesting places

Maybe you don't know what you're looking for. Maybe you're like my teenage sons, who stand in front of the open refrigerator, waiting for the sandwich fairy to hand them a snack. The Maps app features a sort of I-don't-know-what-I-want-but-I-want-something fairy. It's the Places command.

Touch the Places button (refer to Figure 10-1) to see the Places pop-up window. It shows categories of places near you: restaurants, coffee shops, bars, hotels, attractions, and more. Touch an item to see matching locations in your vicinity.

You can also use the Places app to summon the Places pop-up window in the Maps app. You can find the Places app on the Apps Menu.

Locating a contact

You can hone in on where your contacts are located by using the Maps app. This trick works when you've specified an address for the contact — home, work, prison, or another location. If so, the Galaxy Tab can easily help you find that location or even give you directions.

The secret to finding a contact's location is the little Place icon by the contact's address, shown in the margin. Anytime you see this icon, you can touch it to view that location by using the Maps app.

The Galaxy Tab Is Your Copilot

Finding something is only half the job. The other half is getting there. The Galaxy Tab is ever-ready, thanks to the various direction and navigation features nestled in the Maps app.

I don't believe that the Galaxy Tab has a car mount, not like a cell phone does. Therefore, I strongly recommend that if you use your Tab in your auto, have someone else hold it and read the directions. Or use voice navigation and, for goodness sake, don't look at the Tab while you're driving!

Getting directions

One command associated with locations on the map is Get Directions. Here's how to use it:

1. **Touch a location's cartoon bubble displayed by an address, a contact, or a business or from the result of a map search.**

   A pop-up window appears, offering more information, similar to what's shown in Figure 10-3.

2. **Touch the Directions button.**

   A menu appears, offering three choices.

3. **Choose Get Directions from the Please Select menu.**

   A list of directions appears on the left side of the screen, similar to what's shown in Figure 10-5. The list starts with your location and ends at the location you selected. A blue line on the map on the other side of the screen shows your route.

4. **Follow the blue line.**

If you can't constantly look at the Tab to see the map, touch the Navigation button, shown in Figure 10-5. Also see the next section for more details on navigation using the Maps app.

> ✔ The Maps app alerts you to any toll roads on the specified route. As you travel, you can choose alternative, non-toll routes if available. You're prompted to switch routes during navigation; see the next section.

> ✔ You may not get perfect directions from the Maps app, but for places you've never visited, it's a useful tool.

Navigating to your destination

Maps and lists of directions are so 20th century. I don't know why anyone would bother, especially when the Galaxy Tab features a digital copilot in the form of voice navigation.

Change starting or ending points

Choose transportation method Navigation Your location Your destination

Directions   Your route

Figure 10-5: Going from here to there.

To use navigation, choose the Navigation option from any list of directions. Or, touch the Navigation button, as shown earlier, in Figure 10-5. You can also enter the Navigation app directly by choosing it from the Apps Menu, though then you must type (or speak) your destination, so it's just easier to start in the Maps app.

In Navigation mode, the Galaxy Tab displays an interactive map that shows your current location and turn-by-turn directions for reaching your destination. A digital voice tells you how far to go and when to turn, for example, and gives you other nagging advice — just like a backseat driver, albeit an accurate one.

After choosing Navigation, sit back and have the Tab dictate your directions. You can simply listen, or just glance at the Tab for an update of where you're heading.

To stop navigation, touch the Menu icon button and choose the Exit Navigation command.

✔ To remove the navigation route from the screen, exit Navigation mode and return to the Maps app. Touch the Menu icon button and choose the Clear Map command.

✔ When you tire of hearing the navigation voice, touch the Menu icon button and choose the Mute command.

✔ I refer to the navigation voice as *Gertrude*.

✔ You can touch the Menu icon button while navigating and choose Route Info to see an overview of your journey.

✔ When viewing the Route Info screen, touch the Gear button to see a handy pop-up menu. From this menu, you can choose options to modify the route so that you avoid highways or toll roads, for example.

✔ The neat thing about the Navigation feature is that whenever you screw up, a new course is immediately calculated.

✔ In Navigation mode, the Galaxy Tab consumes a lot of battery power. I highly recommend that you plug the Tab into your car's power adapter ("cigarette lighter") for the duration of the trip.

Adding a navigation shortcut to the Home screen

When you visit certain places often — such as the liquor store — you can save yourself the time you would spend repeatedly inputting navigation information: All you need to do is create a navigation shortcut on the Home screen. Here's how:

1. **Touch the Add button in the upper-right corner of the Home screen.**

   You see the Home screen overview, which shows all five Home screen panels plus categories listing items you can add to the Home screen.

2. **Choose the More category.**

3. **Choose Directions & Navigation.**

4. **Type a destination, a contact name, an address, or a business in the text box.**

   As you type, suggestions appear in a list. You can choose a suggestion to save yourself some typing.

5. **Choose a traveling method.**

   Your options are car, public transportation, bicycle, and on foot.

6. **Scroll down a bit to type a shortcut name.**

7. **Choose an icon for the shortcut.**

   You may have to touch the Back icon button to dismiss the onscreen keyboard and see the shortcut icons.

8. **Touch the Save button.**

   The navigation shortcut is placed on the Home screen.

9. **Touch the Home icon button to return to the Home screen.**

To use the shortcut, simply touch it on the Home screen. Instantly, the Maps app starts and enters Navigation mode, steering you from wherever you are to the location referenced by the shortcut.

See Chapter 20 for additional information on creating Home screen shortcuts.

Where Are Your Friends?

A feature in the Maps app is Latitude. It's a layer you can apply to a map, but it's also the name of its own app, Latitude.

Latitude is a social networking service that lets you share your physical location with your friends, also assumed to be using Latitude. Being able to more easily know where your friends are makes it possible to meet up with them — or, I suppose, to avoid them. It's all up to you.

To join Latitude, you touch the Menu icon button when viewing a map and then choose the Join Latitude command. Or, you can just start the Latitude app.

After opening Latitude, read the information and then touch the Allow & Share button to continue. If you don't see the Join Latitude command, you've already joined; start Latitude by choosing the Latitude command.

To make Latitude work, you need to add friends to Latitude, and those friends need to use Latitude. After adding Latitude friends, you can share your location with them as well as view their locations on a map. You can also chat with Google Talk, send them e-mail, get directions to their location, and do other interesting things.

To exit Latitude, touch the Menu icon button when Latitude is active and choose Settings. Choose the Sign Out of Latitude command from the Settings pop-up window.

It's a Big, Flat Camera

C ameras have come a long way since Nicéphore Niépce took a day-long exposure of his backyard using a *camera obscura.* Photography was an analog, real-world thing until the 1990s. Then technology went digital, and in a few decades, it will be old people who refer to a "roll" of film.

What's also changed is the camera. No more do you hold the thing up to your face. Instead, you hold the device at arm's length and peer at a teensy monitor. What's even more strange is holding up a large, flat object such as the Galaxy Tab and using it to take a picture. Sure, it works. It's handy. But it's just very unusual and different enough that I present to you an entire chapter on using your Tab as a camera.

The Galaxy Tab Camera

I admit that the Galaxy Tab isn't the world's best camera. And I'm sure that Mr. Spock's tricorder wasn't the best camera in the *Star Trek* universe, either, but it could take pictures. That comparison is kind of the whole point: Your Galaxy Tab is an incredible gizmo that does many things. One of those things is to take pictures, as described in this section.

Snapping a pic

Picture-taking duties on your Galaxy Tab are handled by the Camera app. It controls both the main camera, which is on the Tab's butt, and the front-facing camera, which is not on the Tab's butt. Like all apps on the Tab, you can find and start the Camera app by touching its icon on the Apps Menu screen.

After starting the Camera app, you see the main Camera screen, as illustrated in Figure 11-1.

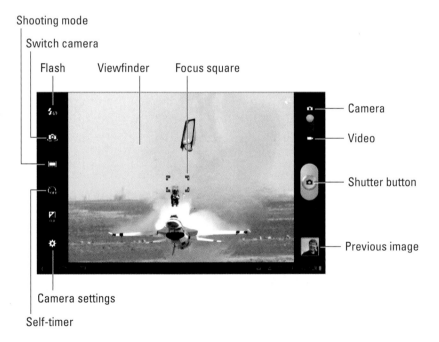

Figure 11-1: Your Tab as a camera.

To take a picture, first ensure that the Camera app is in still picture mode: Check the switch on the upper-right part of the screen to confirm that it's in the Camera position. Then point the camera at the subject and touch the Shutter button, shown in Figure 11-1.

After you touch the Shutter button, the camera will focus, you may hear a mechanical shutter sound play, and the flash may go off. You're ready to take the next picture.

To preview the image you just snapped, touch the little icon that appears in the lower-right corner of the screen, as shown in Figure 11-1.

- The Wi-Fi Tab features an extra button on the bottom left. (Refer to Figure 11-1.) It's the Back button, which is used to exit the Camera app.

- The camera focuses automatically, though you can drag the focus square around the touchscreen to specifically adjust the focus. (Refer to Figure 11-1.)

- The Galaxy Tab camera has a fixed focal-length lens, so there is no zoom feature.

- The Tab can be used as a camera in either landscape or portrait orientation, though the Tab's controls and gizmos are always presented in landscape format. (Refer to Figure 11-1.) The icons rotate when you reorient the Tab.

- You can take as many pictures with your Galaxy Tab as you like, as long as you don't run out of space for them in the Tab's internal storage.

- If your pictures appear blurry, ensure that the camera lens on the back of the Galaxy Tab isn't dirty.

- Use the Gallery app to preview and manage your pictures. See Chapter 12 for more information about the Gallery.

- The Galaxy Tab not only takes a picture but also keeps track of where you were located on Planet Earth when you took it. See the section "Setting the image's location," later in this chapter, for details. Also refer to Chapter 12 for information on reviewing a photograph's location.

- The Galaxy Tab stores pictures in the JPEG image file format. Images are stored in the `DCIM/Camera` folder; they have the `jpg` filename extension. By default, images are stored on the MicroSD card. You can change the storage location by pulling out the Control Drawer and choosing the Settings icon. (Refer to Figure 11-1.) Choose Storage Location and select either Internal Phone Storage or SD Card.

Deleting an image immediately after you take it

Sometimes, you just can't wait to delete an image. Either an irritated person is standing next to you, begging that the photo be deleted, or you're just not happy and you feel the urge to smash into digital shards the picture you just took. Hastily follow these steps:

1. **Touch the image preview that appears in the lower-right corner of the screen. (Refer to Figure 11-1.)**

   After touching the preview, you see the full-screen image.

2. **Touch the Trash icon in the upper-right corner of the screen.**

3. **Choose Confirm Delete to erase the image.**

   The image has been banished to bit hell.

 If necessary, touch the Back icon button to return to the Camera app.

Setting the flash

The camera on the Galaxy Tab has three flash settings, as shown in Table 11-1.

Table 11-1		Galaxy Tab Camera Flash Settings
Setting	*Icon*	*Description*
Auto	🔆	The flash activates during low-light situations but not when it's bright out.
On	🔆	The flash always activates.
Off	🔆	The flash never activates, even in low-light situations.

To change or check the flash setting, look at the Flash button on the left side of the screen, shown earlier, in Figure 11-1. The button's icon confirms the current flash setting, which is Off in the figure. Choose the Flash setting from the pop-up menu that appears.

 A good time to turn on the flash is when taking pictures of people or objects in front of something bright, such as a cute, fuzzy kitten playing with a ball of white yarn in front of an exploding gasoline truck.

Changing the resolution

Proving once again that the Galaxy Tab isn't really a digital camera (it only *has* a digital camera), there are only two resolution settings for the main camera: pitiful and pathetic.

Well, the settings aren't called *pitiful* or *pathetic,* but compared with the high resolutions of mainstream consumer digital cameras, the resolutions aren't going to wow them at the county fair.

To set the resolution in the Camera app, touch the Settings button on the left side of the Camera app's main screen. (Refer to Figure 11-1.) Choose the Resolution command and then select between 2048X1536 (pitiful) and 1024X768 (pathetic).

Touch the Back icon button to dismiss the Settings menu.

- ✔ The Galaxy Tab's front-facing camera has a fixed resolution of 1,600 by 1,200 pixels.

- ✔ A picture's *resolution* describes how many pixels, or dots, are in the image. The more dots, the better the image looks and prints.

- ✔ The 2048X1536 resolution is 2,048 by 1,536 pixels, which works out to a 3.2 megapixel image. That's very low, seeing how most digital cameras — even on cell phones — are in the 8 megapixel range.

- ✔ *Megapixel* is a measurement of the amount of information stored in an image. One megapixel is approximately 1 million pixels, or individual dots that compose an image. It's often abbreviated MP.

- ✔ Even though the camera resolution is low, the quality is just super for taking pictures you plan on uploading to Facebook or sharing via e-mail.

- ✔ See the later section, "Setting video quality," for information on the Video Resolution setting, which applies only to shooting video with the Galaxy Tab.

Doing a self-portrait

Who needs to pay all that money for a mirror when you have the Galaxy Tab? Well, forget the mirror. Instead, think about taking all those self-shots without having to second-guess whether the camera is pointed at your face.

To take your own mug shot, start the Camera app and touch the Switch Camera button, shown earlier, in Figure 11-1. When you see yourself on the screen, you're doing it properly.

Smile. Click. You got it.

Touch the Switch Camera button again to direct the Galaxy Tab to use the main camera again.

Taking a panoramic shot

No, it's not an exotic new alcoholic drink: A *panorama* is a wide shot, like a landscape, a beautiful vista, or a family photograph after a garlic feast. One Galaxy Tab camera mode allows you to crunch several images into a panoramic shot. Obey these steps:

1. **Start the Camera app.**

2. **Touch the Shooting mode button.**

   Refer to Figure 11-1. The button's icon changes, depending on which mode you're using.

3. **Choose Panorama.**

4. **Hold your arms steady.**

5. **Touch the Shutter button.**

   You see a green frame on the screen, which approximates the current shot. Arrows point in the eight directions in which you can pan.

6. **Pivot slightly to your right (or in whatever direction, but you must continue in the same direction).**

   As you move the camera, the green frame adjusts to your new position. The Galaxy Tab beeps as the next image in the panorama is snapped automatically. All you need to do is keep moving.

7. **Continue pivoting as subsequent shots are taken, or touch the Shutter button again to finish the panorama.**

   After the last image is snapped, wait while the image is assembled.

The Camera app sticks the different shots together, creating a panoramic image.

- ✔ To exit Panoramic mode, repeat Steps 1 and 2, but in Step 3 choose Single Shot.

- ✔ The Galaxy Tab camera automatically captures the panoramic shot. You touch the Shutter button only when you're done.

Setting the image's location

The Galaxy Tab not only takes a picture, but also keeps track of where you're located on Planet Earth when you take the picture — if you've turned on that option. The feature is called Geo-Tab or GPS-Tag, and here's how to ensure that it's on:

1. **While using the Camera app, touch the Settings button.**

2. **Choose GPS Tag.**

3. **If the On setting isn't chosen, touch it to activate GPS Tag.**

4. **Touch the Back icon button to close the Settings menu.**

Not everyone is comfortable with having the Tab record a picture's location, so you can turn the option off. Just repeat these steps, but choose Off in Step 3.

See Chapter 12 for information on reviewing a photograph's location.

Adjusting the camera

The Camera app sports various adjustments you can make, two of which are fun to play with: Scene Mode and Effects. Both options are found on the Settings menu, which is displayed when you touch the Settings button on the left side of the screen. (Refer to Figure 11-1.)

Scene Mode: Choosing this item lets you configure the camera for taking certain types of pictures. Choose an option that describes the type of images you're capturing, such as Sports for quick-action, Night for low-light situations, or Text for copying documents. The None setting directs the camera to choose the best scene by guessing.

Effects: Add special visual effects by touching the Effects option. There are only four: None for no effects; Grayscale to shoot in monochrome; Sepia for that old-time look; and Negative, which is how people who watch too much politics on television see the world.

Live from Your Galaxy Tab, It's Video!

When the action is hot — when you need to capture more than a moment (and maybe the sounds) — you switch the Galaxy Tab camera into Video mode. Doing so may not turn you into the next David Fincher, because I hear he uses an iPhone to make his films.

Recording video

Video chores on the Galaxy Tab are handled by the same Camera app that takes still images, as discussed earlier in this chapter. The secret is to switch the Camera app into Video mode. You do that by flipping the switch illustrated in both Figures 11-1 and 11-2.

Adjust white balance

Switch camera

Light on/off

Maximum recording time

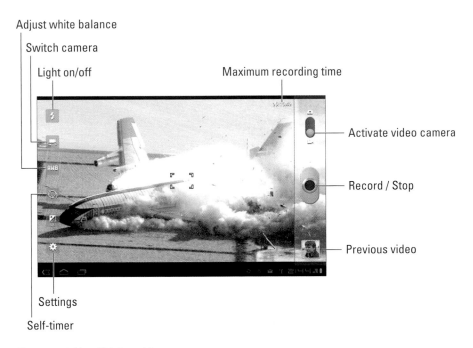

Activate video camera

Record / Stop

Previous video

Settings

Self-timer

Figure 11-2: Your Tab is a video camera.

The video interface on the Camera app is illustrated in Figure 11-2. Start shooting the video by touching the Record button.

While the Tab is recording, the Shutter button changes to the Stop button. A time indicator appears in the upper-right corner of the screen, telling you the video shot duration.

To stop recording, touch the Stop button.

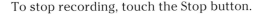

✔ Hold the Tab steady! The camera still works when you whip the Tab around, but wild gyrations render the video unwatchable.

✔ The Camera app restarts itself in video mode if that was the active mode when you last quit.

✔ The video's duration depends on its resolution (see the next section) as well as on the storage available on your Tab. The maximum recording time is shown on the screen before you shoot. (Refer to Figure 11-2.) While you record, elapsed time appears.

✔ As with the single-shot version of the Camera app, there are no zoom controls for shooting video.

✔ Visual effects (the cheap kind, not the Hollywood CGI kind) can be applied to the video. Touch the Settings button and choose Effects.

✔ Chapter 12 covers the Gallery app, used to view and manage videos stored on your Tab. Directions are also found in Chapter 15 for uploading your video to YouTube as well as editing video with the Movie Studio app.

✔ Recorded video is saved in the Tab's internal storage.

✔ The video is stored on the Galaxy Tab using the MPEG-4 video file format. The video files are located in the `DCIM/Camera` folder and have the `mp4` filename extension.

Setting video quality

You might guess that setting the highest video quality would always be best. Not so! For example, video you shoot for YouTube need not be of top quality. Multimedia text messaging (known as *MMS*) video should be of very low quality or else the video doesn't attach to the message. Also, high resolution video uses up a heck of a lot more storage space on the Galaxy Tab.

To set the video quality while using the Camcorder app, touch the Settings icon. (Refer to Figure 11-2.) Choose the Resolution command. There are two settings:

1080X720: The highest-quality setting is best suited for video you plan to show on a large-format TV or computer monitor. It's useful for video editing or for showing important events, such as Bigfoot sightings.

640X480: This setting is good for Internet video or e-mail attachments, though it doesn't enlarge well.

The front-facing camera has no video quality setting; the quality is fixed at 640X480, the same as the lowest setting for the main camera.

Check the video quality *before* you shoot! Especially if you know where the video will end up (on the Internet, on a TV, or in an MMS message), it helps to set the quality first.

Shedding some light on your subject

You don't need a flash when recording video, but occasionally you need a little more light. You can manually turn on the Galaxy Tab's LED flash to help: On the left side of the Camera app screen, touch the Light button. Choose On to turn on the LED light, and choose Off to disable it.

The light comes on only when you start recording your video.

There is no light for shooting video with the front-facing camera.

Turning on the LED light consumes a hefty portion of battery power. Use it sparingly.

Shooting yourself

Put away your crossbow, blow gun, and rubber bands. When I refer to "shooting yourself," I'm writing about the Galaxy Tab's ability to let you record your own image — your face — by using the front-facing video camera. It's cinchy.

The secret to shooting yourself is to touch the Switch Camera button, shown earlier in Figure 11-2. As soon as you see your punum on the touchscreen, you've done things properly.

The front-facing camera uses only 640 by 480 resolution (refer to the preceding section), though it's ideal for attaching to an e-mail or text message.

Also see Chapter 9 for information on video chat, which is a live version of shooting yourself.

Uploading and sharing video

Throughout various Galaxy Tab apps, you can find Upload commands and Share icon buttons. You can use those buttons to instantly capture a video and send it off to the Internet. For example, you can use the Facebook app to capture and upload a video faster than you can say, "Whoa! That was embarrassing."

The secret is to find the Upload or Share command. When you do, choose the option to Capture Video. After that, you see the Camera app in Video mode, where you can quickly capture a few seconds of real life. After you're done recording, you return to the other app, where you can add a title, comments, or do other mischief with your video.

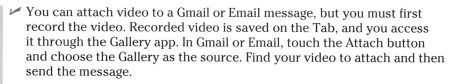

✔ You can attach video to a Gmail or Email message, but you must first record the video. Recorded video is saved on the Tab, and you access it through the Gallery app. In Gmail or Email, touch the Attach button and choose the Gallery as the source. Find your video to attach and then send the message.

✔ Refer to Chapter 6 for information on sending e-mail.

✔ Keep the video message short! Short is good for a video message attachment or an online post.

Galaxy Gallery

In This Chapter

▶ Viewing images and videos stored on your Tab

▶ Finding an image's location

▶ Setting an image for a contact or as wallpaper

▶ Editing images

▶ Deleting pictures and videos

▶ Using Picasa

▶ Printing an image

▶ Publishing a video on YouTube

▶ Sharing images and videos

*T*here's no point in the Galaxy Tab having a camera unless it has a place to store pictures. My inner nerd reminds me that the Tab's internal storage is the place where images and videos dwell, swaddled in a binary blanket called *digital film.* That's all safe and good, but how can you get to those pictures and videos? More importantly, how can you view them, share them with your friends, or send them off to the information superhighway?

The answer lies in an electronic Louvre of sorts. It's the Gallery app, which you can use to view, manage, and manipulate the images you take using the Galaxy Tab's cameras. Further, you can import other images into the Tab, including photos stored on your computer or found on the Internet. All that stuff is covered in this chapter.

Where Your Pictures Lurk

Some people hang their pictures on the wall. Some put pictures on a piano or maybe on a mantle. In the digital realm, pictures are stored electronically, compressed and squeezed into a series of ones and zeroes that mean nothing unless you have an app that lets you view those images. On the Galaxy Tab, that app is the *Gallery*.

Visiting the Gallery

Start the Gallery app by choosing its icon from the Apps Menu, or you might find a Gallery app shortcut icon on the Home screen.

When the Gallery app opens, you see your visual media (pictures and videos) organized into piles, or albums, as shown in Figure 12-1. The number and variety of albums depend on how you synchronize your Tab with your computer, which apps you use for collecting media, or which photo-sharing services you use on the Internet, such as Picasa.

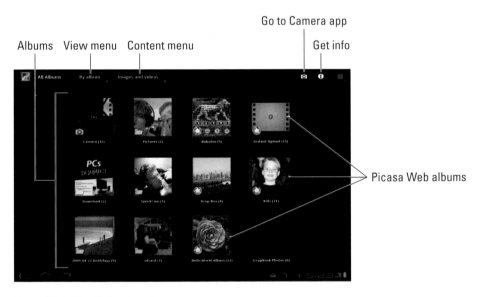

Figure 12-1: The Gallery's main screen.

Touch an album (pile) to open it and view the pictures or videos it contains. The next section describes how to view albums in the Gallery.

✔ The Camera album contains video you've shot using the Tab.

✔ The Download album contains images downloaded from the Internet.

✔ Albums labeled with the Picasa icon have been synchronized between Picasa Web on the Internet and your Galaxy Tab. See the section "Accessing your Picasa account," later in this chapter.

✔ Other albums in the Gallery represent images synchronized between the Galaxy Tab and your computer. See Chapter 18 for information on sharing images between the Tab and your computer.

✔ Various apps may also create their own albums in the Gallery app.

✔ The View menu allows you to control how the images and videos are displayed in the gallery. Figure 12-1 shows the gallery organized by album view.

✔ You can use the Content menu (refer to Figure 12-1) to see pictures, videos, or both displayed in the gallery.

Looking at an album

Touching an album in the Gallery app displays that album's contents, pictures and videos, in a grid of thumbnail previews. Those previews give you an idea of what the images are, similar to what's shown in Figure 12-2.

Figure 12-2: Looking at an album.

When a picture preview features a tiny Play button (refer to Figure 12-2), then it's a video. Otherwise, the thumbnails represent still images.

You can view more images in the album by swiping your finger left and right.

To view all the images in an album, touch the Slideshow button, illustrated in Figure 12-2. Playing a slide show turns the Galaxy Tab into a fancy, animated picture frame.

Viewing a picture or video

To view an image or a video, open an album and then touch a thumbnail with your finger.

Images appear full size on the screen, similar to what's shown in Figure 12-3. You can rotate the Tab horizontally (or vertically) to see the image in another orientation. Later sections describe in more detail what you can do when viewing an image.

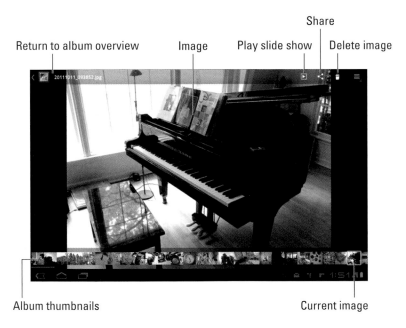

Figure 12-3: Examining an image.

Videos play when you choose them. The Video Playing screen is illustrated in Figure 12-4. To see the controls (illustrated in Figure 12-4), touch the screen while the video is playing.

Current time index   Play / Pause button   Video duration

Video playing   Drag to "scrub"

Figure 12-4: Watching a video.

To return to the main category in the Gallery app, touch the Back icon button. When viewing a still picture, you can choose the Gallery button from the top of the screen, as shown in Figure 12-3.

✔ To quickly find videos, choose the command Videos Only from the Content menu, as shown in Figure 12-1.

✔ Touch a video or an image to redisplay the onscreen controls, as shown in Figures 12-3 and 12-4.

✔ To run a slide show of photos in an album, touch the Slideshow button, shown in Figure 12-3. The slide show starts, displaying one image after another. For videos, only a freeze framc from the video appears. To stop the slide show, touch the screen.

Finding out where you took a picture

When you snap a picture, the Galaxy Tab can save your location. This information is obtained from the Tab's GPS, the same tool used to find your location on a map. In fact, you can use the GPS information saved with a picture to see exactly where the picture was taken.

To see where you've taken a picture, follow these steps in the Gallery app:

1. **View the image.**
2. **Touch the Menu icon button.**
3. **Choose the command Show On Map.**

   The Maps app starts, showing the approximate location where the picture was taken, as shown in Figure 12-5.

Image viewed in the Gallery app.

Image location on the map.

Figure 12-5: Finding where an image was taken.

Not every image has location information. In some cases, the Galaxy Tab cannot read the GPS to store the information. When this happens, location information is unavailable and the Show On Map command doesn't show up on the menu.

✒ Videos also store location information on the Galaxy Tab, though there doesn't appear to be any way to access that information by using the Gallery app.

✒ The Tab's GPS can be disabled for images you capture. Refer to Chapter 11 for information on how to turn GPS on or off when taking pictures.

Assigning an image to a contact

You can set any image for a contact. It doesn't necessarily have to be an image you've taken with the Galaxy Tab; any image you find in the Gallery app will do. Follow these steps:

1. View an image in the gallery.

2. Touch the Menu icon button.

3. Choose Set Picture As.

If the Set Picture As command doesn't appear, you cannot use that image; not every album allows its images to be set for contacts.

4. Choose Contact Photo.

5. Scroll the Tab's Contacts list and choose a particular contact.

You can use the Search command to easily locate a contact when you have an abundance of them.

6. Crop the image.

Refer to the later section, "Cropping an image," for detailed instructions on working the crop-thing.

7. Touch the OK button.

Or, touch the X (Cancel) button to chicken out or change your mind.

The contact's image is set and you're returned to view the image in the gallery.

Images changed for a Google contact are instantly synchronized with your Google account on the Internet.

Setting an image as wallpaper

You can choose as the Galaxy Tab's Home screen background or wallpaper any picture that's viewable in the Gallery app. Basically, you follow the same steps as outlined in the preceding section, but in Step 4, choose Lock Screen or Wallpaper instead of Contact Photo. Then skip to Step 6.

The Lock Screen is the background image you see when the Tab is locked; the Wallpaper is the background displayed behind icons and widgets on the Home screen.

Touch the Home icon button to see the new wallpaper.

You can also change wallpaper by long-pressing the Home screen and choosing the Wallpapers category. See Chapter 20 for details.

Edit and Manage the Gallery

The best tool for image editing is a computer amply equipped with photo-editing software, such as Photoshop or one of its less expensive alternatives. Even so, it's possible to use the Gallery app to perform some minor photo surgery. This section highlights a few of the more useful things you can do.

Cropping an image

One of the few, true image-editing commands available in the Gallery app is Crop. You can use Crop to slice out portions of an image, such as when removing ex-spouses and convicts from a family portrait. To crop an image, obey these directions:

1. **Summon the image you want to crop.**

2. **Touch the Menu icon button.**

   If you can't see the button, touch the screen, and it reappears.

3. **Choose Crop.**

   If the Crop command is unavailable, you have to choose another image. (Not every album lets you modify images.)

4. **Work the crop-thing.**

   You can drag the orange rectangle around to choose which part of the image to crop. Drag an edge of the rectangle to resize the left and right or top and bottom sides. Or, drag a corner of the rectangle to change the rectangle's size proportionally. Use Figure 12-6 as your guide.

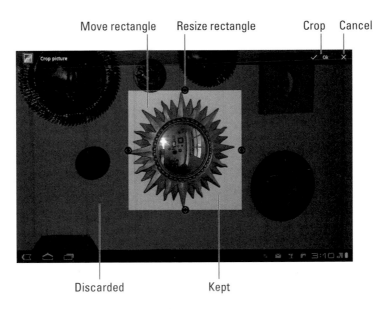

Figure 12-6: Working the crop-thing.

5. **Touch the Ok button when you're done cropping.**

Only the portion of the image within the orange rectangle is saved; the rest is discarded.

There's no way to undo a crop action after you've touched the Ok button.

 Working the rectangle to crop an image can be frustrating. When the image zooms in too small, you may have difficulty zooming back out. At that point, you can touch the X (Cancel) button and start over again.

Deleting pictures and videos

It's entirely possible, and often desirable, to remove unwanted, embarrassing, or questionably legal images and videos from the Gallery.

 To zap a single image, summon the image on the screen and touch the Trash icon that appears in the upper-right corner. Choose the Confirm Delete command. The image is gone.

Deleting a video isn't as easy as removing an image: You have to long-press the video thumbnail in an album. The long-press activates multiple-selection mode, which is covered in the later section, "Selecting multiple pictures and videos." For removing a video, however, just touch the Trash icon that appears in the upper-right corner of the screen. Choose the Confirm Delete command, and the video is gone.

✏ You can't undelete an image or a video you've deleted. There's no way to recover such an image using available tools on the Galaxy Tab.

✏ Some images can't be edited, such as images brought in from social networking sites or from online photo-sharing albums.

✏ You can delete a whole swath of images by selecting a group at a time. See the later section, "Selecting multiple pictures and videos," for details.

Rotating pictures

Which way is up? Well, the answer depends on your situation. For taking pictures with the Galaxy Tab, sometimes images just don't appear "up," no matter how you turn the Tab. To fix that situation, heed these steps:

1. **Choose an image to rotate.**

2. **Touch the Menu icon button.**

3. **Choose the More command.**

4. **Choose Rotate Left to rotate the image counterclockwise; choose Rotate Right to rotate the image clockwise.**

You can rotate a whole slew of images at one time: Select all the images as described in the next section. Choose More and then Rotate Left or Rotate Right. All the images are rotated at one time.

✏ You cannot rotate videos.

✏ You cannot rotate certain images, such as images shared from your Picasa Web Albums.

Selecting multiple pictures and videos

You can apply the Delete and Rotate commands to an entire swath of items in the gallery at once. To do so, you must know the secret, which I carefully divulge in these steps:

1. **Open the album (pile) you want to mess with.**

2. **Long-press an image to select it.**

   Instantly, you activate image-selection mode. (That's my name for it.) The screen changes to look like Figure 12-7.

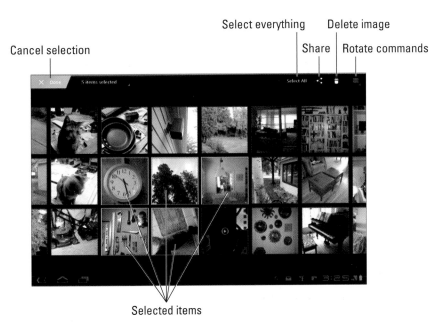

Figure 12-7: Choosing images to mess with.

3. **Continue touching images and videos to select them.**

   Or you can choose the Select All command, shown in Figure 12-7.

4. **Perform an action on the group of images or videos.**

   Later sections describe specifically what you can do.

To deselect items, touch them again. To deselect everything, touch the Done command, shown in Figure 12-7.

The type of commands you can use on a group of items in an album depends on the group. Some commands, such as Delete and Share, can be performed on any old group. Other commands, such as the image rotation commands, work only with pictures, not with videos.

Set Your Pics and Vids Free

Keeping your precious moments and memories in the Galaxy Tab is an elegant solution to the problem of lugging around photo albums. But when you want to show your pictures to the widest possible audience, you need a much larger stage. That stage is the Internet, and you have many ways to send and save your pictures and videos online, as covered in this section.

Refer to Chapter 18 for information on synchronizing and sharing information between the Galaxy Tab and your computer.

Accessing your Picasa account

Part of your Google account includes access to the online photo-sharing website, Picasa Web. If you haven't yet been to the Picasa Web site on the Internet, use your computer to visit this website:

```
http://picasaweb.google.com
```

Configure things by logging into your Google account on that website.

The Picasa account should be synchronized and configured automatically with your Galaxy Tab. So if you've saved pictures on the Picasa Web site, you can find them on the Tab similar to those shown in Figure 12-1. If not, follow these steps to ensure that Picasa is being property synched:

1. **At the Home screen, touch the Apps Menu icon button.**

2. **Open the Settings icon.**

3. **Choose Accounts & Sync.**

4. **Choose your Google account from the list under Manage Accounts.**

5. **Ensure that there's a check mark by the item Sync Picasa Web Albums.**

    That's pretty much it.

Any images you have on Picasa Web are automatically copied to your Galaxy Tab from now on.

Of course if you prefer not to have Picasa synchronize your images, repeat the steps in this section but remove the check mark in Step 5.

✔ Picasa Albums feature the Picasa logo on them, as shown in the margin.

 ✔ The best way to manage Picasa Web images is to go to the Picasa Web site on the Internet.

Printing your pictures

A trick you wouldn't expect to find on a portable gizmo is the ability to print your lovely photos. The Galaxy Tab is more than up to the task, *if* you have a Bluetooth printer and you've survived the ordeal of connecting *(pairing)* the printer to your Tab. That task is covered in Chapter 17, and it's required before the topic of printing pictures can even be whispered around the Galaxy Tab.

When you have the Tab and a Bluetooth printer paired and on speaking terms, obey these steps to print an image in the gallery:

1. **Ensure that the Tab's Bluetooth wireless radio is on.**

   Refer to Chapter 17 for information about Bluetooth.

2. **Ensure that the Bluetooth printer is on, that its Bluetooth radio is on, and that the printer is stocked with ink and paper, ready to print.**

3. **Open the Gallery app and browse to find the image you want to enshrine on paper.**

4. **Touch the Share button.**

   You see a menu of places and methods by which you can share the image.

5. **Choose Bluetooth.**

6. **Choose the Bluetooth printer from the Bluetooth Device Picker window.**

7. **If prompted by the printer, confirm that the image upload is okay.**

   Not every Bluetooth printer has such a prompt; some just go ahead and print the image.

Bluetooth printing isn't perfect. For example, your Galaxy Tab may not recognize the Bluetooth printer. It happens. As an alternative, you can attach an image to an e-mail message, send it to yourself, and then print it from your computer.

Posting your video to YouTube

The best way to share a video is to upload it to YouTube. As a Google account holder, you also have a YouTube account. You can use the YouTube app on the Galaxy Tab along with your account to upload your videos to the Internet, where everyone can see them and make rude comments about them. Here's how:

1. **Ensure that the Wi-Fi connection is activated.**

   The best way to upload a video is to turn on the Wi-Fi connection, which doesn't incur data surcharges like the digital cellular network. In fact, if you opt to use the 4G LTE network for uploading a YouTube video, you'll see a suitable reminder about the data surcharges.

2. **Start the Gallery app.**

3. **Open the album containing the video you want to upload.**

4. **Long-press the video.**

5. **Touch the Share button.**

6. **Choose YouTube.**

   The Upload Video window appears, listing all sorts of options and settings for sending the video to YouTube.

7. **Type the video's title.**

8. **Touch the More Details button.**

9. **Scroll through the list of options.**

   You can type a description, specify whether to make the video public or private, add tags, or change other settings.

10. **Touch the Upload button.**

    You return to the gallery, and the video is uploaded. It continues to upload even if the Galaxy Tab falls asleep.

The uploading notification appears while the video is being sent to YouTube. When the upload has completed, the notification stops animating and becomes the Uploads Finished icon, as shown in the margin.

To view your video, open the YouTube app. It's found on the Apps Menu screen and discussed in detail in Chapter 15.

✔ YouTube often takes awhile to process a video after it's uploaded. Allow a few minutes to pass (longer for larger videos) before the video becomes available for viewing.

✔ *Upload* is the official term to describe sending a file from the Galaxy Tab to the Internet.

✔ See Chapter 15 for more information on using YouTube.

Sharing with the Share menu

Occasionally, you stumble across the Share command when working with photos and videos in the Gallery app. This command is used to distribute images and videos from your Galaxy Tab to your pals in the digital realms.

The menu that appears when you touch the Share icon button contains various options for sharing media. The number and variety of items that appear depend on the apps installed on your Tab, which Internet services you belong to (Facebook and Twitter, for example), and which type of media is being shared.

Here's a quick summary of the various items you may find on the Share or Share Via menu, as well as how they work:

Bluetooth: You can use the Bluetooth networking standard to send images to a Bluetooth printer or to upload the images to a Bluetooth-enabled computer. Printing with Bluetooth is covered earlier in this chapter, in the section "Printing your pictures."

Facebook, Google+, Twitter: Sharing pictures on a social networking site is simple: Choose the image and then choose the social networking site from the Share menu. Fill in the information on the next screen, and soon the image is shared with all your friends and followers. See Chapter 8 for more information on social networking on the Galaxy Tab.

Email and Gmail: Choosing Email or Gmail for sharing sends the media file from your Galaxy Tab as a message attachment. Fill in the To, Subject, and Message text boxes as necessary. Touch the Send button to send the media.

Picasa: The Picasa photo-sharing site is one of those free services you get with your Google account. See the section "Accessing your Picasa account" for details on sharing images with Picasa.

YouTube: The YouTube sharing option appears whenever you choose to share a video from the Gallery app. See the section "Posting your video to YouTube."

13

The Galaxy Is Alive with the Sound of Music

In This Chapter

▶ Finding music on the Galaxy Tab

▶ Enjoying a tune

▶ Turning the Tab into a deejay

▶ Transferring music from your computer to the Tab

▶ Buying music online

▶ Organizing your tunes into a playlist

▶ Listening to streaming music

*1*t has no mouth, but yet it can sing!

The Galaxy Tab's amazing arsenal of features includes its ability to play music. So it effectively replaces any gramophone that you've been lugging around, which is the whole idea behind such an all-in-one gizmo like the Galaxy Tab. You can cheerfully and adeptly transfer all your old Edison cylinders and 78 LPs over to the Galaxy Tab for your listening enjoyment. This chapter tells you how.

Your Hit Parade

The primary source of your musical joy on the Galaxy Tab is an app aptly named Music. You can find that app on the Apps Menu, or there may be a handy shortcut right on the main Home screen.

Browsing your Music library

Songs stored on your Galaxy Tab are accessed through the Music app. After you start that app, you see a screen similar to Figure 13-1. If you just got your Galaxy Tab, you may not yet see any music. That's okay; the later section, "Add Some Music to Your Life," explains how to add music.

Main screen

Category menu

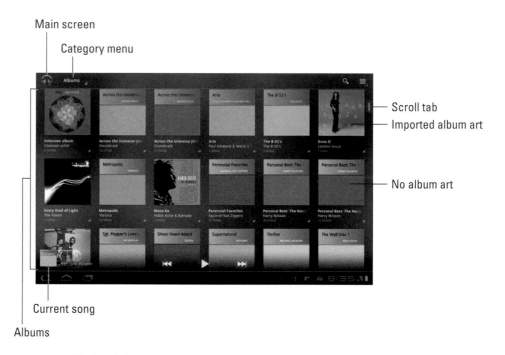

Scroll tab

Imported album art

No album art

Current song

Albums

Figure 13-1: The Music library.

The music stored on your Galaxy Tab is presented in the Music app by category. You choose a category from the Category menu, shown in Figure 13-1. There are several categories:

New and recent: Songs and albums are listed in a cascade in the order you've imported from your computer or purchased online. Scroll the list left or right to find recent items.

Albums: Music is organized by album, as shown in Figure 13-1. Choose an album to list its songs.

Artists: Songs are listed by recording artist or group. Choose Artist to see those songs listed by album.

Songs: All music (songs and audio) is listed individually in alphabetical order.

Playlists: Music you've organized into playlists that you create. Choose a playlist name to view songs organized in that playlist. Included are recently played songs, favorites, and other preset categories.

Genres: Audio is organized by categories such as Rock, Vocal, and Classical.

These categories are merely ways the music is organized — ways to make the music easier to find when you may know an artist's name but not an album title. The Genres category is for those times when you're in a mood for a certain type of music but don't know or don't mind who recorded it.

A *playlist* is a list you create yourself to organize songs by favorite, theme, mood, or whatever other characteristic you want. The section "Organize Your Music," later in this chapter, discusses playlists.

- Music is stored on the Galaxy Tab's internal memory.

- The size of the internal memory limits the total amount of music that can be stored on your Tab. Also, consider that storing pictures and videos horns in on some of the space that can be used to store music.

- Two types of album artwork are used by the Music app. For purchased music, the album artwork represents the original album. That may also happen for music copied (imported) from your computer. Otherwise, the Music app slaps down a generic album cover, as shown in Figure 13-1.

- There's no easy or obvious way to apply album cover artwork to music with a generic album cover.

- When the Galaxy Tab can't recognize an artist, it uses the title Unknown Artist. It usually happens with music you copy manually to your Tab, but it can also apply to audio recordings you make yourself.

Playing a tune

To listen to music by locating a song in your Music library, as described in the preceding section, touch the song title, and the song plays, as shown in Figure 13-2.

While the song plays, you're free to do anything else on the Galaxy Tab. In fact, the song continues to play even when the Tab goes to sleep.

After the song is done playing, the next song in the list plays. The list order depends on how you start the song. For example, if you start a song from the album view, all songs in that album play in the order listed.

Add to playlist

Song is playing   Album cover artwork   Song info

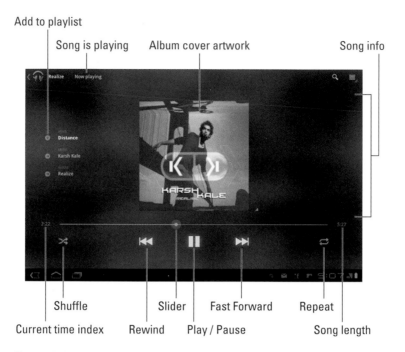

Shuffle   Slider   Fast Forward   Repeat

Current time index   Rewind   Play / Pause   Song length

Figure 13-2: A song is playing.

The next song in the list doesn't play if you have the Shuffle button activated. (Refer to Figure 13-2.) In that case, the Music app randomly chooses another song from the same list. Who knows which one is next?

The next song also might not play when you have the Repeat option on: The three repeat settings are illustrated in Table 13-1, along with the Shuffle settings. To change settings, simply touch either the Shuffle or Repeat button.

Table 13-1		Shuffle and Repeat Button Icons
Icon	*Setting*	*What Happens When You Touch the Icon*
	No Shuffle	Songs play one after the other.
	Shuffle	Songs are played in random order.
	No Repeat	Songs don't repeat.

Icon	Setting	What Happens When You Touch the Icon
	Single Repeat	The same song plays over and over.
	List Repeat	All songs in the list play over and over.

To stop the song from playing, touch the Pause button. (Refer to Figure 13-2.)

A notification icon appears while music is playing on the Galaxy Tab, as shown in the margin. To quickly summon the Music app and see which song is playing, or to pause the song, touch that notification, or pop up the notifications list, to see the name of the song that's playing. You can use the controls in the notification to pause the song or to skip forward or backward.

✔ Volume is set by using the Volume switch on the left side of the Galaxy Tab: Up is louder; down is quieter.

✔ While browsing the Music library, you see the currently playing song displayed at the bottom of the screen, as shown in Figure 13-1.

✔ When you're browsing your Music library, you may see a green song-is-playing icon, similar to the one shown in the margin. This icon flags any song that's playing or paused.

✔ Determining which song plays next depends on how you chose the song that's playing. If you choose a song by artist, all songs from that artist play, one after the other. When you choose a song by album, that album plays. Choosing a song from the entire song list causes all songs in the Music library to play.

✔ To choose which songs play after each other, create a playlist. See the section "Organize Your Music," later in this chapter.

✔ After the last song in the list plays, the Music app stops playing songs — unless you have the List Repeat option set, in which case the list plays again.

✔ You can use the Galaxy Tab's search abilities to help locate tunes in your Music library. You can search by artist name, song title, or album. The key is to touch the Search icon button when you're using the Music app. Type all or part of the text you're searching for and touch the Search button on the onscreen keyboard. Choose the song you want to hear from the list that's displayed.

Being the life of the party

You need to do four things to make your Galaxy Tab the soul of your next shindig or soirée:

- ✔ Connect it to a stereo.
- ✔ Use the Shuffle command.
- ✔ Set the Repeat command.
- ✔ Provide plenty of drinks and snacks.

Hook the Galaxy Tab into any stereo that has a standard line input. You need, on one end, an audio cable that has a mini-headphone jack and, on the other end, an audio input that matches your stereo. Look for such a cable at Radio Shack or any stereo store.

After you connect your Tab, start the Music app and choose the party play-list you've created. If you want the songs to play in random order, touch the Shuffle button.

You might also consider choosing the List Repeat command (see Table 13-1) so that all songs in the playlist repeat.

To play all songs saved on your Galaxy Tab, choose the Songs category and touch the first song in the list.

Enjoy your party, and please drink responsibly.

Add Some Music to Your Life

Odds are good that your Galaxy Tab came with no music preinstalled. It might have: Some cellular providers may have preinstalled a smattering of tunes, which merely lets you know how out of touch they are musically. Regardless, you can add music to your Galaxy Tab in a number of ways, as covered in this section.

Borrowing music from your computer

Your computer is the equivalent of the 20th-century stereo system — a combination tuner, amplifier, and turntable, plus all your records and CDs. If you've already copied your music collection to your computer, or if you use your computer as your main music storage system, you can share that music with your Galaxy Tab.

Many music-playing, or jukebox, programs are available. On Windows, the most common program is Windows Media Player. You can use this program to synchronize music between your PC and the Galaxy Tab. Here's how it works:

1. **Connect the Galaxy Tab to your PC.**

   Use the USB cable that comes with the Tab.

   Over on the PC, an AutoPlay dialog box appears in Windows, prompting you to choose how best to mount the Galaxy Tab into the Windows storage system.

2. **Close the AutoPlay dialog box.**

3. **Start Windows Media Player.**

4. **Click the Sync tab or Sync toolbar button.**

   The Galaxy Tab appears in the Sync list on the right side of the Windows Media Player, as shown in Figure 13-3.

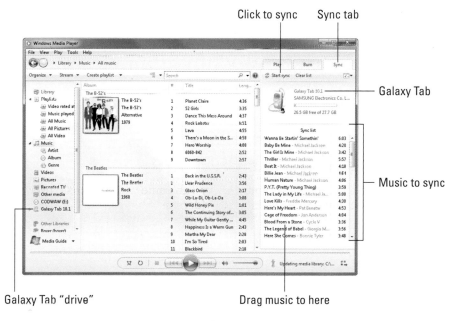

Figure 13-3: Windows Media Player meets Galaxy Tab.

5. **Drag to the Sync Area the music you want to transfer to your Tab. (Refer to Figure 13-3.)**

6. **Click the Start Sync button to transfer the music from your PC to the Galaxy Tab.**

   The Sync button may be located atop the list, as shown in Figure 13-3, or it might be found on the bottom.

7. **Close the Windows Media Player when you're done transferring music.**

   Or, you can keep it open — whatever.

8. **Unplug the USB cable.**

   Or, you can leave the Tab plugged in.

When you have a Macintosh, or you detest Windows Media Player, you can use the doubleTwist program to synchronize music between your Galaxy Tab and your computer. Refer to the section about synchronizing with doubleTwist in Chapter 18 for more information.

✔ You must mount the Galaxy Tab — specifically, its MicroSD card — into your computer's storage system before you can synchronize music.

✔ The Galaxy Tab can store only so much music! Don't be overzealous when copying your tunes. In Windows Media Player (refer to Figure 13-3), a capacity thermometer-thing shows you how much storage space is used and how much is available on your Tab. Pay heed to the indicator!

✔ Windows Media Player complains when you try to sync the Galaxy Tab to more than one PC. If you do, you're warned after Step 6 in this section. It's not a big issue: Just inform Windows Media Player that you intend to sync with the computer for only this session.

✔ You can't use iTunes to synchronize music with the Galaxy Tab.

✔ Okay, I lied in the preceding point: You *can* synchronize music using iTunes but only when you install the *iTunes Agent* program on your PC. You then need to configure the iTunes Agent program to use your Galaxy Tab with iTunes. After you do that, iTunes recognizes the Galaxy Tab and lets you synchronize your music. Yes, it's technical; hence the icon in the margin.

Buying music at the Amazon MP3 store

A more specific solution for buying music for the Galaxy Tab is to use the Amazon MP3 store. It's a universal approach, which works on just about every Android device, including the Galaxy Tab.

The best way to use the Amazon MP3 store is to have an Amazon account. If you don't have one set up, use your computer to visit www.amazon.com and create one. You also need to keep a credit card on file for the account, which makes purchasing music with the Galaxy Tab work O so well.

You also need to download the Amazon MP3 app for your Tab. Scan the barcode in the margin and refer to Chapter 16 for information on obtaining new apps.

Follow these steps to buy music from the Amazon MP3 store:

1. **Ensure that you're using a Wi-Fi or high-speed digital network connection.**

   Activating the Tab's Wi-Fi is described in Chapter 17.

2. **From the Apps Menu, choose the Amazon MP3 app.**

   The Amazon MP3 app connects you with the online Amazon music store, where you can search or browse for tunes to preview and purchase for your Galaxy Tab.

   The Amazon MP3 store presents you with two options for purchasing music: Store and Player. The Store option is where you buy music to download to your Galaxy Tab. The Player option, which I don't cover here, lets you save your music on the Internet, where you can play it from any device connected to the Internet.

3. **Touch the Store button.**

4. **Fill in the Search Amazon MP3 text field to begin your music quest.**

   Or, you can browse by top-selling songs and albums, new releases, or browse by category.

5. **Choose a result.**

   If the result is an album, choosing it displays the album's tracks. Otherwise, an audio preview plays.

   When the result is an album, choose a song in the album to hear the preview.

   Touch the song again to stop the preview.

6. **To purchase the song, touch the big button with the amount in it.**

   Some buttons say *FREE,* for free songs.

   Touching the button doesn't purchase the song. Instead, its text changes into the word *BUY.*

7. **Touch the word *BUY.***

Say "Hello" to the Music Hub

The Wi-Fi Galaxy Tab ships with an app called the Music Hub. If you don't see that app on the cellular Tab, you're not really missing much: The Music Hub is merely a place to browse and shop for music, though it also gives you access to playlists and other features beyond a music-buying app like the Amazon MP3 store, such as the ability to create playlists and a personal page.

---

8. **If necessary, you may need to accept the license agreement.**

   This step happens the first time you buy something from the Amazon MP3 store.

9. **Sign in to your Amazon.com account: Type your account name or e-mail address and password.**

   Your purchase is registered, account authorized, and download started. If they aren't, touch the Retry button to try again.

10. **Wait while the music downloads.**

    Well, actually, you don't have to wait: The music continues to download while you do other things on the Tab.

No notification icon appears when the song or album has finished downloading. Notice, however, that the MP3 Store Downloading icon vanishes from the notification part of the screen. It's your clue that the new music is ready for your ears.

- Amazon e-mails you a bill for your purchase. That's your purchase record, so I advise you to be a good accountant and print it and then input it into your bookkeeping program or personal finance program at once!

- You can review your Amazon MP3 store purchases by touching the bottom Menu icon button in the Amazon MP3 app and choosing the Downloads command.

Organize Your Music

The Music app categorizes your music by album, artist, song, and so forth, but unless you have only one album and enjoy all the songs on it, that configuration probably won't do. To better organize your music, you can create *playlists.* That way, you can hear the music you want to hear, in the order you want, for whatever mood hits you.

Reviewing your playlists

Any playlists you've already created, or that have been preset on the Tab, appear in the Playlists category, which you can choose from the Category menu in Music app. (Refer to Figure 13-1.) Any playlists you've created are displayed on the screen, as shown in Figure 13-4.

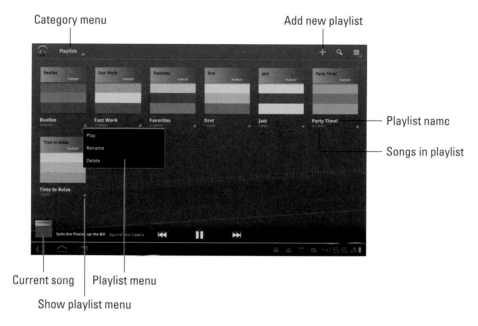

Category menu · Add new playlist · Playlist name · Songs in playlist · Current song · Playlist menu · Show playlist menu

Figure 13-4: Playlists in the Music app.

To see which songs are in a playlist, touch the playlist album icon. To play the songs in the playlist, touch the first song in the list. Or you can choose the Play command from the playlist's menu, as shown in Figure 13-4.

A playlist is a helpful way to organize music when a song's information may not have been completely imported into the Galaxy Tab. For example, if you're like me, you probably have a lot of songs labeled Unknown. A quick way to remedy that situation is to name a playlist after the artist and then add those unknown songs to the playlist. The next section describes how it's done.

Creating your own playlists

Making a new playlist is easy, and adding songs to the playlist is even easier. Follow these steps:

1. **Choose the Playlist category from the Category menu in the Music app.**

   Refer to Figure 13-4 for the location of the Category menu.

2. **Touch the Add button in the upper-right corner of the screen.**

3. **Type a name for your playlist.**

   Short and descriptive names are best.

4. **Touch the OK button to create the playlist.**

   The new playlist is created and placed into the Playlists screen, similar to what's shown in Figure 13-4.

But the playlist is empty! To add songs you need to go out and fetch them, adding each one to a playlist. Here's how you do that:

1. **Hunt down the song you want to add to a playlist.**

   You don't need to play the song, simply display the song in the Music app.

   Likewise, you can hunt down albums, artists, or even genres. The technique described in this set of steps works for every category in the Music app.

2. **Touch the menu triangle by the song (or album or artist).**

3. **Choose the command Add to Playlist.**

4. **Choose a playlist.**

   The song (or album or artist) is added to the playlist's repertoire of music.

Repeat this set of steps to continue adding songs to playlists.

You can have as many playlists as you like on the Galaxy Tab and stick as many songs as you like into them. Adding songs to a playlist doesn't noticeably affect the Tab's storage capacity.

- ✔ To remove a song from a playlist, open the playlist and touch the menu triangle by the song. Choose the Delete command and then touch Ok to confirm.

- ✔ Removing a song from a playlist doesn't delete the song from the Galaxy Tab's Music library.

> ✔ Songs in a playlist can be rearranged: While viewing the playlist, use the tab on the far left end of a song title to drag that song up or down in the list.

> ✔ To delete a playlist, touch the menu triangle in the playlist icon's lower-right corner. (Refer to Figure 13-4.) Choose the Delete command. Touch Delete.

Removing unwanted music

To purge music from your Galaxy, follow these brief, painless steps:

1. **Locate the music that offends you.**

   You can choose any music category except Playlist; deleting music from a playlist doesn't permanently remove it from the Tab. I recommend using the Songs category.

2. **Touch the menu triangle button by the song.**

   Or you can choose the menu triangle button by an artist, album, or just about any other category in the Music app.

3. **Choose Delete.**

   A warning message appears.

4. **Touch Ok to confirm.**

   The music is gone. La, la, la, la: The music is gone.

The music is deleted permanently from the Galaxy Tab's internal storage.

By deleting music, you free up a modicum of storage space, though you can't recover any music you delete. If you want the song back, you have to reinstall it, sync it, or buy it again, as described elsewhere in this chapter.

Soap, No Soap, Galaxy Radio

Though they're not broadcast radio stations, some sources on the Internet — *Internet radio* sites — play music. Lamentably, the Galaxy Tab doesn't come with any Internet radio apps, but that doesn't stop you from finding a few good ones at the Android Market. There are three I can recommend:

✔ TuneIn Radio

✔ Pandora Radio

✔ StreamFurious

The TuneIn Radio app gives you access to hundreds of Internet radio stations broadcasting around the world. They're organized by category, so you can find just about whatever you want. Many of the radio stations are also broadcast radio stations, so odds are good you can find a local station or two, which you can listen to on your Galaxy Tab.

 Pandora Radio lets you select music based on your mood and customizes, according to your feedback, the tunes you listen to. The app works like the Internet site www.pandora.com, in case you're familiar with it. The nifty thing about Pandora is that the more you listen, the better the app gets at finding music you like.

 StreamFurious streams music from various radio stations on the Internet. Though not as customizable as Pandora, StreamFurious uses less bandwidth so you can enjoy your music without having to risk running up digital cellular surcharges.

All these apps are available at the Android Market. They're free, though paid versions might also be available.

 ✔ It's best to listen to Internet radio when your Tab is connected to the Internet via a Wi-Fi connection. Streaming music can use a lot of your cellular data plan's data allotment.

✔ See Chapter 16 for more information about the Android Market.

 ✔ Internet music of the type delivered by the apps mentioned in this section is referred to by the nerds as *streaming music.* That's because the music arrives on your Galaxy Tab as a continuous download from the source. Unlike music you download and save, streaming music is played as it comes in and not stored long-term.

14

Your Digital Library

In This Chapter

▶ Starting your digital library

▶ Using the Kindle app

▶ Buying a book in the Kindle Store

▶ Reading an eBook with Kindle

*B*efore writing was invented, information was stored in the human head and relayed from person to person through stories. After writing was invented, early Cro-Magnon scientists determined that something convenient must be developed on which to write. Stone tablets were okay, but hardly portable. Then came papyrus scrolls, bound books, and then in the 21st century, the eBook.

The eBook, or electronic book, is the latest, best development in the art of storing the written word. Rather than load yourself down with bulky, printed tomes, you can carry something light and electronic like the Galaxy Tab. Armed with eBook reader software, you can have a whole library of reading fun always available to provide entertainment and information.

Why Don't You Read It on the Road?

Welcome to the latest craze in publishing: eBooks, or electronic books. It's important to know that eBooks is pronounced "ee-books," not "eb-ooks," which makes no sense but, honestly, given weird technology jargon, who really knows?

An *eBook* is essentially a digital version of the material you would normally see on paper. The words, formatting, figures, pictures — all that stuff is simply stored digitally so that you can read it on some sort of eBook reader. In the case of the Galaxy Tab, you need eBook software, which is included in the form of the Books app.

The primary advantage of an eBook reader is that you can keep an entire library of books with you. So rather than pay way too much for the latest pot-boiler in an airport bookstore, you can shop online before you leave and take an eBook with you. That way, when you're bored with reading your e-mail, surfing the web, playing games, checking your stocks, or chatting it up with a friend, you can read books on your Galaxy Tab.

- ✒ The Galaxy Tab was supposed to ship with an app called the Reader's Hub. It would have been the Tab's primary eBook reader, library, and book-buying app. It may appear with a future update of the Galaxy Tab's software, but as this book goes to press, the Reader's Hub is not available.

- ✒ Just about any current, popular title you can buy in a bookstore or online is available in the eBook format.

- ✒ You can also use eBook reader software to view periodicals — magazines and newspapers — as long as you pay for the subscription and the eBook-reading software you're using allows for daily updates.

- ✒ eBook titles cost money, though they're generally cheaper than their real-world equivalents.

- ✒ It's easy and free to build up your eBook library with classics and older books. Most of those titles are free, though some compilations have a modest price tag, such as 99 cents.

Google Does Books

Your Galaxy Tab comes with Google's own eBook reader app. It has the clever name Books, and it can be found on the Apps Menu along with all the other apps installed on your Tab.

- ✒ The Books app may come preinstalled with some free books for you to try. If not, getting free books is easy, as described in this section.

- ✒ Because the Books app is from Google, it uses the Android Market as your online bookstore. See Chapter 16 for more information about the Android Market.

Using the Books app

The Books app organizes the books into a library and displays the books for reading on your Galaxy Tab.

Begin your reading experience by opening the Books app, found on the Apps Menu. If you're prompted to turn on Synchronization, touch the Turn On Sync button.

The Books app main screen displays your eBook library, looking similar to Figure 14-1. The library lists any titles you've obtained for your Google Books account. Or, when you're returning to the Books app after a break, you see the current page of the eBook you were last reading.

Buy more books at the Android Market

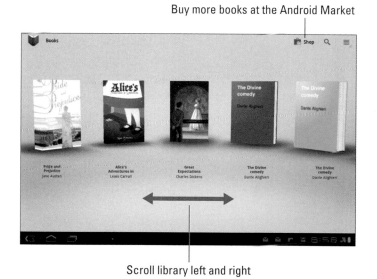

Scroll library left and right

Figure 14-1: The Books library.

Scroll through the library by swiping the screen left or right. To begin reading, touch a book to open it. The next section covers how you read a book using the Books app.

- If you don't see a book in the library, touch the Menu icon button and choose the Refresh command.

- To ensure that your reading material is always available, touch the Menu icon button and choose the Make Available Offline command. That way, the Galaxy Tab doesn't have to access the Internet in order to synchronize and download books from the library. I choose that command specifically before I leave on a trip where an Internet signal may not be available (such as in an airplane).

✔ If you want only a specific eBook to be available offline, long-press it and choose the Make Available Offline command.

✔ To remove a book from the library, long-press the cover and choose the Remove From My eBooks command. There is no confirmation: The book is instantly removed.

✔ Synchronization allows you to keep copies of your Google Books on all your Android devices, as well as on the `http://books.google.com` website.

Reading a Books eBook

The eBook experience on the Galaxy Tab should be familiar to you, especially if you're reading this text in a real book. The entire page-turning and reading operation works the same. The only major difference is that you can read a physical book without batteries and in direct sunlight, but I won't dwell on that.

Touch a book in the Books app library to open it. If you've opened the book previously, you're returned to the page you last read. Otherwise, the first page you see is the book's first page.

Figure 14-2 illustrates the basic book-reading operation in the Books app. You turn pages by swiping left or right, but probably mostly left. You can also turn pages by touching the far left or right sides of the screen.

The Books app also works in a vertical orientation, though when you turn the Tab that way, only one page is shown at a time.

✔ If the onscreen controls (refer to Figure 14-2) disappear, touch the screen to see them again.

✔ The Aa button is used to adjust the display. Touching that button displays a palette of options for adjusting the text on the screen and the brightness.

✔ To return to the library, touch the Books button in the upper-left corner of the screen or touch the Back icon button.

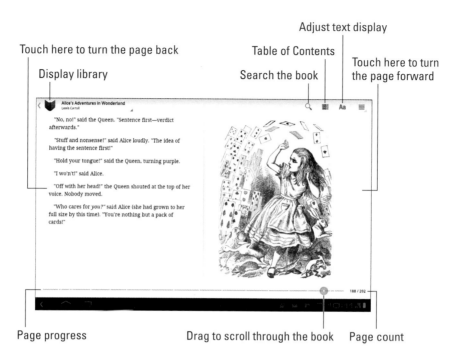

Adjust text display

Touch here to turn the page back

Table of Contents

Display library

Search the book

Touch here to turn the page forward

Page progress

Drag to scroll through the book

Page count

Figure 14-2: Reading an e-book in the Books app.

Buying books

Nothing is more delightful for an author to write about than buying books, especially when he's urging someone else to do it. For the Books app, you obtain new titles — free or paid — from the Android Market, the same place you visit to obtain apps for your Galaxy Tab.

To quickly visit the Android Market's online bookstore, touch the Shop button on the Book app's main screen. (Refer to Figure 14-1.) You can also start the Market app and choose Books from the main screen.

Search for books, browse the categories, or use the Search button to locate a specific title, topic, or author.

- ✔ Books with a price button must be purchased using your Google Checkout account. The process is the same as for buying an app: See Chapter 16 for the specifics.

- ✔ Free books have a Free button.

✔ Books you obtain from the Market, free or paid, can be synchronized with any Android device you have where the Books app is installed. Use the Refresh command, discussed in the earlier section, "Using the Books app," to synchronize books between your various Android gizmos.

The Kindle eBook Reader

The good folks at Amazon recognize that after buying yourself a Galaxy Tab, you'll probably never have use for their fancy eBook reader, the Kindle. Those fools who dare take a Kindle on a transcontinental flight can seethe with jealousy as they sit across the aisle from you, knowing how much better the Galaxy Tab is than the Kindle gizmo.

You'll say, "Hey! I see you have a Kindle." Then you'll snicker.

The Kindle owner will be miffed and will most likely respond, "Well, I see that you don't have an iPad!"

Just chuckle softly to yourself. That's because both you and the silly Kindle owner are probably using the same software to read your Kindle eBooks.

Obtaining the Kindle app

You can pick up a copy of the Kindle app free at the Android Market. Use the QR code in the margin or simply visit the Market and search for *Kindle.* Install the app on your phone, carefully following the directions listed in Chapter 16.

The first time you start the Kindle app, you may be asked to register or sign in to your Amazon account. Do so. By signing in, you can instantly coordinate your Kindle eBook library with any previous purchases you may have made.

The Kindle app's main interface is illustrated in Figure 14-3. It shows a scrolling list of your eBook library, plus it gives you quick access to the Kindle Store to buy even more books. And everyone should buy more books.

Figure 14-3 shows archived books in the Kindle library. Those are titles you've already purchased from the Kindle Store, either online or from another Android or Kindle gizmo. They're archived because they haven't yet been transferred to your Galaxy Tab. To do so, touch the title, as illustrated in Figure 14-3.

Archived title (Touch to download)

List view / Grid view

Shop

Books in the Kindle Library

Figure 14-3: Kindle on the Galaxy Tab.

✔ Consider placing a shortcut to the Kindle app on the Home screen. See Chapter 20 for the complete, scintillating instructions.

✔ If you don't yet have an account on Amazon, get one! Visit www.amazon.com and follow the directions to sign up and create an account. Maybe even buy a nice sweater or some concrete while you're there. Amazon carries everything.

Getting some Kindle reading material

You can get two types of books with the Kindle app: Good and terrible. Regardless of their satisfaction level, the two types of books can be free or paid. Mostly older titles and classics are free; the rest are paid. Shopping for books works like this:

1. **Start the Kindle app on your Galaxy Tab.**

2. **Touch the Kindle Store button.**

   Refer to Figure 14-3 for its location.

You see the Amazon Kindle Store. There are recommended books, categories to browse, plus lists — including lists of the top paid and free titles. It's just like a bookstore, but you can shop in your pajamas.

Well, you can shop in your pajamas at a real-world bookstore as well, but no one notices when you do so at the Kindle Store.

3. **Search for the book you want or browse the categories.**

   As a suggestion, choose the category Free Popular Classics to find something free to download.

4. **Touch to select a title.**

   Free titles have $0.00 listed as their price; otherwise, you see the book's cost displayed.

   If you're timid about paying for an eBook, choose the Try a Sample button instead. A snippet from the book is downloaded, which you can peruse at your leisure at no charge.

5. **Touch the Buy button.**

   Yes, it still says "Buy" even when the title is free.

   After touching the Buy button, the title is downloaded (transferred from the Kindle Store over the Internet and into your Galaxy Tab).

6. **Touch the Read Now button to read your new book, or keep shopping.**

   As an author, I recommend that you keep shopping. Never stop book shopping.

You may be prompted to log in to your Amazon account again after touching the Buy button (Step 5). Do so. You may also be prompted to enter or choose a credit card if you don't have one automatically set up for your Amazon account. That's normal, and it's perfectly safe.

See the next section for information on reading eBooks.

   ✔ You receive an e-mail confirmation message describing your purchase. The e-mail appears even when you "buy" a free eBook.

   ✔ Not every title is available as an eBook.

Reading on your Galaxy Tab

The whole point of getting an eBook is so that you can read the thing, flipping the digital pages just the same as you would in a real book, although I don't recommend that you lick your finger to turn the page. (See Chapter 21 for information on cleaning the Galaxy Tab screen.)

After choosing a book in the Kindle app, you see it open on the touchscreen. The first time you open a book, you see the first page. Otherwise, you see the page you were last reading.

Figure 14-4 illustrates the basic reading maneuvers: You can touch the left or right sides of the screen to flip a page left or right, respectively. You can also swipe the pages left or right.

Turn page back

Kindle Library   Adjust brightness   Adjust text size

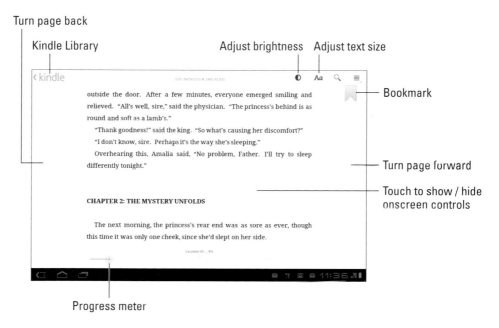

Bookmark

Turn page forward

Touch to show / hide onscreen controls

Progress meter

Figure 14-4: Reading with Kindle.

You can drag the progress meter at the bottom of the screen to skim back and forth through the book. Or, for more precise movement in an eBook, touch the Menu icon button and choose the Go To command.

Long-pressing text selects the text on the screen, similar to selecting any text on the Galaxy Tab, as discussed in Chapter 4. A menu appears atop the screen when you've selected text. You can make a note for that chunk of text, highlight it, or search for text elsewhere in the same book or on Wikipedia or Google.

The Kindle app lacks a quick command to keep the screen from reorienting itself. To turn off screen orientation (rotation) on the Galaxy Tab, refer to Chapter 3.

15

What Else Does It Do?

Most gizmos are designed to solve a single problem. The food processor slices, grates, or chops food, but it doesn't play music (though I'm sure John Cage would argue that point). The lawn mower is good at cutting the grass but terrible at telling time. And if you have a tuba, it can play music, but it's a poor substitute for a hair dryer. That's all well and good because people accept limitations on devices designed with a specific purpose.

The Galaxy Tab is a gizmo with many purposes. Its abilities are limited only by the apps you get for it. To help you grasp this concept, the Tab comes with a slate of apps preinstalled. They can give you an idea of what the Tab is capable of, or you can simply use those apps to make the Galaxy Tab a more versatile and useful device.

It's an Alarm Clock

Your Galaxy Tab keeps constant, accurate track of the time, which is displayed at the bottom of the Home screen as well as on the Lock screen. The display is lovely and informative, but it can't actually wake you up. To have it do that, you need to somehow choose a specific time and apply a noise to that time. This process turns the Galaxy Tab into an alarm clock.

Alarm clock duties are the responsibility of the Clock app. It's the same app you see if you plug the Tab into a docking station. It just displays a large digital clock on the screen, as shown in Figure 15-1.

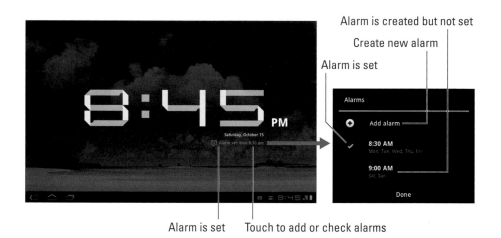

Figure 15-1: The Clock app.

You can create alarms for the Clock app by touching the Set Alarm button, illustrated in Figure 15-1. You see a pop-up window where you can create or set alarms.

Set an alarm by touching the box, which places a green check mark by the alarm time and days. To create a new alarm, follow these steps:

1. **Touch the Set Alarm or Alarm Set button. (Refer to Figure 15-1.)**

   The Alarms screen appears, shown on the right in Figure 15-1.

2. **Choose Add Alarm.**

3. **Touch the check box by Turn Alarm On to activate the alarm.**

4. **Touch Time and use the pop-up window to configure the hour and minute and to specify either AM or PM; touch the Set button to set the time.**

5. **Choose Repeat to set on which days the alarm sounds.**

6. **Choose Ringtone to specify which music plays when the alarm sounds.**

   To set no ringtone, choose the Silent option, found at the top of the Ringtones list. But if you do that, ensure that you also set the Vibrate option. The alarm should signal you somehow.

7. **Place a check mark by the Vibrate option if you want the Tab to vibrate in addition to playing music.**

8. **Touch Label to give the alarm a name.**

   For example, *Wake up,* and *Get to the airport,* and *Annoy my spouse* are excellent examples of good, descriptive labels.

9. **Touch the Done button to create the alarm.**

The alarm you create appears on the Alarms screen, similar to the one shown in Figure 15-1.

Any new alarm you create is automatically set — it goes off when the proper time approaches. To disable an alarm, touch the Alarm icon shown in Figure 15-1.

Alarms must be set or else they don't trigger. To set an alarm, touch the check box by the alarm, as shown in Figure 15-1.

   ✔ Turning off an alarm doesn't delete the alarm.

   ✔ To remove an alarm, long-press it and choose the option Delete Alarm from the menu. Touch the OK button to confirm.

   ✔ The alarm doesn't work when you turn off the Galaxy Tab. The alarm does, however, go off when the Tab is sleeping.

It's a Very Big Calculator

The Calculator is perhaps the oldest of all computer programs. It's probably also the least confusing and frustrating app to use on your Galaxy Tab.

Start the Calculator app by choosing its icon from the Apps Menu. The Calculator appears, as shown in Figure 15-2.

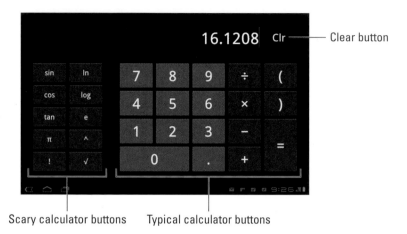

Clear button

Scary calculator buttons   Typical calculator buttons

Figure 15-2: The Calculator.

Type in your equations using the various buttons on the screen. The parenthesis buttons can help you determine which part of a long equation gets calculated first. Use the Clr button to clear input.

> ✔ Long-press the calculator's text (or results) to cut or copy the results.

> ✔ I use the Calculator most often to determine my tip at a restaurant. In Figure 15-2, a calculation is being made for an 18 percent tip on an $89.56 tab.

It's a Calendar

Feel free to take out any datebook you have and throw it away. You never need to buy another one again. That's because your Galaxy Tab is the ideal datebook and appointment calendar. Thanks to the Calendar app and the Google Calendar feature on the Internet, you can manage all your scheduling right on your Galaxy Tab. It's almost cinchy.

> ✔ Google Calendar works with your Google account to keep track of your schedule and appointments. You can visit Google Calendar on the web at
>
>   http://calendar.google.com

> ✔ You automatically have a Google Calendar; it comes with your Google account.

> ✔ I recommend that you use the Calendar app on your Galaxy Tab to access Google Calendar. It's a better way to access your schedule than using the Browser app to reach Google Calendar on the web.

> ✔ Before you throw away your datebook, copy into the Calendar app some future appointments and info, such as birthdays and anniversaries.

Browsing your schedule

To see what's happening next, to peruse upcoming important events, or just to know which day of the month it is, summon the Calendar app. It's located on the Apps Menu along with all the other apps that dwell on your Galaxy Tab, though there might be a shortcut icon on the first Home screen panel to the right of the main Home screen.

Figure 15-3 shows the Calendar app's monthly view. It looks like a typical calendar, with the month and year at the top. Scheduled appointments and events appear on various days.

Choose calendar view   Show current day Add new event

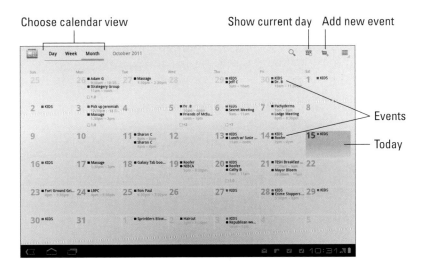

Events

Today

Figure 15-3: The Calendar's Month view.

To view your appointments by week, touch the Week button. Or, you can touch the Day button to see your daily schedule.

> ✔ See the later section, "Creating a new event," for information on reviewing and creating events.

> ✔ Use Month view to see an overview of what's going on, and use Week or Day view to see your appointments.

✔ I check Week view at the start of the week to remind me of what's coming up.

✔ Different colors flag your events, as seen by the teensy squares next to event names in Figure 15-3. The colors represent a calendar category to which the events are assigned. See the later section, "Creating a new event," for information on calendars.

✔ Use your finger to flick the calendar displays left or right to see the next or previous day, week, or month.

Reviewing appointments

To see more detail about an event, touch it. When you're using Month view, touch the date with the event on it to see the Week view. Then choose the event again to see its details.

The information you see depends on how much information was recorded when the event was created. Some events have only a minimum of information; others may have details, such as a location for the event. When the event's location is listed, you can touch that location, and the Maps app pops up to show you where the event is being held.

Birthdays and a few other events on the calendar may be pulled in from your social networking sites. That probably explains why some events are listed twice; they're pulled in from two sources.

Creating a new event

The key to making the calendar work is to add events: appointments, things to do, meetings, or full-day events such as birthdays or colonoscopies. To create a new event, follow these steps in the Calendar app:

1. **Select the day for the event.**

   Or if you like, you can switch to Day view, where you can touch the starting time for the new event.

2. **Touch the Add New Event button. (Refer to Figure 15-3.)**

   The New Event screen appears. Your job now is to fill in the blanks to create the new event.

   The more information you supply, the more detailed the event, and the more you can do with it on your Galaxy Tab as well as on Google Calendar on the Internet.

3. Type an event name.

Sometimes I simply write the name of the person I'm meeting.

4. Choose a calendar category for the event.

Calendars are created on the Google Calendar website. You can choose which calendar to assign an event to only by using the Galaxy Tab's Calendar app. It's the calendars that are color-coded.

5. Set the meeting duration using the From and To buttons.

Because you followed Step 1, you don't have to set the date (unless the event is longer than a day). Touch the time buttons, if necessary, to adjust when the event starts and stops.

When the event lasts all day, such as a birthday or your mother-in-law's visit that was supposed to last for an hour, touch the All Day check mark.

Steps 6 and 7 are optional:

6. Type a location for the event in the Where field.

7. Type a description.

Or you can use the Description field to type in notes about the event, such as whether to wear a tie or just show up naked.

8. Specify whether the event repeats.

Touch the Repeat button to set up a recurring schedule.

9. Set whether the event has a Reminder.

The Calendar app is configured to automatically set a reminder 10 minutes before an event begins. If you prefer not to have a reminder, touch the minus button by the Reminders item. You can set additional reminders by using the plus button. Change the reminder time by touching the triangle menu button and choosing a new time value.

10. Touch the Done button to create the new event.

The Done button has a check mark by it, and it's located in the upper-right corner of the screen.

You can change an event at any time: Simply touch the event to bring up more information and then touch the Details button. Choose Edit from the top of the screen to modify the event.

To remove an event, touch the event to bring up more information and touch the Delete button at the top right of the screen. Touch the OK button to confirm.

🔹 Adding an event location not only tells you where the event will be located, but also hooks that information into the Maps app. My advice is to type information into the event's Where field just as though you're typing information to search for in the Maps app. When the event is displayed, the location is a clickable link; touch the link to see where it is on a map.

🔹 Use the Repetition item to create repeating events, such as weekly or monthly meetings, anniversaries, and birthdays.

🔹 Reminders can be set so that the Tab alerts you before an event takes place. The alert can show up as a notification icon (shown in the margin), or it can be an audio alert or a vibrating alert. Pull down the notifications and choose the calendar alert. You can then peruse pending events.

🔹 To deal with an event notification, choose the notification as described in Chapter 3.

🔹 You can also create events by using the Google Calendar on the Internet. Those events are instantly synced with the calendar on your Galaxy Tab.

It's Your Video Entertainment

It's not possible to watch "real" TV on the Galaxy Tab, but a few apps come close. The YouTube app is handy for watching random, meaningless drivel, which I suppose makes it a lot like TV. And then there's Media Hub, which lets you buy and rent real movies and TV shows. And when you tire of those apps, you can create your own movies by using the Android Movie Studio.

Enjoying YouTube

YouTube is the Internet phenomenon that proves that real life is indeed too boring and random for television. Or is that the other way around? Regardless, you can view the latest videos on YouTube — or contribute your own — by using the YouTube app on your Galaxy Tab. The main YouTube screen is depicted in Figure 15-4.

To view a video, touch its name or icon in the list.

Touch the full-screen button to view the video in a larger size.

Browse for videos by choosing the Browse category, as shown in Figure 15-4. Or you can search for videos by using the Search YouTube text box, also shown in the figure. As a suggestion, type a search term for something you'd like to see, such as *plane crashes,* or *people-eating bugs,* or *disappointing politicians.*

Return to main YouTube screen

Browse for videos   Search for videos

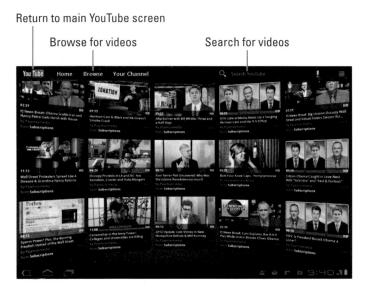

Figure 15-4: YouTube.

Touch the Back icon button to return to the main YouTube screen after watching a video or if you tire of a video and need to return to the main screen out of boredom.

- Use the YouTube app to view YouTube videos, rather than use the Browser app to visit the YouTube website.

- Because you have a Google account, you also have a YouTube account. I recommend that you log in to your YouTube account when using YouTube on the Galaxy Tab: Touch the Menu icon button and choose the command My Account. Log in if you haven't already. Otherwise, you see your account information, your videos, and any video subscriptions.

- Not all YouTube videos are available for viewing on mobile devices.

- To create and upload a video you've already shot to YouTube, touch the Your Channel button at the top of the main screen (refer to Figure 15-4); then touch the Upload button in the upper-right corner of the screen. Use the Gallery to locate a video to send to YouTube.

- Also see Chapter 11 for information on shooting video with your Galaxy Tab.

Buying and renting movies

The Amazon Market not only lets you buy apps and books for your Galaxy Tab, but you can also use it to rent movies. Further, the cellular tab comes with an app that allows you to buy or rent films and television shows. It's called the Media Hub. You can use both apps to boost the entertainment potential for your Tab.

Use either app, Market or Media Hub, to browse or search for movies and TV shows to rent or buy. Purchasing a movie at the Market works just like purchasing an app, so if you've already set up your Galaxy Tab with a Google Checkout account, you're ready to go. With the Media Hub, you need to supply credit card or other information to make your first purchase. The app remembers that information for future purchases.

- Movies rented at the Market are available for viewing up to 30 days after you pay the rental fee. After you start the movie, you can pause and watch it again and again during a 24-hour period.

- To view movies rented at the Market, you need to get the Videos app. Don't fret: You're prompted to download and install the app if you don't yet have a copy on your Galaxy Tab.

- One of the best ways to view movies is to connect the Tab to an HDMI monitor or TV set. That way you get the Big Screen experience, and can share the movie with several friends without having you all crowd around the Galaxy Tab. To get HDMI output on the Tab, you need to purchase a special HDMI dongle or use the Multimedia Dock.

Making your own movies

Forget Hollywood! The Galaxy Tab comes with the Movie Studio app, which you can use to craft your own epic productions. You can mix in still images and videos you've already shot (which are stored in the Gallery app), or you can shoot new footage right from within the Movie Studio app itself.

Figure 15-5 illustrates the Movie Studio app's main screen.

The Movie Studio app is actually quite sophisticated for a tablet. Aside from stitching together video and still images, there are filters you can add (called Effects in the program), text overlays, and transitions between shots. You can even add in music tracks and other audio. It's pretty impressive.

- Touch the Menu icon button and choose Export Movie to save your project.

- Touch the Add Music button (refer to Figure 15-5) to pluck out an audio track from the Music app, or from any other music-like app on the Galaxy Tab.

- See Chapter 11 for information on using your Galaxy Tab as both a still and video camera. Chapter 12 covers the Gallery, where images and videos are stored.

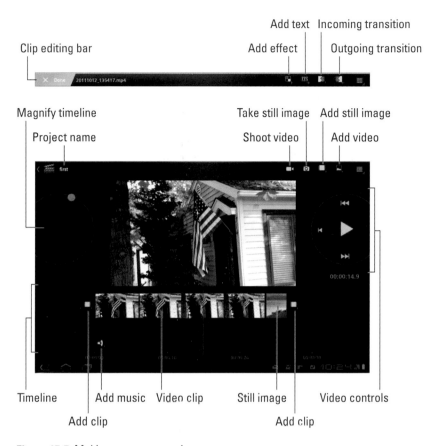

Figure 15-5: Making your own movies.

It's Your Game Machine

One of the best ways to put expensive, high-tech gizmos to work is to play games. Don't even sweat the thought that you have too much "business" or "work" or other important stuff you can do on a Galaxy Tab. The more advanced the mind, the more the need for play, right? So indulge yourself.

Lamentably, there are no sample games that ship with the Galaxy Tab. That may change in the future, but for now you're left to hunt down games at the Market just like everyone else in the Android Kingdom.

Just to be a tease, Figure 15-6 shows a game on the Galaxy Tab. It's one of many, so don't think I'm recommending anything, though I did play Jet Car Stunts on my Galaxy Tab for hours on end during an intercontinental flight.

Figure 15-6: A game on the Galaxy Tab.

See Chapter 16 for information on using the Android Market.

16

A Galaxy of Apps

In This Chapter

▶ Shopping at the Android Market

▶ Downloading a free app

▶ Buying an app

▶ Sending an app suggestion to a friend

▶ Updating your apps

▶ Removing an app

*W*ithout apps, your Galaxy Tab would be nothing more than a pricey frame without a picture. There must be apps!

A moderate assortment of apps was preinstalled by Samsung, and perhaps another few apps were installed by your cellular provider. Beyond that, you can add more apps to your Tab, which extends the list of things you can do in the mobile universe. Adding new apps and managing all your Tab's apps are the topics of this chapter.

Welcome to the Market

People love to shop when they're buying something they want or when they're spending someone else's money. You can go shopping for your Galaxy Tab, and I'm not talking about going back to your local Phone Store to buy overpriced accessories. I'm talking about software, programs, applications — or just plain old apps.

The Android Market may sound like the place where you can go buy an R2-D2 or a Robby the Robot. Instead, it's an online place where you go to pick up new apps, buy books, and rent movies for your Galaxy Tab. You can browse, you can get free apps or books, or you can pay. It all happens at the Android Market.

- ✔ Officially, the Android Market is called the Market. The name of the app is Market. I still like to call it the Android Market.

- ✔ *App* is short for application. It's a program, or software, you can add to your Galaxy Tab to make it do new, wondrous, or useful things.

- ✔ Because the Galaxy Tab uses the Android operating system, it can run nearly all applications written for Android.

- ✔ You can be assured that all apps that appear in the Android Market can be used with the Galaxy Tab. There's no way to download or buy something that's incompatible with your Tab.

- ✔ All apps you download can be found on the Apps Menu screen. Further, apps you download have shortcut icons placed on the Home screen. See Chapter 20 for information on moving apps on the Home screen.

- ✔ You obtain items from the Market by *downloading* them into your Tab. That file transfer works best at top speeds; therefore:

- ✔ I highly recommend that you connect your cellular Tab to a Wi-Fi network if you plan to obtain apps, books, or movies at the Android Market. Not only does Wi-Fi give you speed, but it also helps avoid data surcharges. See Chapter 17 for details on connecting the Galaxy Tab to a Wi-Fi network.

- ✔ The Market app is frequently updated, so its look may change from what you see in this chapter. They may also add a Music category in the near future. Updated information on the Market is available on my website:

    `www.wambooli.com/help/galaxytab`

Browsing the Android Market

You access the Android Market by opening the Market app, found on the Apps Menu screen but also on the main Home screen.

After opening the Market app, you see the main screen, similar to the one shown in Figure 16-1. You can browse for apps, games, books, or movie rentals. The categories are listed on the top-left part of the screen, with the other parts of the screen highlighting popular or recommended items. Those recommendations are color-coded to let you know what they are: green for apps, blue for books, and red for video rentals.

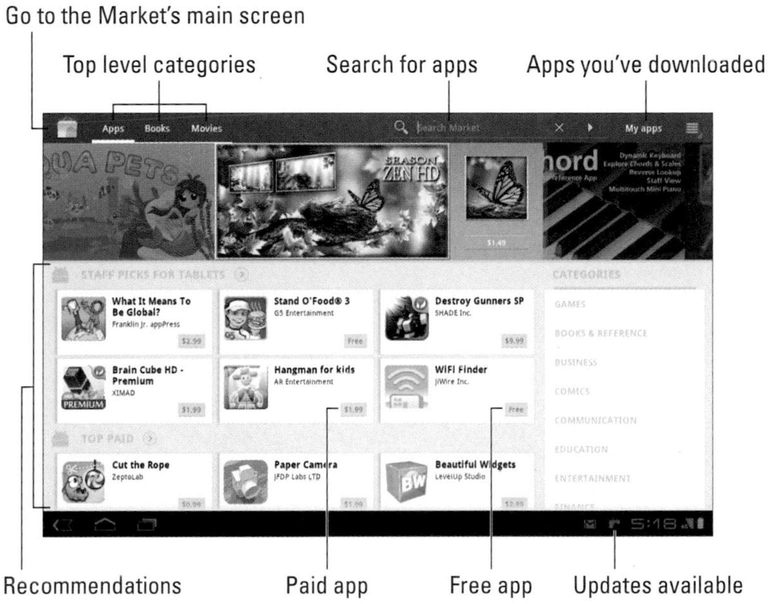

Go to the Market's main screen

Top level categories   Search for apps   Apps you've downloaded

Recommendations   Paid app   Free app   Updates available

Figure 16-1: The Android Market.

Find items by choosing a category from the top of the screen. (Refer to Figure 16-1.) The next screen lists popular and featured items plus categories you can browse by swiping the screen right to left. The category titles appear toward the top of the screen.

When you have an idea of what you want, such as an app's name or even what it does, searching works fastest: Touch the Search Market button at the top of the Market screen. (Refer to Figure 16-1.) Type all or part of the app's name, the book or movie title, or perhaps a description. Touch the keyboard's Search or Go button to begin your search.

To see more information about an item, touch it. Touching something doesn't buy it but instead displays a more detailed description, screen shots, a video preview, comments, plus links to similar items.

Return to the main Android Market screen at any time by touching the Market icon in the upper-left corner of the screen.

- The first time you enter the Android Market, you have to accept the terms of service; touch the Accept button.

- Pay attention to an app's ratings. Ratings are added by people who use the apps — people like you and me. Having more stars is better. You can see additional information, including individual user reviews, by choosing the app.

- Another good indicator of an app's success is how many times it's been downloaded. Some apps have been downloaded over ten million times. That's a good sign.

- Apps you download are added to the Apps Menu, made available like any other app on your Tab. They also appear as Home screen shortcut icons.

- In addition to getting apps, you can download widgets for the Home screen as well as wallpapers for the Galaxy Tab. Just search the Market for *widget* or *live wallpaper.*

- See Chapter 20 for more information on widgets and live wallpapers.

- Books and videos you get from the Market are viewed using the Books and Videos apps, respectively. See Chapter 14 for information on Google Books; Chapter 15 for information on videos.

Getting a free app

After you locate an app you want, the next step is to download it. Follow these steps:

1. **If possible, activate the Wi-Fi connection to avoid incurring data overages.**

   See Chapter 17 for information on connecting your Galaxy Tab to a Wi-Fi network.

2. **Open the Market app.**

3. **Locate the app you want and open its description.**

   You can browse for apps or use the Search button to find an app by name or what it does.

4. **Touch the Install button.**

   Free apps feature an Install button. Paid apps have a button with the app's price on it. (See the next section for information on buying an app.)

After touching the Install button, you're alerted to any services that the app uses. The list of permissions isn't a warning, and it doesn't mean anything bad. It's just that the Market is telling you which of your Tab's features the app uses.

5. **Touch the OK button to accept the conditions and begin the download.**

6. **Touch the Open button to run the app.**

Or, if you were doing something else while the app was downloading and installing, choose the Installed App notification, as shown in the margin. The notification features the app's name with the text `Successfully Installed` beneath it.

At this point, what happens next depends on the app you've downloaded. For example, you may have to agree to a license agreement. If so, touch the I Agree button. Additional setup may involve setting your location, signing in to an account, or creating a profile, for example.

After you complete the initial setup, or if no setup is necessary, you can start using the app.

  ✔ Peruse the list of services an app uses (in Step 4) to look for anything unusual or out of line with the app's purpose. For example, an alarm clock app that uses your contact list and the text messaging service would be a red flag, especially if it's your understanding that the app doesn't need to text message any of your contacts.

  ✔ Chapter 24 lists some Android apps that I recommend, all of which are free.

Buying an app

Some great free apps are available, but many of the apps you dearly want probably cost money. It's not a lot of money, especially compared with the price of computer software. In fact, it seems odd to sit and stew over whether paying 99 cents for a game is "worth it."

I recommend that you download a free app first to familiarize yourself with the process.

When you're ready to pay for an app, follow these steps:

1. **Activate the Galaxy Tab's Wi-Fi connection.**

2. **Open the Market app.**

3. **Browse or search for the app you want and then choose the app to display its description.**

   Review the app's price.

4. **Touch the Buy button.**

   That app's price is listed above the button.

   The next window, titled Purchase & Allow Access, displays the services the app uses, such as Storage to keep high scores or other data, Networking Communication to access the Internet, and so on.

5. **Choose your credit card.**

   The credit card information is at the top of the Purchase & Allow Access window, on the right. The card must be on file with Google Checkout. If you don't yet have a card on file, choose the option Add Payment Method. Choose Add Card and then fill in the fields on the Credit Card screen to add your payment method to Google Checkout.

6. **Touch the OK button.**

   Your payment method is authorized, and the app is downloaded and installed.

The app can be accessed from the Apps Menu, just like all other apps available on your Galaxy Tab. Or if you're still at the app's screen in the Market, touch the Open button.

Eventually, you receive an e-mail message from the Android Market, confirming your purchase. The message contains a link you can click to review the refund policy should you change your mind on the purchase.

Be quick on that refund: Some apps allow you only 15 minutes to get your money back. Otherwise, the standard refund period is 24 hours. You know when the time is up because the Refund button changes its name to Uninstall.

Also see the section "Removing downloaded apps," later in this chapter.

Never buy an app twice

Any apps you've already purchased in the Android Market, say for an Android phone or other mobile device, are available for download on your Galaxy Tab at no charge. Simply find the app and touch the Install button.

You can review any already-purchased apps in the Market: Choose My Apps from the top of the screen. At the bottom of the list of apps, under the heading Not Installed, you find any apps you've already purchased at the Market.

App Management 101

The Market is not only where you buy apps — it's also the place you return to for performing app management. That task includes reviewing apps you've downloaded, updating apps, organizing apps, and removing apps you no longer want or that you severely hate.

Reviewing your apps

To peruse the apps you've downloaded from the Android Market, follow these steps:

1. **Start the Market app.**
2. **Choose My Apps from the top of the screen.**
3. **Scroll your downloaded apps.**

The list of downloaded apps should look similar to the one shown in Figure 16-2. Instantly, you can see any apps that are in need of an update, as shown in the figure.

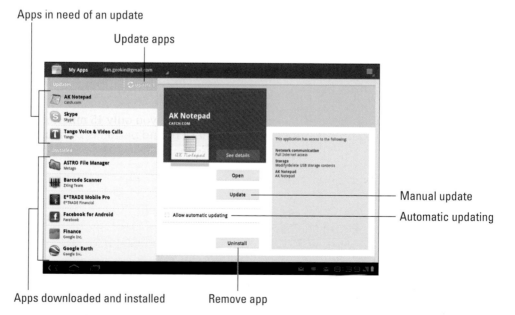

Figure 16-2: The My Apps list.

Touch an app to see details about the app, such as the details for the AK Notepad shown in Figure 16-2. You can touch the See Details button to read more about the app, though the most handy thing to do is to use the Open button to run the app.

You can place a check mark by the option Allow Automatic Updating, which assists in keeping your apps current. Also, there's that Uninstall button, which removes the app from your Tab. Later sections in this chapter describe the details on updating and uninstalling apps.

✔ The list of installed apps shows all the apps you've downloaded on your Galaxy Tab.

✔ Some apps on the My Apps screen might not be installed on your Galaxy Tab. For example, they could have been downloaded and then removed. They appear at the bottom of the app list under the heading Not Installed.

✔ Uninstalled apps remain on the My Apps list because you did, at one time, download the app. To reinstall them (and without paying a second time for paid apps), choose the app from the Not Installed list.

Sharing an app

When you love an app so much that you just can't contain your glee, feel free to share that app with your friends. You can easily share a link to the app in the Market by obeying these steps:

1. View the My Apps list.

Refer to the preceding section. Actually, the app doesn't have to be on your list of downloaded apps; you can share any app in the Market.

2. Choose the app from the list to display information about the app.

For example, in Figure 16-2, information about the AK Notepad is displayed.

3. Touch the See Details button.

4. Touch the Share button.

A menu appears listing various apps and methods for sharing the app's Market link with your pals.

5. Choose a sharing method.

For example, choose Gmail to send a link to the app in an e-mail message.

6. **Use the chosen app to send the link.**

What happens next depends on which sharing method you've chosen.

The end result of these steps is that your friend receives a link. They can touch that link on their phone, or other mobile Android device, and be whisked instantly to the Market, where they can view the app and easily install it.

Methods for using the various items on the Share menu are found throughout this book.

Updating an app

One nice thing about using the Android Market to get new software is that the market also notifies you of new versions of the programs you download. Whenever a new version of any app is available, you see it flagged for updating, as shown in Figure 16-2. Updating the app to get the latest version is cinchy.

From the My Apps list (refer to Figure 16-2), touch the Update button to update all the apps for which automatic updating is allowed.

Some apps must be updated individually. To do so, touch the app in the Update part of the My Apps list. Then touch the Update button (also shown in Figure 16-2) to manually update the app.

To make updating easier, you can place a green check mark by the item Allow Automatic Updating. Refer to Figure 16-2 for that check mark box's location.

✔ The updating process often involves downloading and installing a new version of the app. That's perfectly fine; your settings and options aren't changed by the update process.

✔ Update to apps might also be indicated by the Updates Available notification icon, shown in the margin as well as in Figure 16-1. Choose the Updates Available notification to be instantly whisked to the My Apps screen, where you can update your apps as described in this section.

Removing downloaded apps

I can think of a few reasons to remove an app. It's with eager relish that I remove apps that don't work or somehow annoy me. It's also perfectly okay to remove redundant apps, such as when you have multiple eBook readers that you don't use. And if you're desperate for an excuse, removing apps frees up a modicum of storage in the Galaxy Tab's internal storage area.

Whatever the reason, remove an app by following these directions:

1. **Start the Market app.**

2. **Choose My Apps from the top of the screen.**

3. **Touch the app that offends you.**

4. **Touch the Uninstall button.**

   The app is removed.

The app continues to appear on the Downloads list even after it's been removed. After all, you downloaded it once. That doesn't mean that the app is installed.

✔ In most cases, if you uninstall a paid app right away, your credit card or account is fully refunded. The definition of "right away" depends on the app and is stated on the app's description screen. It could be anywhere from 15 minutes to 24 hours.

✔ You can always reinstall paid apps that you've uninstalled. You aren't charged twice for doing so.

✔ You can't remove apps that are preinstalled on the Tab by either Samsung or your cellular service provider. I'm sure there's probably a technical way to uninstall the apps, but seriously: Just don't use the apps if you want to remove them and discover that you can't.

Part IV
Nuts & Bolts

*T*here's a lot you can do with your Galaxy Tab that doesn't qualify as communications or a whatever-else it can do. Yes, those things are impressive, but there's more to the Tab than just being the ultimate gizmo.

For example, you can connect the Tab to a wireless network or a computer. You can customize the Tab. You can perform maintenance and configuration settings. None of those things have the glamour of, say, video chat, but they're necessary, important, and covered in this part of the book.

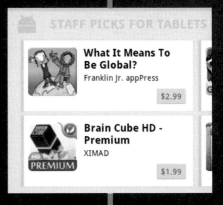

17

It's a Wireless Life

In This Chapter

▶ Using the cellular data network

▶ Accessing a Wi-Fi network

▶ Using the Galaxy Tab as a mobile hotspot

▶ Tethering the Galaxy Tab connection

▶ Using Bluetooth

▶ Printing with your Galaxy Tab

What exactly is *portable?* Back in the olden days, the boys in Marketing would say that bolting a handle to just about anything made it portable. Even a rhinoceros would be portable if he had a handle. Well, and the legs, they kind of make the rhino portable, I suppose. But my point is that to be portable requires more than just a handle; it requires a complete lack of wires.

The Galaxy Tab's battery keeps it away from a wall socket. The digital cellular signal keeps your gizmo away from a phone line. Other types of wireless communications are available to the Tab, including Wi-Fi and Bluetooth. Both of those features ensure the Tab's portability, and they're both covered in this chapter.

Wireless Networking Wizardry

You know that wireless networking has hit the big-time when you see people asking Santa Claus for a wireless router at Christmas. Such a thing would have been unheard of years ago because routers were used primarily for woodworking back then. Today, wireless networking is what keeps gizmos like the Galaxy Tab connected to the Internet.

The primary reason for wireless networking on the Galaxy Tab is to connect to the Internet. For exchanging and synchronizing files, refer to Chapter 18.

Using the cellular data network

The cellular Galaxy Tab is designed to connect to the Internet by using the digital cellular network. This signal is the same type used by cell phones and cellular modems to wirelessly connect to the Internet.

Several types of digital cellular networks are available:

4G LTE: The fourth generation of wide-area data network is as much as ten times faster than the 3G network and is the latest craze in cellular networking. Verizon is busily covering the country in a coat of 4G LTE paint; if the signal isn't available in your area now, it will be soon.

3G: The third generation of wide-area data networks is several times faster than the previous generation of data networks. This type of wireless signal is the most popular in the United States.

1X: There are several types of original, slower cellular data signals available. They all fall under the 1X banner. It's slow.

Your Galaxy Tab always uses the best network available. So, if the 4G LTE network is within reach, that network is used for Internet communications. Otherwise, the 3G network is chosen.

- A notification icon for the type of network being used appears in the status area, right next to the Signal Strength icon.

- Accessing the digital cellular network isn't free. Your Galaxy Tab most likely has some form of subscription plan for a certain quantity of data. When you exceed that quantity, the costs can become prohibitive.

- See Chapter 19 for information on how to avoid cellular data overcharges when taking your Galaxy Tab out and about.

- A better way to connect your Galaxy Tab to the Internet is to use the Wi-Fi signal, covered in the next section. The digital cellular network signal makes for a great fallback because it's available in more places than Wi-Fi is.

- Wi-Fi–only Galaxy Tabs can't access the digital cellular network.

Understanding Wi-Fi

The digital cellular connection is nice, and it's available pretty much all over, but it will cost you moolah. A better option, and one you should seek out when it's available, is *Wi-Fi*, or the same wireless networking standard used by computers for communicating with each other and the Internet.

To make Wi-Fi work on the Galaxy Tab requires two steps. First, you must activate Wi-Fi, by turning on the Tab's wireless radio. The second step, covered in the following section, is connecting to a specific wireless network.

Wi-Fi stands for *wireless fidelity*. It's also known by various famous numbers, including 802.11g and 802.11n.

Activating and deactivating Wi-Fi

Follow these carefully written directions to activate Wi-Fi networking on your Galaxy Tab:

1. **Touch the Apps Menu button.**
2. **Open the Settings app.**
3. **Choose Wireless & Networks.**
4. **Touch the square by Wi-Fi to place a green check mark by that option.**

The Tab's Wi-Fi radio is activated. If you've already configured your Tab to connect to an available wireless network, it's connected automatically. Otherwise, you have to connect to an available network, which is covered in the next section.

To turn off Wi-Fi, repeat the steps in this section. Turning off Wi-Fi disconnects the Tab from any wireless networks.

✔ From the And-Now-He-Tells-Us Department, you can quickly get to the Wi-Fi Settings window from the Quick Settings screen. See Chapter 3 for more information on the Quick Settings screen.

✔ If you place a check mark by the option Network Notification on the Wi-Fi Settings window, the Tab alerts you to the presence of available Wi-Fi networks whenever you're in range and not connected to a network. This option is a good one to have set when you're frequently on the road. That's because:

✔ Using Wi-Fi to connect to the Internet doesn't incur data usage charges.

✔ The Galaxy Tab Wi-Fi radio places an extra drain on the battery, but it's truly negligible. If you want to save a modicum of juice, especially if you're out and about and don't plan to be near a Wi-Fi access point for any length of time, turn off the Wi-Fi radio as described in this section.

Connecting to a Wi-Fi network

After you've activated the Galaxy Tab's Wi-Fi radio, you can connect to an available wireless network. Heed these steps:

1. **Touch the Apps Menu button on the Home screen.**

2. **Open the Settings app.**

3. **Choose Wireless & Networks.**

4. **Choose Wi-Fi Settings.**

5. **Ensure that Wi-Fi is on.**

   When you see a green check mark next to the Wi-Fi option, Wi-Fi is on.

6. **Choose a wireless network from the list.**

   Available Wi-Fi networks appear at the bottom of the screen, as shown in Figure 17-1. When no wireless networks are listed, you're sort of out of luck regarding wireless access from your current location.

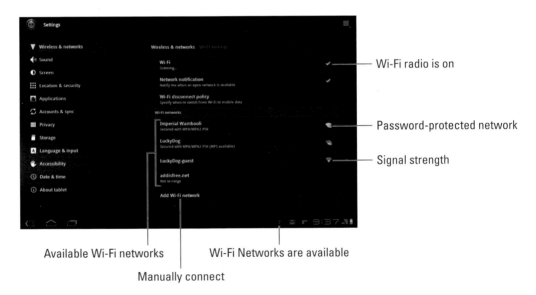

Available Wi-Fi networks   Wi-Fi Networks are available

Manually connect

Figure 17-1: Finding a wireless network.

In Figure 17-1, I chose the Imperial Wambooli network, which is my office network.

7. **Optionally, type the network password.**

Touch the Password text box to see the onscreen keyboard.

Touch the Show Password check box so that you can see what you're typing; some of those network passwords can be *long*.

8. **Touch the Connect button.**

You should be immediately connected to the network. If not, try the password again.

When the Galaxy Tab is connected to a wireless network, you see the Wi-Fi status icon, shown in the margin. This icon replaces the cellular data signal icon. It means that the Tab's Wi-Fi is on, connected, and communicating with a Wi-Fi network.

Some wireless networks don't broadcast their names, which adds security but also makes connecting more difficult. In those cases, choose the command Add Wi-Fi Network (refer to Figure 17-1) to manually add the network. You need to type the network name, or *SSID*, and choose the type of security. You also need the password if one is used. You can obtain this information from the girl with the pink hair who sold you coffee or from whomever is in charge of the wireless network at your location.

 ✔ Not every wireless network has a password.

 ✔ Some public networks are open to anyone, but you have to use the Browser app to find a login page that lets you access the network: Simply browse to any page on the Internet, and the login page shows up.

 ✔ The Galaxy Tab automatically remembers every Wi-Fi network it has ever been connected to and automatically reconnects upon finding the same network again.

 ✔ To disconnect from a Wi-Fi network, simply turn off Wi-Fi. See the preceding section.

 ✔ Unlike a cellular data network, a Wi-Fi network's broadcast signal goes only so far. My advice is to use Wi-Fi whenever you plan to remain in one location for a while. If you wander too far away, your Tab loses the signal and is disconnected.

A Connection Shared

Your Galaxy Tab has no trouble sniffing out a digital cellular signal, so it can access the Internet just about anywhere. Your laptop might not be so lucky. But hey: You're already paying for the digital cellular signal, right? So why should you bother getting a digital cellular modem for the laptop, as well as buying into another cellular contract, when you could just use the Galaxy Tab as a portable modem?

Sharing the Galaxy Tab's Internet connection is not only possible, but also relatively easy. You can go about sharing in one of two ways: The wireless way is to create a mobile hotspot; the wired way is to use the *tethering* technique. Both methods are covered in this section.

Creating a mobile hotspot

You can direct the Galaxy Tab to share its digital cellular connection with as many as five other wireless gizmos. This process is referred to as *creating a mobile, wireless hotspot,* though no heat or fire is involved.

To set up a mobile hotspot with your Galaxy Tab, heed these steps:

1. **Turn off the Galaxy Tab's Wi-Fi radio.**

   You can't be using a Wi-Fi connection when you create a Wi-Fi hotspot. Actually, the notion is kind of silly: If the Galaxy Tab can get a Wi-Fi signal, other gizmos can too, so why bother creating a Wi-Fi hotspot in the first place?

   See the earlier section, "Activating and deactivating Wi-Fi," for information on disabling Wi-Fi on your Galaxy Tab.

2. **If you can, plug in the Galaxy Tab.**

   It's okay if you don't find a power outlet, but running a mobile hotspot draws a lot of power. The Tab's battery power drains quickly if you can't plug in.

3. **From the Apps screen, open the Settings app.**

   Touch the Apps Menu button to get to the Apps screen.

4. **Choose Wireless & Networks.**

5. **Choose Tethering & Portable Hotspot.**

   The Tethering & Portable Hotspot window appears.

6. **Touch the box to place a green check mark by Portable Wi-Fi Hotspot.**

   Yep, that's about all there is to it.

 When the hotspot is activated, you see the Tethering or Hotspot Active status icon displayed, as shown in the margin. You can continue to use the Galaxy Tab while it's sharing the digital cellular connection, but other devices can now use their Wi-Fi radio to access your Tab's shared connection.

To turn off the mobile hotspot, choose the Tethering or Mobile Hotspot Active notification and remove the green check mark by Portable Wi-Fi Hotspot.

✔ One of the easiest ways to disable the Wi-Fi radio is to use the Quick Settings. See Chapter 3 for more information on Quick Settings.

✔ You can change the mobile hotspot configuration by choosing the Configure Wi-Fi Hotspot command in the Tethering & Portable Hotspot window. Use the Configure Wi-Fi Hotspot dialog box to change the Wi-Fi network name (SSID) and set security (add a password), if you like.

✔ The range for the mobile hotspot is about 30 feet.

✔ Some cellular providers may not allow you to create a mobile hotspot, and of course, you cannot create a mobile hotspot when your Galaxy Tab doesn't use the cellular data network.

✔ Don't forget to turn off the mobile hotspot when you're done using it. Those data rates can certainly add up!

Sharing the Internet via tethering

Another, more personal way to share your Galaxy Tab's digital cellular connection, and to get one other device on the Internet, is *tethering*. This operation is carried out by connecting the Tab to another gizmo, such as a laptop computer, via its USB cable. Then you activate USB tethering, and the other gizmo is suddenly using the Galaxy Tab like a modem.

To set up tethering on your Galaxy Tab, heed these directions:

1. **Turn off the Tab's Wi-Fi radio.**

   You cannot share a connection with the Wi-Fi radio on; you can share only the digital cellular connection.

2. **Connect the Tab to a PC using its USB cable.**

   Specifically, the PC must be running Windows 7 or Windows Vista or some flavor of the Linux operating system.

3. **At the Home screen, touch the Apps Menu button.**

4. **Open the Settings app.**

5. **Choose Wireless & Networks.**

6. **Choose Tethering & Portable Hotspot.**

7. **Place a green check mark by the option USB Tethering.**

   The option is disabled when you're using a Wi-Fi connection, which means that you ignored Step 1, or when the Galaxy Tab isn't connected to a PC via the USB cable, which means that you ignored Step 2.

8. **On the PC, choose Public when prompted to specify the type of network to which you've just connected.**

 Though the Galaxy Tab's digital cellular network is being shared, you see the Tethering Active notification, shown in the margin. You can choose that notification to turn off tethering: Simply remove the check mark by the USB Tethering option.

   ✔ Sharing the digital network connection incurs data usage charges against your cellular data plan. Be careful with your data usage when you're sharing a connection.

   ✔ You may be prompted on the PC to locate and install software for the Galaxy Tab. Do so: Accept the installation of new software when prompted by Windows.

The Bluetooth Experience

Computer nerds have long had the desire to connect high-tech gizmos to one another. The Bluetooth standard was developed to sate this desire in a wireless way. Though Bluetooth is wireless communication, it's not the same as wireless networking. It's more about connecting peripheral devices, such as keyboards, mice, printers, headphones, and other gear. It all happens in a wireless way, as described in this section.

Understanding Bluetooth

Bluetooth is a peculiar name for a wireless communications standard. Unlike Wi-Fi networking, with Bluetooth you simply connect two gizmos. Here's how the operation works:

1. **Turn on the Bluetooth wireless radio on each gizmo.**

   There are two Bluetooth gizmos: the peripheral and the main device to which you're connecting the gizmo, such as the Galaxy Tab.

2. **Make the gizmo you're trying to connect to discoverable.**

   By making a device discoverable, you're telling it to send a signal to other Bluetooth gizmos, saying, "Here I am!"

3. **On the Galaxy Tab, choose the peripheral gizmo from the list of Bluetooth devices.**

   This action is known as *pairing* the devices.

4. **Optionally, confirm the connection on the peripheral device.**

   For example, you may be asked to input a code or press a button.

5. **Use the device.**

   What you can do with the device depends on what it does.

When you're done using the device, you simply turn it off. Because the Bluetooth gizmo is paired with the Galaxy Tab, it's automatically reconnected the next time you turn it on (that is, if you have Bluetooth activated on the Tab).

 Bluetooth devices are marked with the Bluetooth icon, shown in the margin. It's your assurance that the gizmo can work with other Bluetooth devices.

 Bluetooth was developed as a wireless version of the old RS-232 standard, the serial port on early personal computers. Essentially, Bluetooth is wireless RS-232, and the variety of devices you can connect to and the things you can do with Bluetooth are similar to what you could do with the old serial port standard.

Activating Bluetooth

To make the Bluetooth connection, you turn on the Galaxy Tab's Bluetooth radio. Obey these directions:

1. **On the Apps screen, open the Settings icon.**

2. **Choose Wireless & Networks.**

3. **Place a green check mark by the Bluetooth option.**

 When Bluetooth is on, the Bluetooth status icon appears, as shown in the margin.

To turn off Bluetooth, repeat the steps in this section: Remove the check mark in Step 3.

Connecting to a Bluetooth device

To make the Bluetooth connection between the Galaxy Tab and some other gizmo, follow these steps:

1. **Ensure that Bluetooth is on.**

   Refer to the preceding section.

2. **Turn on the Bluetooth gizmo or ensure that its Bluetooth radio is on.**

   Some Bluetooth devices have separate power and Bluetooth switches.

3. **On the Galaxy Tab, touch the Apps Menu button on the Home screen and run the Settings app.**

4. **Choose Wireless & Networks.**

5. **Choose Bluetooth Settings.**

   The Bluetooth Settings window appears.

6. **If the other device has an option to become visible, select it.**

   For example, some Bluetooth gizmos have a tiny button to press that makes the device visible to other Bluetooth gizmos. (You don't need to make the Galaxy Tab visible unless you're accessing it from another Bluetooth gizmo.)

7. **Choose Find Nearby Devices.**

   Eventually, the device should appear on the Bluetooth Settings window, as shown in Figure 17-2.

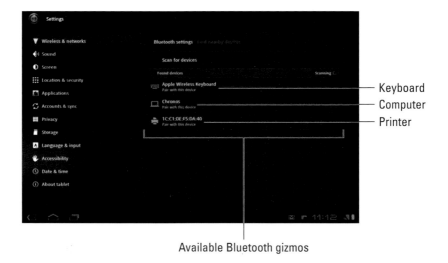

Available Bluetooth gizmos

Figure 17-2: Finding Bluetooth gizmos.

8. **Choose the device.**

9. **If necessary, input the device's passcode or otherwise acknowledge the connection.**

   Not every device has a passcode. If prompted, acknowledge the passcode on either the Galaxy Tab or the other device.

After you acknowledge the passcode (or not), the Bluetooth gizmo and your Galaxy Tab are connected and communicating. You can begin using the device.

Connected devices appear on the Bluetooth Settings window, at the bottom under the heading Paired Devices.

To break the connection, you can either turn off the gizmo or disable the Bluetooth radio on your Galaxy Tab. Because the devices are paired, when you turn on Bluetooth and reactivate the device, the connection is instantly reestablished.

✔ How you use the device depends on what it does. For example, the keyboard in Figure 17-2 can be used for text input, the computer can be accessed for sharing files, and the printer can be used for printing documents or pictures, which is covered in the next section.

✔ You can unpair a device by choosing it from the Bluetooth Settings window. Choose the Unpair command to break the Bluetooth connection and stop using the device.

✔ Only unpair devices you don't plan on using again in the future. Otherwise, simply turn off the Bluetooth device.

✔ Bluetooth can use a lot of power. Especially for battery-powered devices, don't forget to turn them off when you're no longer using them with the Galaxy Tab.

Printing to a Bluetooth printer

Perhaps the only, and most crazy, way to print something on your Galaxy Tab is to connect to a Bluetooth printer and *upload* a document or image for printing. It's not an obvious thing to do, and Bluetooth printers are kind of rare. Still, it works, and reading this section helps make it work.

Before you can print, ensure that your Galaxy Tab is paired with the Bluetooth printer. You may have to make the printer discoverable, and then you need to choose it from the list of devices, as shown in Figure 17-2. You may also have to type the printer's PIN into the Galaxy Tab; the PIN should be displayed on the printer's screen or available in its documentation. (My printer uses the PIN code 0000.)

When the printer and the Bluetooth printer are properly paired, you see the printer listed under Bluetooth Devices on the Bluetooth Settings screen. Even if it says "Paired but not connected," you're ready to go.

Assuming that the Bluetooth printer is on and ready to print, obey these steps to print something on your Galaxy Tab:

1. **View the document, web page, or image you want to print.**

2. **Choose the Share command.**

   If a Share button isn't visible in the app, press the Menu button to look for the Share command.

3. **Choose Bluetooth from either the Share or Share Via menu.**

4. **Choose your Bluetooth printer from the list of items on the Bluetooth Device Picker screen.**

5. **If a prompt appears on the printer, confirm that the Galaxy Tab is printing a document.**

   The document is uploaded (sent from the Tab to the printer), and then it prints. You can view the uploading status by checking the notifications in the lower-right corner of the screen.

Not everything on your Galaxy Tab can be printed on a Bluetooth printer. When you can't find the Share command or the Bluetooth item isn't available on the Share menu, you can't print using Bluetooth.

Bluetooth printers sport the Bluetooth logo somewhere.

18

Connect and Share

he Galaxy Tab is adept at communicating wirelessly. It can connect to the Internet using the digital cellular signal or over a Wi-Fi connection. Beyond that, you can use the USB cable to connect your Tab to another gizmo. No, you cannot use the USB cable to connect the Galaxy Tab to the couch, or the toaster, or the time machine. You can, however, use the USB cable to connect the Galaxy Tab to a computer. This chapter describes all the wonderful things that can happen after you make that connection.

The USB Connection

The most direct way to connect a Galaxy Tab to a computer is by using a wire — specifically, the wire nestled cozily in the heart of a USB cable. There are lots of things you can do after making the USB connection. Before doing those things, you need to connect the cable.

Yeah, it may seem excessive to write an entire section on what's apparently a simple operation. But if you've used the Galaxy Tab and already tried to make a USB connection, you probably discovered that it's not so simple.

Connecting the Galaxy Tab to your PC

The USB connection between the Galaxy Tab and your computer works fastest when both devices are physically connected. You make this connection happen by using the USB cable that comes with the Tab. Like nearly every computer cable in the Third Dimension, the USB cable has two ends:

- ✔ The A end of the USB cable plugs into the computer.
- ✔ The other end of the cable plugs into the bottom of the Galaxy Tab.

The connectors are shaped differently and cannot be plugged in either backward or upside down. (The end that inserts into the Galaxy Tab has the *SAMSUNG* text facing you when you plug it in.)

After you understand how the cable works, plug the USB cable into one of the computer's USB ports. Then plug the USB cable into the Galaxy Tab.

- ✔ As far as I can tell, you cannot connect the Galaxy Tab to a Macintosh and have it be recognized as an external storage device or media player.
- ✔ You can, however, use Bluetooth to send and receive files between the Galaxy Tab and a Mac. It's not the fastest way to exchange information, but it works. See the later section, "Using Bluetooth to copy a file."
- ✔ Even if you don't use the USB cable to communicate with the computer, the Galaxy Tab's battery charges when it's connected to a computer's USB port — as long as the computer is turned on, of course.

Dealing with the USB connection

Upon making the USB connection between the Galaxy Tab and a PC, a number of things happen. Don't let any of these things cause you undue alarm.

First, you may see the MTP application screen appear on the Galaxy Tab. That screen indicates that the Tab is actively looking for the Samsung Kies program, which it can use to automatically synchronize information between the Tab and your PC.

Second, you may see some activity on the PC, some drivers being installed and such. That's normal behavior any time you first connect a new USB gizmo to a Windows computer.

Third, you may witness the AutoPlay dialog box. That dialog box helps you deal with the Galaxy Tab connection, to transfer music, pictures, files, and so on.

Choose an option from the AutoPlay dialog box, such as Sync Digital Media Files to This Device. From that point on, you'll use Windows or a program on your computer to work with the files on your Galaxy Tab.

Don't be surprised if the AutoPlay dialog box doesn't appear; many PCs are configured to ignore new gizmos. That's okay: You can always manually summon the various options displayed in the AutoPlay dialog box, as discussed elsewhere in this chapter.

 Fourth, the Galaxy Tab is added to your computer's storage system. You see it listed as a device in the Computer window. On my PC, the Tab is assumed to be a portable music player; its icon is shown in the margin.

Bottom line: When you make the USB connection, you can exchange information between your computer and the Galaxy Tab.

- When the Galaxy Tab is connected to a computer using the USB connection, the USB notification appears at the bottom of the screen, as shown in the margin. Choosing that notification does nothing.

- Unlike other Android devices you may be familiar with, there is no configuration option for the USB connection. The Tab always connects as a portable media player.

- You can obtain a copy of the Samsung Kies program for your computer from the `http:\\samsungapps.com` website. I don't specifically cover using Samsung Kies in this book. That's because a lot of people dislike the program, and there are better ways to move files back and forth.

- The Galaxy Tab icon in the Computer window may be named Galaxy Tab, or it could be given the device's technical name, something delightfully cryptic like SCH-I905 or GT-P7510.

- It's actually the Galaxy Tab's internal storage that's mounted into your computer's storage system.

- If you're nerdy, you can open the Galaxy Tab's icon in the Computer window. You see another window that lists the Tab's storage, named *Tablet*. You can open that icon to browse files and folders on the Tab just as you can browse them on your computer. The later section, "Files from Here, Files to There," describes how it works.

Disconnecting the Tab from your computer

This process is cinchy: When you're done transferring files, music, or other media between your PC and the Tab, close all the programs and folders you have opened on the PC, specifically those you've used to work with the Tab's storage. Then you can disconnect the USB cable. That's it.

It's a Bad Idea to unplug the Tab while you're transferring information or while a folder window is open on the PC. Doing so could damage the Galaxy Tab's internal storage, rendering some of the information kept there unreadable. So just to be safe, close those programs and folder windows you've opened before disconnecting.

Files from Here, Files to There

The point of making the USB connection between your Galaxy Tab and the computer is to exchange files. You can't just wish the files over. Instead, I recommend following the advice in this section, which also covers transferring files using Bluetooth.

A good understanding of basic file operations is necessary before you attempt file transfers between your computer and the Galaxy Tab. You need to know how to copy, move, rename, and delete files. It also helps to be familiar with what folders are and how they work. The good news is that you don't need to manually calculate a 64-bit cyclical redundancy check on the data, nor do you need to know what a parity bit is.

Transferring files to the Galaxy Tab

There are plenty of reasons you would want to copy a file from your computer to the Galaxy Tab. You can copy over your pictures and videos, and you can copy over music or audio files. You can even copy vCards that you export from your e-mail program, which helps you build your Contacts list.

Follow these steps to copy a file from your computer to the Galaxy Tab:

1. **Connect the Galaxy Tab to the computer by using the USB cable.**

   Specific directions are offered earlier in this chapter.

2. **If the AutoPlay dialog box appears, choose the option Open Folder/ Device to View Files. Otherwise, open the Computer window, then open the Galaxy Tab's icon, and then open the Tablet icon.**

   The AutoPlay dialog box is shown in Figure 18-1.

   The folder window you see looks like any other folder in Windows. The difference is that the files and folders in that window are on the Galaxy Tab, not on your computer.

Figure 18-1: The AutoPlay dialog box for the
Galaxy Tab.

3. **Locate the files you want to copy to the Galaxy Tab.**

   Open the folder that contains the files, or somehow have the file icons visible on the screen.

4. **Drag the File icon from its folder on your computer to the Galaxy Tab window.**

   If you want to be specific, drag the file to the `download` folder; otherwise, you can place the file into the Galaxy Tab's root folder, as shown in Figure 18-2. Try to avoid dragging the file into other, specific folders, which would make the file more difficult to locate in the future.

5. **Close the folder windows and disconnect the USB cable when you're done.**

   Refer to specific instructions earlier in this chapter.

Any files you've copied are now stored on the Galaxy Tab. What you do with them next depends on the reasons you copied the files: to view pictures, use the Gallery, import vCards, use the Contacts app, listen to music, or use the Music app, for example.

Specific folders on the Galaxy Tab

Drag files here to copy to the 'root'

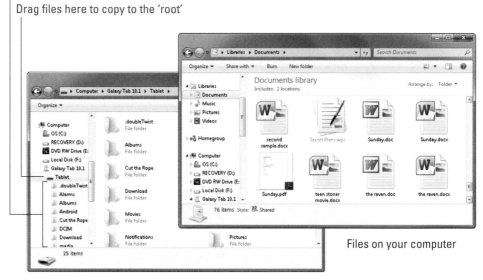

Files on your computer

Files on the Galaxy Tab

Figure 18-2: Copying files to the Galaxy Tab.

  ✔ The best way to move music and pictures over to your Galaxy Tab from
     the computer is to synchronize them. See the later section, "Synchronize
     with doubleTwist."

  ✔ Also refer to Chapter 13 for information on synchronizing music using
     the Windows Media Player.

  ✔ The name of the cellular Galaxy Tab device is SCH-I905; the Wi-Fi version
     is GT-P7510. You may see those names when mounting the Tab into your
     computer's storage system.

Copying files to your computer

After you've survived the ordeal of copying files from your computer to the
Galaxy Tab, copying files in the other direction is a cinch: Follow the steps
in the preceding section, but in Steps 3 and 4 you're dragging the File icons
from the Galaxy Tab folder window to your computer.

My advice is to drag the files to your computer's desktop, unless you know of
another location where you want the files copied.

- ✏ Files you've downloaded on the Galaxy Tab are stored in the download folder.

- ✏ Pictures and videos on the Galaxy Tab are stored in the DCIM/Camera folder.

- ✏ Music on the Galaxy Tab is stored in the Music folder, organized by artist.

- ✏ Files transferred via Bluetooth are stored in the bluetooth folder. See the next section.

- ✏ Quite a few files can be found in the *root folder,* the main folder on the Galaxy Tab, which you see when the Tab is mounted into your computer's storage system and you open its folder.

Using Bluetooth to copy a file

Here's a great way to give yourself a headache: Use the Bluetooth networking system to copy a file between your Galaxy Tab and a Bluetooth-enabled computer. It's slow and painful, but it works.

Get started by pairing the Galaxy Tab with the Bluetooth computer. See Chapter 17 for details on the whole pairing-discovery thing. When your Tab and computer are paired and connected, how the file transfer works depends on whether you're using a PC or a Macintosh.

Send a file from the PC to the Galaxy Tab

On a PC, follow these steps to copy a file to the Galaxy Tab:

1. **Right-click the Bluetooth icon in the Notification Area.**

   The icon looks like the Bluetooth logo, shown in the margin. The Notification Area dwells on the far-right end of the taskbar.

2. **Choose Send a File from the pop-up menu.**

3. **Choose the Galaxy Tab from the list of Bluetooth devices.**

   If you don't see the Tab listed, ensure that the Bluetooth radio is on for both devices and that they're paired.

4. **Click the Next button.**

5. **Click the Browse button to locate files to send to the Tab.**

6. **Use the Browse dialog box to locate and select one or more files.**

7. **Click the Open button to choose the file(s).**

8. **Click the Next button.**

9. **On the Galaxy Tab, touch the Accept button to receive the file.**

   The Tab may play a notification alert, which lets you know that the file is coming over.

10. **On the PC, touch the Finish button.**

   The transfer is complete.

- ✒ Images sent to the Galaxy Tab from a PC can be found in the Gallery app, in the Bluetooth album.

- ✒ Not all PCs are equipped with Bluetooth. To add Bluetooth to a PC, you need a Bluetooth adapter. Inexpensive USB Bluetooth adapters are available at most computer and office supply stores.

Receive a file on a PC from the Galaxy Tab

To send a file from the Tab to a PC, you need to use the Bluetooth item found on the Share menu in various apps. Follow these steps:

1. **On the Galaxy Tab, locate the media or file you want to send to the PC.**

2. **Choose the Share command.**

3. **From the Share or Share Via menu, choose Bluetooth.**

   A list of Bluetooth devices appears.

4. **Choose the PC from the list.**

5. **On the PC, click the Notification Area icon that appears, indicating that a Bluetooth file transfer request is pending.**

6. **On the PC, click the OK button in the Access Authorization dialog box.**

   The file is sent to the PC.

On my PC, the received files are stored in the Bluetooth Exchange Folder, found in the Documents or My Documents folder.

Send a file from a Macintosh to the Tab

On a Macintosh, to copy a file to the Galaxy Tab by using Bluetooth, follow these steps:

1. **Use the Bluetooth menu on the Mac to choose the Galaxy Tab and then Send File, as shown in Figure 18-3.**

   You can find the Bluetooth menu at the far-right end of the menu bar. The Galaxy Tab is probably named SCH-I905, which is Samsung's super secret code name for the cellular Tab.

Galaxy Tab   Bluetooth menu

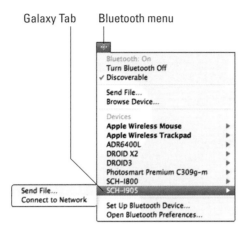

Figure 18-3: Copying a file using Bluetooth on the Mac.

2. **Use the Select File to Send dialog box to browse for the file you want to send from the Mac to the Galaxy Tab.**

3. **On the Galaxy Tab, choose the Bluetooth notification.**

4. **In the dialog box that appears on the Tab, touch the Accept button to receive the file.**

Sadly, I cannot get the Mac to accept a file sent to it using the Bluetooth item from the Share menu. That method may work in the future, in which case the steps should work similar to those described in the earlier section, "Receive a file on a PC from the Galaxy Tab."

Synchronize with doubleTwist

Perhaps the most effective and easy way to move information between the Galaxy Tab and your computer is to use a synchronization utility. One of the most popular is the free program doubleTwist, available at `www.double twist.com`.

doubleTwist isn't an Android app. You use it on your computer. It helps you synchronize picture, music, videos, and web page subscriptions between your computer and its media libraries and any portable device, such as the Galaxy Tab. Additionally, doubleTwist gives you the ability to search the Android Market and obtain new apps for your phone.

To use doubleTwist, connect the Galaxy Tab to your computer as described earlier in this chapter. Use the USB cable to make the PC-Tab connection.

If the doubleTwist program doesn't start automatically after you connect the Tab, start it manually. The doubleTwist interface is illustrated in Figure 18-4.

View local media

Look for apps   Choose items to sync   Items to sync

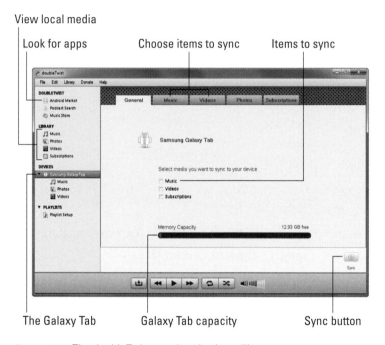

The Galaxy Tab   Galaxy Tab capacity   Sync button

Figure 18-4: The doubleTwist synchronization utility.

To best use doubleTwist, place a check mark by the items you want to sync on the General tab. (Refer to Figure 18-4.) Or, you can choose a tab, such as Videos or Pictures, as shown in Figure 18-4, to select specific items to synchronize. Click the Sync button to copy those files to the Galaxy Tab.

Another way to use doubleTwist is to copy media items to the Galaxy Tab by selecting and then dragging their icons. Choose a media category on your computer, as shown on the left side of the doubleTwist window in Figure 18-4. Drag media from your computer to the Galaxy Tab's icon to copy over those files.

✔ doubleTwist doesn't synchronize contact information.

✔ Some media organization programs on your computer, such as Windows Music Player or Windows Photo Gallery, may allow you to synchronize your media with the Galaxy Tab just as well as or perhaps better than doubleTwist.

The Galaxy Tab's Internal Storage

Somewhere, deep in the bosom of your Galaxy Tab, there lies a storage device. It's like the hard drive in your computer. The thing can't be removed, but that's not the point. The point is that the storage is used for your apps, music, videos, pictures, and a host of other information. This section describes what you can do to manage that storage.

- The Galaxy Tab comes with either 16GB or 32GB of internal storage.

- A GB is a gigabyte, or one billion bytes (characters) of storage. A typical 2-hour movie occupies about 4GB of storage, but most things you store on the Tab — music and pictures, for example — take up only a sliver of storage. Those items do, however, occupy more storage space the more you use your Tab.

Reviewing storage stats

You can see how much storage space is available on your Galaxy Tab's internal storage by following these steps:

1. **At the Home screen, touch the Apps Menu icon button.**

2. **Open the Settings app and choose Storage.**

   You see a screen similar to Figure 18-5. It details information about storage space on the Galaxy Tab's internal storage.

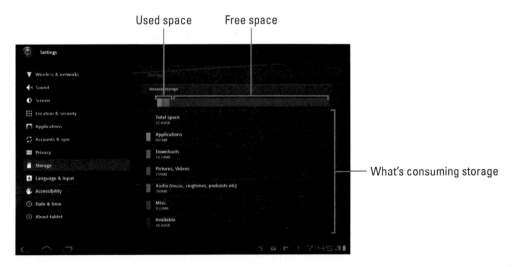

Figure 18-5: Galaxy Tab storage information.

You can choose a category to see more information, or to launch a program. For example, touching the Misc. category (refer to Figure 18-5) displays a list of Misc. Files, including apps and files you've downloaded. Touching the Pictures, Videos category starts the Gallery app.

✔ Things that consume the most storage space are videos, music, and pictures, in that order.

✔ To see how much storage space is left, refer to the Available item.

✔ Don't complain that the Total Space value is far less than the capacity of your Galaxy Tab. In Figure 18-5, it shows 27.89GB total space, even though the Galaxy Tab has 32GB of storage. The missing space is considered overhead, as are several gigabytes taken by the government for tax purposes.

Managing files

You probably didn't get a Galaxy Tab because you enjoy managing files on a computer and wanted another gizmo to hone your skills. Even so, you can practice the same type of file manipulation on the Tab as you would on a computer. Is there a need to do so? Of course not! But if you want to get dirty with files, you can.

The main tool for managing files is the Quickoffice app. You may have seen that app used to display a Microsoft Office document download or file attachment. It can also be used to view PDF files. But when you choose the Quickoffice app from the Apps Menu, it opens as a sort of file manager, as shown in Figure 18-6.

Quickoffice can also be used to create new documents: Touch the New button, as shown in Figure 18-6. Further, it can synchronize with Google Docs, Dropbox, or a number of online file-sharing websites to help coordinate files you may store on the Internet. But for this section's topic, it makes for a modest file-management app.

✔ Another file-management app I can recommend is ASTRO. Its QR code is shown in the margin. Scan that code to download a copy of ASTRO on your Tab, or just search for ASTRO in the Market, as discussed in Chapter 16.

✔ Some file-management apps may appear on various menus as you use the Tab. For example, if you choose an image, you may see a prompt asking you to select either the Gallery or the File Management app to view that image.

✔ If you simply want to peruse files you've downloaded from the Internet, open the Downloads app, found on the Apps Menu screen.

Online file-sharing sites

Create a new document

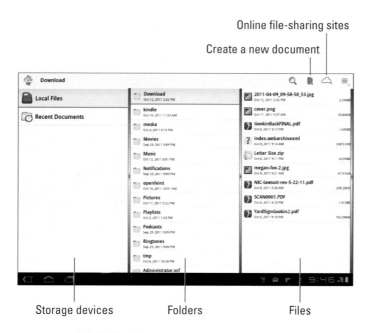

Storage devices   Folders   Files

Figure 18-6: Quickoffice file management.

The HDMI Connection

Tired of that boring 10.1-inch screen on the Galaxy Tab? How large a screen do you want to have? The answer depends on how large of a television set is available. As long as the TV has an HDMI input, you can connect your Galaxy Tab to see the Big Picture.

To make the HDMI connection, you need the Multimedia Dock or HDMI dongle. Yep: The Tab doesn't do HDMI straight out of the box. I'm sure the friendly folks at the Phone Store would be happy to sell you the proper HDMI equipment.

When you have that HDMI connection, plus an HDMI cable, you can hook up the Tab to an HDMI computer monitor or TV set. Simply plug the thing in. Both sound and video can be transferred from the Tab to the monitor (providing that the monitor is equipped with speakers).

Respond to the HDMI notification or pop-up and choose what information the external monitor should display and how you want it displayed. I choose the mirror option so that information displayed on the Tab is echoed on the HDMI screen. Then I can watch a movie or slide show and not have a crowd of people pressing against me. Welcome to the Big Screen.

I've played Angry Birds on a 52-inch plasma TV. It's awesome.

19

Taking Your Tab with You

*L*ast time I checked, the Galaxy Tab didn't come with legs. It doesn't even have a rolling tread, like a tank. That would be nifty, and I'm sure that more Real Men would buy a Galaxy Tab with a tank tread, but it's not my point: The Galaxy Tab is a mobile device. It's wireless. It runs on battery power. You can take the Galaxy Tab with you everywhere you go and not get those peculiar looks you get when you take the washing machine with you.

How far can you go with the Galaxy Tab? As far as you want. As long as you can carry the Tab with you, it goes where you go. How it functions may change depending on your environment, and you can do a few things to prepare before you go, which are all covered in this chapter.

Before You Go

Unless the house is on fire, you should prepare several things before leaving on a trip with your Galaxy Tab. First and most important, of course, is to charge the thing. I plug my Tab in overnight before I leave the next day.

Another good thing to do is to synchronize media with your computer. This operation isn't so much for taking media with you, but rather, it's to ensure that you have a backup of the Tab's media on your computer. See Chapter 18 for synchronization information.

Consider getting some eBooks for the road. I prefer to sit and stew over the Kindle online library before I leave, as opposed to wandering aimlessly in some airport sundry store, trying hard to focus on the good books rather than on the salty snacks. Chapter 14 covers reading eBooks on your Galaxy Tab.

Another nifty thing to do is save some web pages for later reading. I usually start my day by perusing online articles and angry editorials in the local paper. Because I don't have time to read that stuff before I leave, and I do have time on the plane, and I'm extremely unwilling to pay for in-flight Wi-Fi, I save my favorite websites for later reading. Here's how to save a web page by using the Browser app:

1. **Navigate to the page you want to save for later reading.**

2. **Touch the Menu icon button.**

3. **Choose the Save Page command.**

    The page is downloaded, saved to the Tab's internal storage.

Repeat these steps for each web page you want to read when offline.

To view the page, open the Downloads app on the Apps Menu. You see the web page listed, along with other items you've downloaded. Unfortunately, web pages are saved using the page's original name, plus the long link name to that page. The name isn't too cryptic, so even if you choose the wrong page from the Downloads list, you're still reading a web page you've previously saved.

Downloaded web pages will be missing some information; only the text and formatting are saved; pictures might be missing. Though this arrangement may not look pretty, at least you'll have some reading material on the plane — specifically, stuff you're used to reading that day anyway.

- ✔ You can also download Google Books books using the Books app, though Kindle is my personal favorite.

- ✔ See Chapter 7 for more information on the Browser app and browsing the web on the Galaxy Tab.

Galaxy Tab Travel Tips

I'm not a frequent flier, but I am a nerd. The most amount of junk I've carried with me on a flight is two laptop computers and three cell phones. I know that's not a record, but it's enough to warrant my list of travel tips, all of which apply to taking the Galaxy Tab with you on an extended journey:

- ✔ Take the Galaxy Tab's AC adapter and USB cable with you. Put them in your carry-on luggage. Many airports feature USB chargers, so you can charge the Tab in an airport if you need to.

- ✔ At the security checkpoint, place your Galaxy Tab in a bin by itself or with other electronics.

- ✔ Use the Calendar app to keep track of your flights. The event title serves as the airline and flight number. For the event time, use the takeoff and landing schedules. For the location, list the origin and destination airport codes. And, in the Notes field, put the flight reservation number. If you're using separate calendars (categories), specify the Travel calendar for your flight.

- ✔ See Chapter 15 for more information on the Calendar app.

- ✔ Some airlines feature Android apps you can use while traveling. At the time this book went to press, American Airlines, Southwest, United, Continental, and a host of other airlines feature apps. You can use the apps to not only keep track of flights but also to check in: Eventually, printed tickets will disappear, and you'll merely show your "ticket" on the Galaxy Tab screen, which is then scanned at the gate.

- ✔ Some apps you can use to organize your travel details are similar to, but more sophisticated than, the Calendar app. Visit the Android Market and search for *travel* or *airlines* to find a host of apps.

Into the Wild Blue Yonder

It truly is the most trendy of things to be aloft with the latest mobile gizmo. Like taking a cell phone on a plane, however, you have to follow some rules. Though the Galaxy Tab isn't a cell phone, you still have to heed the flight crew's warnings regarding cell phones.

First and foremost, turn off the Galaxy Tab when instructed to do so. This direction is given before takeoff and landing, so be prepared.

Before takeoff, you'll most likely want to put the Tab into Airplane or Flight mode. Yep, it's the same Airplane mode you see on a cell phone: The various scary and dangerous wireless radios on the Tab are disabled in that mode. With Airplane mode active, you're free to use the Tab in-flight, and you can rest assured that with Airplane mode active, you face little risk of the Galaxy Tab causing the plane's navigational equipment to fail and the entire flight to end as a fireball over Wyoming.

To enter Airplane mode on the Galaxy Tab, follow these steps just before takeoff:

1. **At the Home screen, touch the current time to pop up the list of notifications.**

2. **Touch the Quick Settings button.**

3. **Choose Airplane Mode to turn that option on.**

   On the Wi-Fi Tab, the option is titled Flight Mode. Same thing.

When the Galaxy Tab is in Airplane mode, a special icon appears by the current time at the bottom right of the screen. You might also see the text No Internet Connection appear because it's true!

And now, for the quick shortcut: To put the Galaxy Tab into Airplane mode, press and hold the Power button and choose the Airplane Mode command.

To exit Airplane mode, repeat the steps in this section but remove the green check mark by touching the square next to Airplane Mode.

- ✔ Officially, the Galaxy Tab must be powered off when the plane is taking off or landing. See Chapter 2 for information on turning off the Tab.

- ✔ You can compose e-mail while the Tab is in Airplane mode. The messages aren't sent until you disable Airplane mode and connect again with a data network.

- ✔ Bluetooth networking is disabled in Airplane mode. Even so:

- ✔ Many airlines now feature wireless networking onboard, which you can use with the Galaxy Tab — if you're willing to pay for the service. Simply activate Wi-Fi on the Tab, per the directions in Chapter 17, and then connect to the in-flight wireless network when it's available.

The Galaxy Tab Goes Abroad

You have no worries taking the Wi-Fi Galaxy Tab abroad. Because it uses Wi-Fi signals, your biggest issue is simply finding that type of Internet access so that you can use your Tab's communications abilities. That rule also holds true for the cellular Tab, which can also use Wi-Fi abroad. But for the digital cellular signal, more precautions need to take place. After all, you don't want to incur any data roaming charges, especially when they're priced in *zloty* or *pengö*.

Traveling overseas with the Tab

The Tab works overseas. The two resources you need to heed are a way to recharge the battery and access Wi-Fi. As long as you have both of them, you're pretty much set. (Data roaming is covered in the next section.)

The Tab's AC plug can easily plug into a foreign AC adapter, which allows you to charge the Tab in outer Wamboolistan. From personal experience, I can tell you that I charged my Tab nightly while I spent time in France, and it worked like a charm.

Wi-Fi is pretty universal, and as long as your location offers this service, you can connect the Tab and pick up your e-mail, browse the web, or do whatever other Internet activities you desire. Even if you have to pay for Wi-Fi access, I believe that you'll find it less expensive than paying a data roaming charge.

Even when you have Wi-Fi, you need to set up international credit on Skype. See Chapter 9 for more information on making Skype calls.

Disabling data roaming

When I've taken my cellular Galaxy Tab abroad, I've kept it in Airplane mode. If you do that, there's no chance of data roaming charges, and you can still enable Wi-Fi. Even so, and just to be sure, you can disable data roaming on the Galaxy Tab by obeying these steps:

1. **On the Home screen, touch the Apps Menu icon button.**
2. **Open the Settings app.**
3. **Choose Wireless & Networks.**
4. **Choose Mobile Networks.**
5. **Choose Global Data Roaming Access.**
6. **Choose Deny Data Roaming Access.**

Of course, you don't need to disable data roaming or keep the Tab stuck in Airplane mode if you simply want to use your Tab overseas and see what comes in the mail regarding a data bill. I prefer not to have such a surprise.

✔ Contact your digital cellular provider when you're traveling abroad to ask about overseas data roaming. A subscription service or other options may even be available, especially when you plan to stay overseas for an extended length of time.

✔ You can determine whether the Tab is roaming by looking at the Status screen: Run the Settings app, choose About Tablet, and then choose Status. The Roaming item in the list describes whether or not the Tab is data roaming.

20

Customize Your Galaxy Tab

In This Chapter

▶ Changing the background image

▶ Putting apps and widgets on the Home screen

▶ Rearranging things on the Home screen

▶ Removing the screen lock

▶ Adding a pattern lock, PIN, or password

▶ Changing the notification ringtone

▶ Adjusting the brightness

*I*t's entirely possible to own the amazing Galaxy Tab for the rest of your life and never even once bother to customize the gizmo. It's not only possible, it's sad. That's because there exists great potential to create your own Tab. You can change so many things, from the way it looks to the way it sounds. The reason isn't simply to change things because you can, but to make the Tab work best for how you use it. After all, it's *your* Galaxy Tab.

Home Screen Decorating

Lots of interesting doodads are on the Galaxy Tab Home screen. Items such as icons, widgets, and shortcuts adorn the Home screen like olives in a festive salad. All that stuff can change, even the background images. You must simply know the key.

The key to modifying the Home screen lies in the Customize button, found in the upper-right corner of the screen. Yes, it's the standard Add button, shown in the margin, but in this case you're adding things to the Home screen.

After touching the Customize button, you see what I call the Customize screen, shown in Figure 20-1. That's where you begin your Home screen decorating adventure, as discussed in this section.

Home screen panel overview

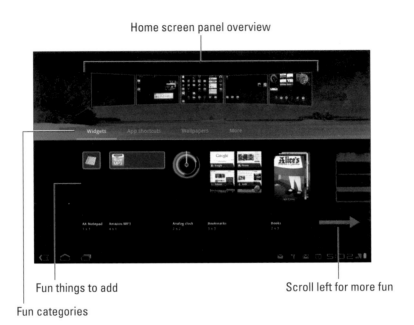

Fun things to add   Scroll left for more fun

Fun categories

Figure 20-1: The Customize screen.

You can touch any panel in the Home screen panel overview to instantly display that panel. This trick isn't really a shortcut, but it's handy.

Hanging new wallpaper

The Home screen has two types of backgrounds, or *wallpapers:* traditional and live. A *live* wallpaper is animated. A not-so-live *(traditional)* wallpaper can be any image, such as a picture you've taken and stored in the Gallery app.

To set a new wallpaper for the Home screen, obey these steps:

1. **Touch the Customize button on the Home screen.**

   The Add to Home Screen menu appears, as shown in Figure 20-1.

2. **Choose Wallpapers.**

   You have three options:

Gallery: Choose a still image from those you've taken, stored in the Gallery app.

Live Wallpapers: Choose an animated or interactive wallpaper from a list.

Wallpapers: Choose a wallpaper from a range of images preinstalled on the Galaxy Tab.

3. **Select a wallpaper type.**

4. **For the Gallery of Wallpapers item, choose whether you want the image to adorn the Home screen or the Lock screen.**

   Live wallpapers can be applied only to the Home screen.

5. **Choose the wallpaper you want from the list.**

   For the Gallery option, you see a preview of the wallpaper where you can select and crop part of the image.

   For certain live wallpapers, a Settings button may appear. The settings let you customize certain aspects of the interactive wallpaper.

6. **Touch the OK or Set Wallpaper button to confirm your selection.**

   The new wallpaper takes over the Home screen or Lock screen.

Live wallpaper features some form of animation, which can often be interactive. Otherwise, the wallpaper image scrolls slightly as you swipe from one Home screen panel to another.

✔ The Zedge app has some interesting wallpaper available. It's an über-repository of wallpaper images, collected from Android users all over the world. Check out Zedge at the Android Market; see Chapter 16.

✔ See Chapter 12 for more information about the Gallery app, including information on how cropping an image works.

Adding apps to the Home screen

The first thing I did on my Galaxy Tab was to place my most favorite apps on the Home screen. Here's how that works:

1. **Touch the Apps Menu icon button on the Home screen.**

   To take a shortcut, you can also long-press any blank part of the Home screen.

2. **Long-press the app icon you want to add to the Home screen.**

   After a moment, you see the Home screen panel overview displayed at the bottom of the screen, as shown in Figure 20-2.

Choose an app icon

Drag the icon to a
Home screen panel

Home screen
panel overview

Figure 20-2: Stick an app on the Home screen.

3. **Drag the app down to one of the Home screen panels.**

The app icon remains stuck under your finger tip. Lift your finger after
you drag the icon all the way to a Home screen panel.

4. **Touch the Home screen panel to see a preview of your icon.**

Don't worry if it isn't in the exact spot. The later section, "Moving and
removing icons and widgets," describes how to rearrange icons on the
Home screen.

The app hasn't moved: What you see is a copy. You can still find the app on
the Apps Menu screen, but now the app is — more conveniently — available
on the Home screen.

✔ Keep your favorite apps, those you use most often, on the Home screen.

✔ Icons on the Home screen are aligned to a grid. You can't stuff more icons
on the Home screen than will fit in the grid, so when a Home screen
is full of icons (or widgets), use another Home screen, as described in
Chapter 3.

✔ You can also add app icons by using the Customize screen. (Refer to
Figure 20-1.) After touching the Customize button on the Home screen,
choose App Shortcuts. Touch an app icon to add it to a Home screen
panel, or you can drag the icon up to the Home screen panel overview.

Slapping down widgets

A *widget* works like a tiny, interactive or informative window, often providing a gateway into another app on the Galaxy Tab. Just as you can add apps to the Home screen, you can also add widgets.

The Galaxy Tab comes with a smattering of widgets preaffixed to the Home screen, possibly just to show you how they can be used. You can place even more widgets on the Home screen by following these steps:

1. **Touch the Customize icon button on the Home screen.**
2. **Choose Widgets.**
3. **Scroll the list to find the widget you want to add.**
4. **Drag the widget to a Home screen panel.**

    The widget is plopped on the Home screen.

The variety of available widgets depends on the applications you have installed. Some applications come with widgets, some don't. Some widgets come independently of any application.

 ✔ More widgets are available at the Android Market. See Chapter 16.

 ✔ You cannot install a widget when the Home screen has no room for it. Choose another panel or remove icons or widgets to make room.

 ✔ To remove a widget, see the later section, "Moving and removing icons and widgets."

Creating shortcuts

A *shortcut* is a doodad you can place on the Home screen that's neither an app nor a widget. Instead, a shortcut is a handy way to get at a feature or an informational tidbit stored in the Galaxy Tab without having to endure complex gyrations.

For example, I have a shortcut on my Home screen that uses the Maps app Navigation feature to help me return to my house. I have the shortcut there in case of a zombie attack so that I can return home to my hardy stock of power tools.

To add a shortcut, touch the Customize icon button on the Home screen and choose the More category on the Customize screen. (Refer to Figure 20-1.) Choose an item to add from the list. What happens next depends on which shortcut you choose.

For example, when you choose a bookmark, you add a web page bookmark to the Home screen. Touch that shortcut to open the Browser app and pluck the web page from your list of bookmarks.

Choose a Contact shortcut to display contact information for a specific person.

A nerdy shortcut to add is the Settings shortcut. After choosing this item, you can select from a number of on–off options or status items that can appear on the Home screen as widgets.

Moving and removing icons and widgets

Icons and widgets are fastened to the Home screen by something akin to the same glue they use on sticky notes. You can easily pick up an icon or a widget, move it around, and then restick it. Unlike sticky notes, the icons and widgets never just fall off, or so I'm told.

To move an icon or a widget, long-press it. Eventually, the icon seems to lift and break free, as shown in Figure 20-3.

Delete icon

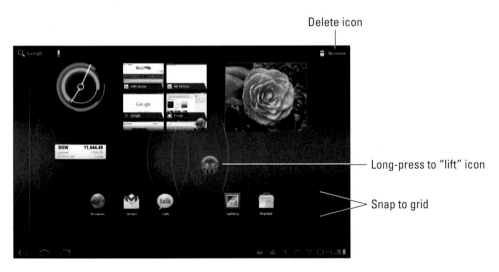

Long-press to "lift" icon

Snap to grid

Figure 20-3: Moving an icon about.

You can drag a free icon to another position on the Home screen or to another Home screen panel, or you can drag it to the Remove (trash can) icon that appears at the top right of the Home screen, shown in Figure 20-3.

Widgets can be moved around or deleted in the same manner as icons.

- ✔ Dragging a Home screen icon or widget to the Trash icon removes the icon or widget from the Home screen. It doesn't uninstall the app or widget, which is still found on the Apps Menu screen. In fact, you can always add the icon or widget to the Home screen again, as described earlier in this chapter.

- ✔ When an icon hovers over the Remove icon, ready to be deleted, its color changes to red.

- ✔ See Chapter 16 for information on uninstalling applications.

- ✔ Your clue that an icon or widget is free and clear to navigate is that the Trash icon appears. (Refer to Figure 20-3.)

Lock Your Galaxy Tab

The Galaxy Tab features a basic lock screen: Simply slide the Unlock button outside of the locking ring, and the Tab is unlocked and ready to use. If you prefer to have a lock that's not so easy to pick, you can choose from one of three types of lock screens: Pattern, PIN, and Password, as described in this section.

Finding the locks

Lock screen security is set on the Set Screen Lock window. Here's how to get there:

1. **From the Home screen, touch the Apps Menu button.**

2. **Choose the Settings app.**

3. **Choose Location & Security.**

4. **Choose Configure Screen Lock.**

5. **If a screen lock is already set, you must trace the pattern or input the PIN or password to continue.**

The Configure Screen Lock window lists five types of lock settings:

Off: The screen doesn't lock. Even the Unlock button and locking ring doesn't show up. Choosing this option disables all locks.

Not Secured: The Tab simply uses the standard locking screen: Slide the Unlock button to the unlocking ring, as described in Chapter 2. Choosing this option disables the Pattern, PIN, and Password locks.

Pattern: To unlock the Tab, you must trace a pattern on the touchscreen.

PIN: The Tab is unlocked by typing a personal identification number (PIN).

Password: You must type a password to unlock the Galaxy Tab.

To set or remove a lock, refer to the following sections.

- ✒ The security you add affects the way you turn on and wake up your Galaxy Tab. See Chapter 2 for details.
- ✒ The security lock can be overridden when USB Debugging is enabled. Unless you're writing software for the Galaxy Tab, however, odds are good that you'll never have USB Debugging turned on.

Removing a lock

You use the Configure Screen Lock window not only to place a lock on the Galaxy Tab, but also to remove any existing locks.

After visiting the Configure Screen Lock window, as described in the preceding section, you can choose the Off or Not Secured option.

To remove all screen locks, choose Off.

To restore the original Unlock button/unlocking ring screen lock, choose Not Secured.

Creating an unlock pattern

One of the most common ways to lock the Tab is to apply an *unlock pattern:* The pattern must be traced exactly as it was created to unlock the device and get access to your apps and other Galaxy Tab features.

1. **Summon the Configure Screen Lock screen.**

   Refer to the earlier section, "Finding the locks."

2. **Choose Pattern.**

   If you've not yet set a pattern lock, you may see a tutorial describing the process; touch the Next button to skip over the dreary directions.

3. **Trace an unlock pattern.**

   Use Figure 20-4 as your inspiration. You can trace over the dots in any order, but you can trace over a dot only once. The pattern must cover at least four dots.

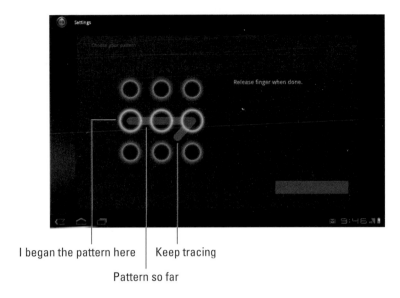

I began the pattern here | Keep tracing

Pattern so far

Figure 20-4: Setting an unlock pattern.

4. **Touch the Continue button.**

5. **Redraw the pattern.**

   You need to prove to the doubtful Galaxy Tab that you know the pattern.

6. **Touch the Confirm button.**

   And the pattern lock is set.

 Ensure that a check mark appears by Use Visible Pattern on the Location & Security window. The check mark ensures that the pattern shows up. For even more security, you can disable the option, but you have to be sure to remember how — and where — the pattern goes.

   ✒ To remove the pattern lock, set either Off or Not Secured as the type of lock, as described in the earlier section, "Finding the locks."

   ✒ The unlock pattern can be as simple or complex as you like. I'm a big fan of simple.

   ✒ Wash your hands! Smudge marks on the display can betray your pattern.

Delaying the screen lock

You may notice that the screen lock shows up right away whenever you sleep the Galaxy Tab. It doesn't have to: You can assign a delay to the screen lock, telling it to kick in after a given amount of time. That way you can wake up the Tab and not have to toil with a lock. It's a feature that comes in handy if you find your Tab always falling asleep on you, and it works better than coffee.

To see the screen lock delay, choose the Timeout item on the Location & Security screen. Choose a timeout value from the scrolling list. The Tab comes configured with the Immediately value set. Other values you can choose range from 5 seconds up to 30 minutes.

Setting a PIN

I suppose that using a PIN, or personal identification number, is more left-brained than using a pattern lock. What's yet another number to memorize?

A *PIN lock* is a code between 4 and 16 numbers long. It contains only numbers, 0 through 9. To set a PIN lock for your Galaxy Tab, follow the directions in the earlier section, "Finding the locks," to reach the Configure Screen Lock window. Choose PIN from the list of locks.

Use the onscreen keyboard to type your PIN once, and touch the Continue button. Type the PIN again to confirm that you know it. The next time you turn on or wake up the Tab, you'll need to type that PIN to get access.

To disable the PIN, reset the Galaxy Tab security level as described in the section "Removing a lock," earlier in this chapter.

Assigning a password

The most secure way to lock the Galaxy Tab is to apply a full-on password. Unlike a PIN (refer to the preceding section), a *password* can contain numbers, symbols, and both upper- and lowercase letters.

Set a password by choosing Password from the Configure Screen Lock window; refer to the earlier section, "Finding the locks," for information on getting to that screen. The password you select must be at least four characters long. Longer passwords are more secure.

You're prompted to type the password whenever you unlock the Galaxy Tab or whenever you try to change the screen lock. Touch the OK button to accept the password you've typed.

See the earlier section, "Removing a lock," for information on resetting the password lock.

Various Galaxy Tab Adjustments

You have plenty of things to adjust, tune, and tweak on the Galaxy Tab. The Settings app is the gateway to all those options, and I'm sure you could waste hours there if you had hours to waste. My guess is that your time is precious; therefore, this section highlights some of the more worthy options and settings.

Singing a different tune

The Sound screen is where you control which sound the Galaxy Tab plays as a ringtone, but it's also where you can set volume and vibration options.

To display the Sound screen, choose Sound from the list of categories on the left side of the Settings app screen.

Here are the worthy options on the Sound Settings screen:

Vibrate: Choose the Vibrate item to see the Vibrate menu. You have four options for vibrating the Galaxy Tab:

Always: The Tab always vibrates when it issues an alert.

Never: The Tab never vibrates.

Only in Silent Mode: The Tab vibrates when you activate Silent mode.

Only When Not in Silent Mode: The Tab vibrates all the time unless Silent mode is activated.

Volume: Though you can set the Galaxy Tab volume using the Volume buttons on the side of the gizmo, the Volume command on the Sound Settings screen lets you set the volume for a number of sound events, as shown in Figure 20-5. Table 20-1 describes what the various volume items control.

General

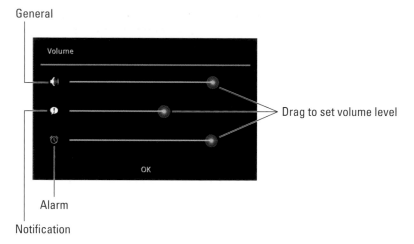

Drag to set volume level

Alarm

Notification

Figure 20-5: Various volume settings.

Table 20-1	Various Noisy Things
Volume Setting	*Sounds It Controls*
General	Sounds generated by the Android operating system (such as when locking the screen or connecting the dock or USB cable) plus media sounds for videos, YouTube, the Internet, games, and other apps
Notification	New notifications, such as new e-mail messages, calendar appointments, or whatever else produces an alert
Alarm	Warnings set by the Alarm Clock app, as well as other alerts

For example, if you want the alarms to be loud, and all those notification sounds to be rather mute, adjust the sliders (refer to Figure 20-5) accordingly.

Notification Ringtone: Choose which sound you want to hear for a notification alert. The list of preset sounds for the Galaxy Tab is shown on the Alarm Tones menu. Choose a sound or choose Silent (at the top of the list) for no sound.

Haptic Feedback: Though the Haptic Feedback item doesn't make noise, you can activate it to have the Galaxy Tab vibrate slightly as you manipulate items on the touchscreen.

✔ You can put the Galaxy Tab in Silent mode by pressing the Down Volume button all the way down until the sound is set to zero, or silence.

✔ Unlike on a cell phone, you cannot assign music or your own audio to a Galaxy Tab ringtone.

Changing visual settings

Probably the key thing you want to adjust visually on the Galaxy Tab is screen brightness. This task is deftly handled by the Quick Settings panel:

1. **Touch the time in the lower-right corner of the screen to pop up the list of notifications.**

2. **Touch the Quick Settings button.**

 3. **Adjust the Brightness slider right (brighter) or left (dimmer).**

You can also touch the Auto button next to the slider to have the Tab automatically adjust its brightness based on ambient light.

Brightness can also be set using the Settings app: On the main Settings app screen, choose the Screen category and then choose Brightness.

Another item worthy of note is the Timeout setting. Choose this option to see the Timeout menu, from which you can set the inactivity duration, after which the Galaxy Tab touchscreen turns itself off. I prefer a value of 1 Minute, which is how the Tab is preconfigured.

✔ The Screen Timeout setting is the setting that the Galaxy Tab uses to put itself into Sleep mode.

✔ See Chapter 3 for more information on Quick Settings.

21

Galaxy Tab Health, Happiness, and Maintenance

I hear that the maintenance on the Eiffel Tower is arduous. Once a year, the French utterly disassemble the landmark; individually scrub every girder, nut, and bolt; and then put it all back together. The entire operation is performed early in the morning, so when Paris wakes up, no one notices. Well, the Tower is cleaner, but no one notices that it was completely disassembled, cleaned, and rebuilt. Truly, the French are amazing.

Fortunately, maintenance for your Galaxy Tab isn't as consuming as maintenance on one of the world's great monuments. For example, cleaning the Tab takes mere seconds, and no disassembly is required. It's cinchy! Beyond covering maintenance, this chapter offers suggestions for using the battery, plus it gives you some helpful tips and Q&A.

Please connect charger

The battery is getting low
15% remaining

OK

Regular Galactic Maintenance

Relax. Maintenance of the Galaxy Tab is simple and quick. Basically, I can summarize it in three words: Keep it clean. Beyond that, another maintenance task worthy of attention is backing up the information stored on your Tab.

Keeping it clean

You probably already keep your Galaxy Tab clean. Perhaps you're one of those people who use their sleeves to wipe the touchscreen. Of course, better than your sleeve is something called a *microfiber cloth*. This item can be found at any computer- or office-supply store.

- ✔ Never use any liquid to clean the touchscreen — especially ammonia or alcohol. Those substances damage the touchscreen, rendering it unable to read your input. Further, such harsh chemicals can smudge the display, making it more difficult to see.

- ✔ If the screen keeps getting dirty, consider adding a screen protector. This specially designed cover prevents the screen from getting scratched or dirty but also lets you use your finger on the touchscreen. Be sure that the screen protector is designed for use with the Galaxy Tab.

- ✔ The screen protectors I picked up at the Verizon Store also came with a handy microfiber cloth.

Backing up your stuff

A *backup* is a safety copy of information. For your Galaxy Tab, the backup copy includes contact information, music, photos, video, and apps you've installed, plus any settings you've made to customize your Tab. Copying that information to another source is one way to keep the information safe in case anything happens to your Galaxy Tab.

Yes, a backup is a good thing. Lamentably, there's no universal method of backing up the stuff on your Galaxy Tab.

Your Google account information is backed up automatically. That information includes your Contacts list, Gmail inbox, and Calendar app appointments. Because that information automatically syncs with the Internet, a backup is always present.

To confirm that your Google account information is being backed up, heed these steps:

1. **At the Home screen, touch the Apps Menu icon button.**

2. **Choose Settings.**

3. **Choose Accounts and Sync.**

4. **Touch the green Sync button by your Google account name.**

5. **Ensure that check marks appear by every item in the list.**

   On my Galaxy Tab, the list includes Books, Calendar, Contacts, Gmail, Google+, and Picasa Web Albums.

6. **Touch the Back icon button.**

7. **Optionally, ensure that your other accounts are being synchronized as well.**

   When you have more than one Google account synchronized with your Galaxy Tab, repeat Steps 1 through 6 for each account.

8. **Touch the Back icon button to return to the main Settings screen.**

9. **Choose Privacy.**

10. **Ensure that a check mark appears by the item Back Up My Data.**

    You should see a check mark there. If not, touch the square to add one.

Beyond your Google account, which is automatically backed up, the rest of the information can be manually backed up. You can choose to either synchronize information on the Galaxy Tab with your computer using an app such as doubleTwist, or you can manually copy files from the Tab's internal storage to the computer as a form of backup.

Yes, I agree: Manual backup isn't an example of technology making your life easier.

 ↳ See Chapter 18 for information about exchanging files between your computer and the Galaxy Tab.

 ↳ A backup of the data stored on the Galaxy Tab would include all data, including photos, videos, and music. Specifically, the folders you should copy are DCIM, Download, and Music. Additional folders to copy include folders named after apps you've downloaded, such as Aldiko, Kindle, Kobo, layar, and other folders named after the apps that created them.

Updating the system

Every so often, a new version of the Galaxy Tab's operating system becomes available. It's an *Android* update because Android is the name of the operating system, not because the Galaxy Tab thinks that it's some type of robot.

When an automatic update occurs, you see an alert or a message appear, indicating that a system upgrade is available. You usually have three options:

- Install Now
- Install Later
- More Info

My advice is to choose Install Now and get it over with — unless you're doing something urgent, in which case you can put off the update until later by choosing Install Later.

- You can manually check for updates: In the Settings app, choose About Tablet and then choose System Updates. When your system is up-to-date, the screen tells you so. Otherwise, you find directions for updating the Android operating system.

- Non-Android system updates might also be issued. For example, Samsung may send out an update to the Galaxy Tab's guts. This type of update is often called a *firmware* update. As with Android updates, my advice is to accept all firmware updates.

Battery Care and Feeding

Perhaps the most important item you can monitor and maintain on your Galaxy Tab is its battery. The battery supplies the necessary electrical juice by which the device operates. Without battery power, your Tab is basically an expensive trivet. Keep an eye on the battery.

Monitoring the battery

You can find information about the Galaxy Tab's battery status at the bottom right of the screen, in the status area, next to the time. The icons used to display battery status are shown in Figure 21-1.

Battery is fully charged, the Tab is happy.

 Battery is starting to drain.

 Battery is low; you're urged to charge soon.

 Battery is very low; stop using and charge at once!

 Battery is being charged.

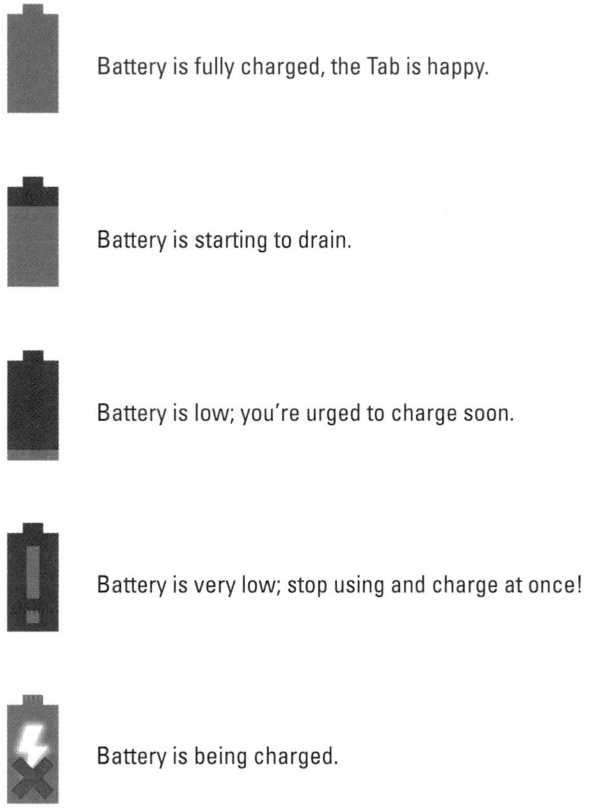

Figure 21-1: Battery status icons.

You might also see an icon for a dead battery, but for some reason I can't get my Galaxy Tab to turn on and display that icon.

When you find the teensy battery icons (refer to Figure 21-1) too vague, you can check the specific battery level by viewing the notification pop-up: At the Home screen, touch the time. You see the notifications displayed, but above that is the Tab's current status. Listed are the date, time, Wi-Fi or cellular data network, and the percentage of battery life remaining.

The next section describes features that consume battery power and how to deal with battery issues.

 Heed those low-battery warnings! The Galaxy Tab alerts you whenever the battery level gets low, as shown in Figure 21-2.

Another warning shows up when the battery level gets seriously low, though I've never seen that warning because I find the message in Figure 21-2 serious enough to move me to action: I either plug in the Tab or turn it off.

Figure 21-2: A low-battery warning.

✔ When the battery level is too low, the Galaxy Tab shuts itself off.

✔ The best way to deal with low battery power is to connect the Tab to a power source: Either plug it into a wall socket or connect it to a computer by using a USB cable. The Galaxy Tab begins charging itself immediately; plus, you can use the device while it's charging.

✔ You don't have to fully charge the Galaxy Tab to use it. When you have only 20 minutes to charge and you get only a 70 percent battery level, that's great. Well, it's not great, but it's far better than a lower battery level.

✔ Battery percentage values are best-guess estimates. The Galaxy Tab has a hearty battery that can last for hours. But when the battery meter gets low, the battery drains faster. So, if you get 8 hours of use from the Tab and the battery meter shows 20 percent left, those numbers don't imply that 20 percent equals 2 more hours of use. In practice, the amount of time you have left is much less than that. As a rule, when the battery percentage value gets low, the battery appears to drain faster.

Determining what is sucking up power

The Galaxy Tab is smart enough to know which of its features use the most battery power. You can check it out for yourself:

1. **At the Home screen, touch the Apps Menu icon button.**
2. **Choose Settings.**
3. **Choose About Tablet.**
4. **Choose Battery Use.**

   You see a screen similar to the one shown in Figure 21-3.

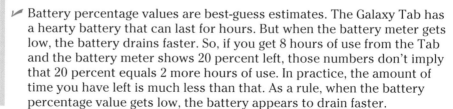

Figure 21-3: Things that drain the battery.

The number and variety of items listed on the Battery Use screen depend on what you've been doing between charges and how many apps you're using.

Carefully note which applications consume the most battery power. You can curb your use of these programs to conserve juice — though, honestly, your savings are negligible. See the next section for battery-saving advice.

Not everything you've done shows up on the Battery Use screen. (Refer to Figure 21-3.) For example, even after I read a Kindle book for about half an hour, Kindle didn't show up. Also, I've seen the Gallery app show up from time to time, even though I've not used it.

At the time this book went to press, no feature could control power management on the Galaxy Tab. A future update of the Android operating system may offer this type of management, in which case you can control how the Galaxy Tab uses power, set timeouts, and adjust power-saving features.

Extending battery life

A surefire way to make a battery last a good long time is to never turn on the device in the first place. That's kind of impractical, so rather than let you use your Galaxy Tab as an expensive paperweight, I offer a smattering of suggestions you can follow to help prolong battery life in your Galaxy Tab:

Turn off vibration options: The Tab's vibration is caused by a teensy motor. Though you don't see much battery savings by disabling the vibration options, it's better than no savings. See Chapter 20 for information on disabling vibration options.

Lower the volume: Additionally, consider lowering the volume for the various noises the Galaxy Tab makes, especially notifications. Information on setting volume options is also found in Chapter 20.

Dim the screen: If you look at Figure 21-3 (earlier in this chapter), you see that the display (labeled Screen) sucks down quite a lot of battery power. Though a dim screen can be more difficult to see, especially outdoors, it definitely saves on battery life.

Turn off Bluetooth: When you're not using Bluetooth, turn it off. See Chapter 17 for information on Bluetooth, though you can turn it off easily from the quick actions at the top of the notification panel.

Turn off Wi-Fi: It's a major trade-off, but while Wi-Fi networking keeps the Galaxy Tab on the Internet, it does drain the battery. Because I tend to use Wi-Fi in only one spot, I keep the Tab plugged in. Away from a single location, however, Wi-Fi "wanders" and isn't useful for an Internet connection anyway. So why not turn it off? Refer to Chapter 17 for information on Wi-Fi.

Help and Troubleshooting

Wouldn't it be great if you could have an avuncular, Mr. Wizard-type available at a moment's notice? He could just walk in and, with a happy smile on his face and a reassuring hand on your shoulder, let you know what the problem is and how to fix it. Never mind that such a thing would be creepy — getting helpful advice is worth it.

Fixing random and annoying problems

Here are some typical problems you may encounter on the Galaxy Tab and my suggestions for a solution:

General trouble: For just about any problem or minor quirk, consider restarting the Galaxy Tab: Turn it off and then turn it on again. This procedure will most likely fix a majority of the annoying problems you encounter.

Check the cellular data connection: As you move about, the cellular signal can change. In fact, you may observe the status bar icon change from 4G LTE to 3G to even the dreaded E or — worse — nothing, depending on the strength and availability of the cellular data service.

My advice for random signal weirdness is to wait. Oftentimes, the signal comes back after a few minutes. If it doesn't, the cellular data network might be down, or you may just be in an area with lousy service. Consider changing your location.

Check the Wi-Fi connection: For Wi-Fi connections, you have to ensure that the Wi-Fi is set up properly and working. This process usually involves pestering the person who configured the Wi-Fi router or, in a coffee shop, bothering the cheerful person with the bad haircut who serves you coffee.

Reset the Wi-Fi connection: Perhaps the issue isn't with the Galaxy Tab at all, but rather with the Wi-Fi network. Some networks have a "lease time" after which your Tab might be disconnected. If so, follow the directions in Chapter 17 for turning off the Tab's Wi-Fi and then turn it on again. That often solves the issue.

Music is playing and you want it to stop: It's awesome that the Galaxy Tab continues to play music while you do other things. Getting the music to stop quickly, however, requires some skill. Primarily, you need skill at popping up the notifications and touching the Pause button that appears in the currently playing song's notification.

An app has run amok: Sometimes, apps that misbehave let you know. You see a warning on the screen announcing the app's stubborn disposition, such as the warning shown in Figure 21-4. When that happens, touch the Force Close button to shut down the errant app.

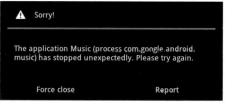

⚠ Sorry!

The application Music (process com.gongle.android. music) has stopped unexpectedly. Please try again.

Force close   Report

Figure 21-4: Halting an app run amok.

When you don't see a warning or when an app appears to be unduly obstinate, you can shut 'er down the manual way, by following these steps:

1. **From the Apps Menu, choose the Settings icon.**

2. **Choose Applications.**

3. **Choose Manage Applications.**

   If you touch the Running item at the top of the Applications screen, you see only the apps that are running. That helps narrow the list.

4. **Choose the application that's causing you distress.**

   For example, a program doesn't start or says that it's busy or has some other issue.

5. **Touch the Stop button.**

   The program stops.

After stopping the program, try opening it again to see whether it works. If the program continues to run amok, contact its developer: Open the Market app. At the main Market app screen, choose My Apps. Choose the app you're having trouble with, and touch the See Details button. Scroll to the bottom of the details screen, and choose Send Email to Developer. Send the developer a message describing the problem.

Reset the Galaxy Tab software: When all else fails, you can do the drastic thing and reset all Tab software, essentially returning it to the state it was in when it first popped out of the box. Obviously, you need not perform this step lightly. In fact, consider finding support (see the next section) before you start the following process:

1. **Start the Settings app, found in the Apps Menu.**
2. **Choose Privacy.**
3. **Choose Factory Data Reset.**
4. **Touch the Reset Tablet button.**
5. **Touch the Erase Everything button to confirm.**

    All the information you've set or stored on the Galaxy Tab is purged. That includes apps you've downloaded, music, synchronized accounts, everything.

Again, do not follow these steps unless you're certain that they will fix the problem or you're under orders to do so from someone in Tech Support.

You can also choose to reset the Galaxy Tab's software and erase everything should you ever return or sell your Galaxy Tab. Of course, you probably love your Galaxy Tab so much that the mere thought of selling it makes you blanch.

Getting support

You can use two sources for support for your Galaxy Tab. For cellular Tabs, the first source of support is your cellular provider. The second source, or only source if you have a Wi-Fi Tab, is Samsung. Or, perhaps, if you were suckered into a long-term service agreement at some Big Box store, you can try getting support from it.

Before you contact someone about support, you need to know the device's ID:

1. **From the Home screen, touch the Apps Menu icon button.**
2. **Choose Settings.**

3. Choose About Tablet.

The Galaxy Tab's model number is listed, as well as the Android version.

Jot down the model number and Android version! Do it right here:

Model Number: _____

Android Version: _____

In the United States, you can contact Verizon for support at (800) 922-0204. You can also visit the Verizon website:

```
http://support.vzw.com
```

For hardware and other issues, you have to contact Samsung. The support number is (800) 726-7864. The Samsung support website is

```
www.samsung.com/us/support
```

 No one likes wading through bottomless automatic customer support systems. Odds are good that you merely want to speak to a human. I've found that the fastest way to do that is to keep pressing the Zero key after you phone into the system. This process eventually turns you over to a live person who, hopefully, can either deal with your problem or connect you with someone who can.

Valuable Galaxy Tab Q&A

I love Q&A! That's because not only is it an effective way to express certain problems and solutions, but some of the questions might also cover things I've been wanting to ask.

"I can't turn the Tab on (or off)!"

Yes, sometimes the Galaxy Tab locks up. I even asked Samsung about this issue specifically, and the folks there told me it's impossible for the Galaxy Tab to seize. Despite this denial, I've discovered that if you press and hold the Power button for about 8 seconds, the Tab turns either off or on, depending on which state it's in.

I've had a program lock the Galaxy Tab tight when the 8-second Power switch trick didn't work. In that case, I waited 12 minutes or so, just letting the Tab sit there and do nothing. Then I pressed and held the Power button for about 8 seconds, and it turned itself back on.

"The touchscreen doesn't work!"

A touchscreen, such as the one used on the Galaxy Tab, requires a human finger for proper interaction. The Tab interprets the static potential between the human finger and the device to determine where the touchscreen is being touched.

You cannot use the touchscreen when you're wearing gloves, unless they're specially designed, static-carrying gloves that claim to work on touchscreens.

The touchscreen might also fail when the battery power is low or when the Galaxy Tab has been physically damaged.

I've been informed that there is an Android app for cats. That implies that the touchscreen can also interpret a feline paw for proper interaction. Either that, or the cat can hold a human finger in its mouth and manipulate the app that way. Because I don't have the app, I can't tell for certain.

"The battery doesn't charge!"

Start from the source: Is the wall socket providing power? Is the cord plugged in? The cable may be damaged, so try another cable.

When charging from a USB port on a computer, ensure that the computer is turned on. Most computers don't provide USB power when they're turned off.

"The Tab gets so hot that it turns itself off!"

Yikes! An overheating gadget can be a nasty problem. Judge how hot the Galaxy Tab is by seeing whether you can hold it in your hand: When it's too hot to hold, it's too hot. If you're using the Galaxy Tab to cook an egg, it's too hot.

Turn off the Galaxy Tab and let the battery cool.

If the overheating problem continues, have the Galaxy Tab looked at for potential repair. The battery might need to be replaced, and as far as I can tell, there's no way to remove and replace the Galaxy Tab battery by yourself.

Do not continue to use any gizmo that's too hot! The heat damages the electronics. It can also start a fire.

"The Tab doesn't do Landscape mode!"

Not every app takes advantage of the Galaxy Tab's ability to orient itself in Landscape mode, or even upside-down mode. For example, many games set their orientations one way and refuse to change, no matter how you hold the Tab. So, just because the app doesn't go into Landscape mode, that doesn't mean anything is broken.

Confirm that the orientation lock isn't on: Pull up the notifications and touch the Quick Settings button at the top of the notification panel. Ensure that the Auto-Rotate Screen item is on; otherwise, the screen doesn't reorient itself.

Part V
The Part of Tens

The 5th Wave   By Rich Tennant

"Okay, antidote, antidote, what would an antidote app look like?"

*W*elcome to the last part of the book, assuming that you've read this book sequentially, which I warned you not to do in the Introduction. Contrary to widely held belief, this part of the book does not contain leftovers. Well, that is, unless it's *Home Cooking For Dummies,* which contains the chapter "Ten Exciting Ways to Make Week-Old Meatloaf Appealing." And this part of the book doesn't hold meaningless drivel, unless you're reading *Congress For Dummies.* No, this part of the book contains chapters that hold ten items each. They range from the interesting to the necessary to the boldly obtuse.

Alarms

 Add alarm

 8:30 AM
Mon, Tue, Wed, Thu, Fri

9:00 AM
Sat, Sun

Done

Ten Tips, Tricks, and Shortcuts

In This Chapter

▶ Finding out which way is up

▶ Reviewing your recent apps

▶ Halting services

▶ Putting a Settings shortcut on the Home screen

▶ Removing the vocal dirty word filter

▶ Telling the Tab what to do

▶ Using contact screen shortcuts

▶ Finding your wayward Galaxy Tab

▶ Setting locations for your schedule

▶ Turning off the 4G LTE signal

A tip is a small suggestion, a word of advice often spoken from experience or knowledge. A *trick,* which is something not many know, usually causes amazement or surprise. A *shortcut* is a quick way to get home, even though it crosses the old grave-yard and you never quite know whether Old Man Witherspoon is the groundskeeper or a zombie.

I'd like to think that just about everything in this book is a tip, trick, or shortcut for using the Galaxy Tab. Even so, I've distilled a list of items in this chapter that are definitely worthy of note.

Discover Which Way Is Up

Maybe I'm the only one who has this issue: The Galaxy Tab is pretty plain. It's difficult for me to tell which edge is the top edge, especially given that the screen auto-rotates into an up position no matter how I hold the Tab.

Normally such an issue shouldn't be a problem, but I like to know which edge has the camera and which edge has the data connector.

To solve the problem, I stuck a tiny strip of white tape along the top, front edge of the Tab. It's just a sliver of white tape, which I pared back using an X-ACTO knife. That way I can always tell which edge of the Tab is the top. Life with my Galaxy Tab has been far less frustrating with that tiny piece of tape in place.

Summon a Recently Opened App

 I have to kick myself in the head every time I return to the Apps Menu screen to, once again, page through the panels o' icons to dig up an app I just opened. Why bother? Because I can summon the list of recently opened apps by touching the Recent Apps button at the bottom left of the Home screen.

 Using the Recent Apps button is the best way you can switch between two running apps. So when you need to switch, for example, between Email and the Browser, just touch the Recent Apps button and choose the bottom item on the list. It's effectively the same thing as the Alt+Tab key combination in Windows.

Stop Unneeded Services

Some things may be going on in your Galaxy Tab that you don't need or even suspect. These activities include the monitoring of information, apps that update, or tiny programs that check on the device's status. The technical term for these activities is *services*.

When a service has started that you don't want, or have been requested to stop, you can halt the service. You can also halt programs that may be spinning away in the background when there's no other apparent way to stop the thing. Here's how:

1. **While at the Home screen, touch the Apps Menu icon button.**
2. **Choose Settings.**
3. **Choose Applications.**
4. **Choose Running.**

    You see the Running Applications screen, similar to Figure 22-1.

The app's name

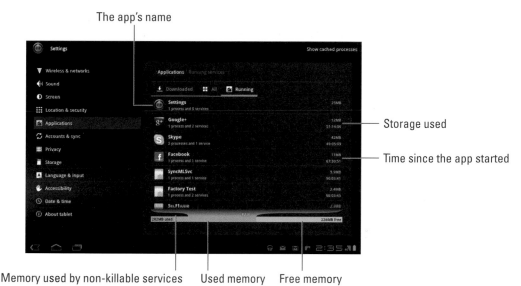

Storage used

Time since the app started

Memory used by non-killable services   Used memory   Free memory

Figure 22-1: Services running on the Galaxy Tab.

5. **Touch an app.**

    Most likely, it's an app you recognize that you don't need running or something you need to stop because it's doing something unwanted or — heaven forbid — unsavory.

6. **On the app's Running Services screen, touch the Stop button.**

When you stop a service, you free resources used by that service. These resources include memory and processor power. The result of stopping unneeded services can be improved performance.

The service you stopped will most likely start up again the next time you start the Galaxy Tab, or if you run the app. The only way to halt a specific service for all eternity is to uninstall the program associated with that service, which is a drastic step. Even then, not every app can be removed; preinstalled apps and phone company apps are stuck to your Galaxy Tab like August ticks on a hound dog.

✔ Do not randomly disable services. Many of them are required for the Galaxy Tab to do its job or for the apps you use to carry out their tasks. If you disable a service you don't recognize and the device begins to act funny, turn the Galaxy Tab off and then on again. That should fix the problem.

✔ You can use the Running Services screen to stop applications run amok, but don't use it to quit an app you can otherwise quit. Most apps have an Exit or Sign Out command. Use the Menu icon button to locate that command and use it instead of killing the app on the Running Services screen.

✔ The weird bar graph at the bottom of the Running Services screen (refer to Figure 22-1) illustrates memory usage in your Galaxy Tab. The black area represents services that cannot be stopped or killed. The gray area represents memory used by the Android system or your apps. The green area shows free, or unused, memory.

Add Settings Shortcuts to the Home Screen

Unlike Android cell phones I love and use, the Galaxy Tab seems to lack a handy way to get to the Settings app screen. It's not that you need to get there often, but I find having a speedy way to do so can really help, especially with some common tasks.

The answer is to place Settings app shortcuts on the Home screen. Here's how it works:

1. **While at the Home screen, touch the Customize icon button.**

2. **Choose the More category.**

3. **Choose Select Settings.**

   A menu of shortcuts appears. It's a scrolling list, so there are several more items than you see initially.

4. **Choose an item to place on the Home screen.**

   A Settings shortcut icon is placed on the screen.

The shortcut icon looks like the Settings icon, but it's not: Instead it's a direct link to the item you chose in Step 4. So although the shortcut doesn't turn something on or off, it quickly gets you to that screen in the Settings app.

✔ Don't worry about where the shortcut icon is placed. You can move shortcut icons just like anything else on the Home screen. See Chapter 20.

✔ I placed a Bluetooth Settings shortcut on my Tab's Home screen. That's because I turn Bluetooth on and off frequently and there's no Bluetooth item on the Quick Settings screen.

✔ If you can't decide which Settings item to place on the Home screen, just put a shortcut to the Settings app itself. I find myself using that app often enough that a shortcut is warranted.

Add Spice to Dictation

I feel that too few people use dictation, despite how handy it can be. Whether or not you use it, you might notice that it occasionally censors some of the words you utter. Perhaps you're the kind of person who won't put up with that kind of s***.

Relax, b******. You can lift the vocal censorship ban by following these steps:

1. **At the Home screen, touch the Apps Menu icon button.**
2. **Choose Settings.**
3. **Choose Language & Input.**
4. **Choose Voice Recognition Settings.**
5. **Remove the check mark by the option Block Offensive Words.**

And just what are offensive words? I would think that *censorship* would be an offensive word. But no, apparently the words s***, c***, and even innocent little old a****** are deemed offensive by Google Voice. What the h***?

Command the Tab with Your Voice

I just tried this trick for my son, and he was really impressed: I touched the Dictation button on the Home screen and uttered, "Listen to the Beatles." In less than five seconds, the Galaxy Tab began playing the White Album.

 You can use the Dictation button (shown in the margin) to bark orders at your Tab. Or, if you can't find the Dictation button, start the Voice Search app from the Apps menu.

Here are just a few of the phrases you can utter into the Tab when you see the Speak Now prompt:

- Watch a video.
- Listen to *(artist, album, song)*.
- Send e-mail to *(contact)*.
- Set alarm for *(time)*.
- Go to *(address, map location)*.

Alas, try as I might, the Tab never responds when I say, "Make me a sandwich!"

Create a Contact Screen Shortcut

The people you contact most often are deserving of their own contact short-cuts on the Home screen. You just don't realize how useful such a thing is until you have one.

To create a contact screen shortcut, follow these steps:

1. **Long-press the Home screen.**

   The Customize screen appears.

2. **Choose the More category.**

3. **Choose Contact.**

4. **Choose a contact from the Contacts list.**

   Preferably, choose someone whom you frequently and electronically contact.

An icon representing the contact appears on the screen. If the contact has an associated picture, you see the picture. Otherwise, you see a generic contact icon, but it has a teeny menu indicator in the lower-right corner. If you touch the contact, that menu appears, displaying a list of quick tasks for the contact, as shown in Figure 22-2.

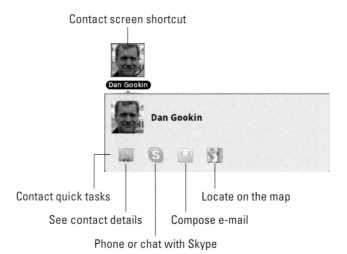

Figure 22-2: Quick tasks for a contact screen shortcut.

Choose a quick task for a contact by touching the task's icon, as shown in Figure 22-2. For some contacts with lots of quick tasks, you may have to scroll the quick tasks left or right to see them all.

The number of quick task icons that appears for a contact depends on how much information you have available for the contact, such as e-mail address; cell phone number (for texting); or linked contacts for Facebook, Skype, Twitter, and so on.

- ✒ When multiple sources, such as e-mail addresses, exist for a contact, you may also see a settings or wrench icon. Choose that icon to select which accounts to use for the quick tasks.

- ✒ To hide the quick contact information, simply touch another part of the Home screen or press the Back icon button.

- ✒ A contact's Facebook status may appear beneath the name, which isn't shown in Figure 22-2.

- ✒ Just touch the contact screen shortcut to see the quick tasks. When you long-press the shortcut, the Galaxy Tab believes that you want to move or delete the icon.

Find Your Lost Galaxy Tab

Someday you may lose your Galaxy Tab. It might be for a panic-filled few seconds, or it might be for forever. The hardware solution is to weld a heavy object to the Tab, such as a bowling ball or furnace, yet that kind of defeats the entire mobile/wireless paradigm. The software solution is to use a cell phone locator service.

Even though the Galaxy Tab isn't a cell phone, you can use the same apps that cell phones use to help find a wayward Galaxy Tab. Those apps use the cellular signal as well as the Tab's GPS to help locate a missing gizmo.

Many apps available on the Android Market can help locate your Galaxy Tab. I've not tried them all. Here are some suggestions:

- ✒ Plan B from Lookout Mobile Security
- ✒ Norton Mobile Security
- ✒ Security Pro

Most of these services require that you set up a web page account to assist in locating your Galaxy Tab. They also enable services that send updates to the Internet. The updates assist in tracking your Galaxy Tab, in case it becomes lost or is stolen.

Enter Location Information for Your Events

When you create an event for the Calendar app, be sure to enter the event location. You can type either an address (if you know it) or the name of the location. The key is to type the text as you would type it in the Maps app when searching for a location. That way, you can touch the event location and the Galaxy Tab displays it on the touchscreen. Finding an appointment couldn't be easier.

✏ See Chapter 10 for more information about the Maps app.

✏ See Chapter 15 for details about the Calendar.

Disable 4G LTE Service

With the über-speed of the 4G LTE network, it's very easy to blow by your monthly data plan allowance. If you're cheap (like me), you probably have an allowance of only 2GB (gigabytes) of data per month before another charge pops up on your bill. To help avoid that, you can get a higher-capacity data plan, or you can just choose to forego the 4G LTE experience.

To limit the Galaxy Tab to use only the 3G (or slower) networks, follow these steps:

1. **At the Home screen, touch the Apps Menu icon button.**
2. **Choose Settings.**
3. **Choose Wireless & Networks.**
4. **Choose Mobile Networks, then System Selection.**
5. **Choose CDMA Mode.**
6. **Choose Automatic.**

To reactivate the 4G LTE network, repeat these steps but choose LTE Automatic in Step 4.

Changing the network doesn't alter your cell phone plan's data service limit. All it does is ensure that you'll take longer to get to that limit.

Ten Things to Remember

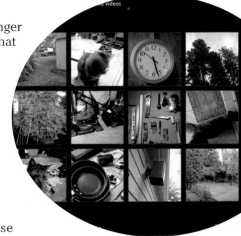

*H*ave you ever tried to tie string around your finger to remember something? I've not attempted that technique just yet. The main reason is that I keep forgetting to buy string and have no way to remind myself.

For your Galaxy Tab, some things are definitely worth remembering. Out of the long, long list, I've come up with ten good ones.

Use Dictation

It's such a handy feature, yet I constantly forget to use it: Rather than type short text messages, use dictation. You can access dictation from any onscreen keyboard by touching the Microphone button. Speak the text; the text appears. Simple.

See Chapter 4 for information on Dictation and also how to put the Microphone button on the onscreen keyboard.

Portrait Orientation

I enjoy the occasional portrait view. Apps such as the Browser, Kindle, and even Email can look much better in a vertical orientation. It's easier to read a conversation in the chatting apps, such as Talk and Skype, when things are narrow. Simply turn the Tab over on its side and start reading.

Not every app supports portrait orientation. Some apps, specifically some games, appear only in landscape orientation.

Orientation Lock

The opposite of remembering that the Galaxy Tab has portrait orientation (see the preceding section) is forgetting that it has an orientation lock feature. When engaged, the orientation lock prevents the screen from adjusting between Landscape and Portrait modes: The screen stays fixed in whichever orientation it was in when you set the orientation lock.

To set the orientation lock, ensure that the Auto-Rotate Screen item is set to Off in the Quick Settings screen. See Chapter 3 for more information about the Quick Settings.

Use the Keyboard Suggestions

Don't forget to take advantage of the suggestions that appear above the onscreen keyboard when you're typing text. In fact, you don't even need to touch a suggestion; to replace your text with the highlighted suggestion, simply touch the onscreen keyboard's Space key. Zap! The word appears.

To ensure that suggestions are enabled, follow these steps:

1. **Start the Settings app.**
2. **Choose Language & Input.**
3. **Choose Configure Input Methods.**

4. **Choose the Settings item in the Samsung Keypad section.**

5. **Ensure that a check mark appears by XT9, the predictive text option.**

Also refer to Chapter 4 for additional information on using the keyboard suggestions.

Things That Consume Lots of Battery Juice

Three items on the Galaxy Tab suck down battery power faster than a massive alien fleet is defeated by a plucky antihero who just wants the girl:

- Wi-Fi networking
- Bluetooth
- Navigation

Both Wi-Fi networking and Bluetooth require extra power for their wireless radios. The amount isn't much, but it's enough that I would consider shutting them down when battery power gets low.

Navigation is certainly handy, but because the Galaxy Tab touchscreen is on the entire time and dictating text to you, the battery drains rapidly. If possible, try to plug the Tab into the car's power socket when you're navigating.

See Chapter 21 for more information on managing the Galaxy Tab's battery.

Use a Docking Stand

I tend to keep my Galaxy Tab in one spot when I'm not on the road. The multimedia stand is a helpful way to hold the Tab, to keep it propped up and easy to use. Because I use the stand as home base for the Tab, I always know where the Tab is, and because I don't have the cleanest of desktops, I can always find the Tab despite ominous swells in seas of paper.

Given the choice of multimedia stand or keyboard dock, I prefer the multimedia stand. The keyboard stand is nice, but it takes up some room, and I don't do much typing on my Tab. (Refer to the section "Use Dictation," earlier in this chapter.)

The Galaxy Tab Can Make Phone Calls

Yeah, I know: It's not a phone. I wish it were (and I'm sure Samsung does as well), but the Galaxy Tab lacks a native ability to use the cellular system for making phone calls. Even so, with apps such as Talk and Skype, you can make phone calls and even video chat with others. Refer to Chapter 9 for details.

Keep Up with Your Schedule

The Calendar app can certainly be handy to remind you of upcoming dates and generally keep you on schedule. A great way to augment the calendar is to employ the Calendar widget on the Home screen.

The Calendar widget lists the current date and then a long list of upcoming appointments. It's a great way to check your schedule, especially when you use your Tab all the time. I recommend sticking the Calendar widget right on the main Home screen.

See Chapter 20 for information on adding widgets to the Home screen; Chapter 15 covers the Calendar app.

Snap a Pic of That Contact

Here's something I always forget: Whenever you're near one of your contacts, take the person's picture. Sure, some people are bashful, but most folks are flattered. The idea is to build up your Contacts list so that all contacts have photos.

When taking a picture, be sure to show it to the person before you assign it to the contact. Let them decide whether it's good enough. Or, if you just want to be rude, assign a crummy-looking picture. Heck, you don't even have to do that: Just take a random picture of anything and assign it to a contact: A plant. A rock. Your cat. But, seriously, keep in mind that the Tab can take a contact's picture the next time you meet up with that person.

See Chapter 11 for more information on using the Galaxy Tab's camera and assigning a picture to a contact.

The Search Command

Google is known worldwide for its searching abilities. By gum, the word *Google* is now synonymous with searching. So please don't forget that the Galaxy Tab, which uses the Google Android operating system, has a powerful Search command.

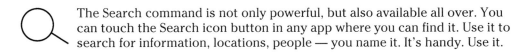 The Search command is not only powerful, but also available all over. You can touch the Search icon button in any app where you can find it. Use it to search for information, locations, people — you name it. It's handy. Use it.

Ten Great Apps

In This Chapter

▶ AK Notepad
▶ Angry Birds
▶ Gesture Search
▶ Google Finance
▶ Google Sky Map
▶ Movies
▶ SportsTap
▶ TuneIn Radio
▶ Voice Recorder
▶ Zedge

There are more than 100,000 apps available at the Android Market — so many that it would take you more than a relaxing evening to discover them all. Rather than list every single app, I've culled from the lot some apps that I find exceptional — that show the diversity of the Android Market but also how well the Galaxy Tab can run Android apps.

Every app listed in this chapter is free; see Chapter 16 for directions on finding them using the Android Market, or scan the barcodes in the margin using your Tab to download the apps quickly. (See the sidebar, "Get thee a barcode–scanner app," to get started.)

AK Notepad

One program that the Galaxy Tab is missing out of the box is a notepad. A good choice for an app to fill that void is AK Notepad: You can type or dictate short messages and memos, which I find handy.

For example, before a recent visit to the hardware store, I made (dictated) a list of items I needed by using AK Notepad. I also keep some important items as notes — things that I often forget or don't care to remember, such as frequent flyer numbers, my dress shirt and suit size (like I ever need that info), and other important notes I might need handy but not cluttering my brain.

Perhaps the most important note you can make is one containing your contact information. A note labeled *In Case You Find This Tablet* on my Tab contains information about me in case I ever lose my gizmo and someone is decent enough to search it for my information. (Also see Chapter 22 for information on finding a wayward Galaxy Tab.)

Angry Birds

The birds may be angry at the green piggies for stealing eggs, but you'll be crazy for this addictive game. Like most popular games, Angry Birds is simple. It's easy to learn, fun to play. The best part is that on the Galaxy Tab, with its awesome 10.1-inch display, the Angry Birds game is beautiful.

Gesture Search

The Gesture Search app provides a new way to find information on your Galaxy Tab. Rather than use a keyboard or dictate, you simply draw on the touchscreen the first letter of whatever you're searching for.

Start the Gesture Search app to begin a search. Use your finger to draw a big letter on the screen. After you draw a letter, search results appear on the screen. You can continue drawing more letters to refine the search or touch a search result.

Gesture Search can find contacts, music, apps, and bookmarks in the Browser app.

TIP

Get thee a barcode-scanner app

Many apps from the Android Market can be quickly accessed by scanning their barcode information. Scanning with what? Why, your Galaxy Tab, of course!

By using a barcode-scanner app, you can instantly read in and translate barcodes into links to that app at the Android Market.

Plenty of barcode apps are out there, though I use one called Barcode Scanner. It's easy:

Run the app. Point the Tab's camera at a barcode and, in a few moments, you see a link or an option for what to do next. To get an app, choose the Open Browser option, which opens the Android Market app right to that app's page.

You can use the Barcode Scanner app to take advantage of the various QR code icons that appear in this chapter, as well as throughout this book. To install an app, choose the option Open Browser.

Google Finance

 The Google Finance app is an excellent market-tracking tool for folks who are obsessed with the stock market or want to keep an eye on their portfolios. The app offers you an overview of the market and updates to your stocks as well as links to financial news.

To get the most from this app, configure Google Finance on the Web, using your computer. You can create lists of stocks to watch, which is then instantly synchronized with your Galaxy Tab. You can visit Google Finance on the Web at

```
www.google.com/finance
```

As with other Google services, Google Finance is provided to you for free, as part of your Google account.

Google Sky Map

 Ever look up into the night sky and say, "What the heck is that?" Unless it's a bird, an airplane, a satellite, or a UFO, the Google Sky Map can help you find what it is. You may discover that a particularly bright star in the sky is, in fact, the planet Jupiter.

The Google Sky Map app is elegant. It basically turns the Galaxy Tab into a window you can look through to identify things in the night sky. Just start the app and hold the Galaxy Tab up to the sky. Pan the Tab to identify planets, stars, and constellations.

 Google Sky Map promotes using the Galaxy Tab without touching it. For this reason, the screen goes blank after a spell, which is merely the Tab's power-saving mode. If you plan extensive stargazing with the Google Sky Map, consider resetting the screen timeout. Refer to Chapter 2 for information on this topic.

Movies

 The Movies app is the Galaxy Tab's gateway to Hollywood. It lists currently running films and films that are opening, and it has links to your local theaters with showtimes and other information. The app is also tied into the popular Rotten Tomatoes website for reviews and feedback. If you enjoy going to the movies, you'll find the Movies app a valuable addition to your Galaxy Tab's app library.

SportsTap

 I admit to not being a sports nut, so it's difficult for me to identify with the craving to have the latest scores, news, and schedules. The sports nuts in my life, however, tell me that the very best app for that purpose is a handy thing named SportsTap.

Rather than blather on about something I'm not into, just take my advice and obtain SportsTap. I believe you'll be thrilled.

Avoiding Android viruses

How can you tell which apps are legitimate and which might be viruses or evil apps that do odd things to your phone? Well, you can't. In fact, most people can't, because most evil apps don't advertise themselves as such.

The key to knowing whether an app is evil is to look at what it does, as described in Chapter 16. If a simple grocery-list app uses the phone's text messaging service and the app doesn't need to send text messages, it's suspect.

In the history of the Android operating system, only a handful of malicious apps have been distributed, and most of them were found in Asia. Google routinely removes these apps from the Android Market, and a feature of the Android

operating system even lets Google remove apps from your tablet. So, you're pretty safe.

Generally speaking, avoid "hacker" apps and porn and apps that use social engineering to make you do things on your Galaxy Tab that you wouldn't otherwise do, such as text an overseas number to see racy pictures of politicians or celebrities.

Also, I highly recommend that you abstain from obtaining apps from anything but the official Android Market. The Amazon Market is okay, but some other markets are basically distribution points for illegal or infected software. Avoid them.

TuneIn Radio

I know I mentioned this app back in Chapter 13, but I really do recommend it. One of my favorite ways that the Galaxy Tab entertains me is as a little radio I keep by my workstation. I use the TuneIn Radio app to find a favorite Internet radio station, and then I sit back and work.

While TuneIn Radio is playing, you can do other things with your Tab, such as check Facebook or answer an e-mail. You can return to the TuneIn Radio app by choosing the triangle notification icon. Or just keep it going and enjoy the tunes.

Voice Recorder

The Galaxy Tab can record your voice or other sounds, and the Voice Recorder is a good app for performing this task. It has an elegant and simple interface: Touch the big Record button to start recording. Make a note for yourself or record a friend doing his Daffy Duck impression.

Previous recordings are stored in a list on the Voice Recorder's main screen. Each recording is shown with its title, the date and time of the recording, and the recording duration.

Zedge

 The Zedge program is a helpful resource for finding wallpapers and ringtones — millions of them. It's a sharing app, so you can access wallpapers and ringtones created by other Android users as well as share your own. If you're looking for a specific sound or something special for Home screen wallpaper, Zedge is the best place to start your search.

Index